D1565811

FIELDING'S
AMAZON

Fielding Titles

Fielding's Amazon

Fielding's Australia

Fielding's Bahamas

Fielding's Belgium

Fielding's Bermuda

Fielding's Borneo

Fielding's Brazil

Fielding's Britain

Fielding's Budget Europe

Fielding's Caribbean

Fielding's Europe

Fielding's Far East

Fielding's France

Fielding's Guide to the World's Most Dangerous Places

Fielding's Guide to the World's Great Voyages

Fielding's Guide to Kenya's Best Hotels, Lodges & Homestays

Fielding's Guide to the World's Most Romantic Places

Fielding's Hawaii

Fielding's Holland

Fielding's Italy

Fielding's London Agenda

Fielding's Los Angeles Agenda

Fielding's Malaysia and Singapore

Fielding's Mexico

Fielding's New York Agenda

Fielding's New Zealand

Fielding's Paris Agenda

Fielding's Portugal

Fielding's Scandinavia

Fielding's Seychelles

Fielding's Southeast Asia

Fielding's Spain

Fielding's Vacation Places Rated

Fielding's Vietnam

Fielding's Worldwide Cruises

Fielding's Cruise Insider

FIELDING'S AMAZON

The Adventurer's Guide To The Mysteries Of The Amazon

Pamela Bloom

Fielding Worldwide, Inc.
308 South Catalina Avenue
Redondo Beach, California 90277 U.S.A.

Fielding's Amazon
Published by Fielding Worldwide, Inc.
Text Copyright ©1995 Pamela Bloom

FIELDING WORLDWIDE INC.

PUBLISHER AND CEO	Robert Young Pelton
PUBLISHING DIRECTOR	Paul T. Snapp
ELECTRONIC PUBLISHING DIRECTOR	Larry E. Hart
PROJECT DIRECTOR	Tony E. Hulette
ADMINISTRATIVE COORDINATOR	Beverly Riess
ACCOUNT SERVICES MANAGER	Christy Harp

EDITORS

Linda Charlton   Kathy Knoles

PRODUCTION

Gini Martin   Chris Snyder

Craig South

COVER DESIGNED BY	Digital Artists, Inc.
COVER PHOTOGRAPHERS — Front Cover	Steve Violet/Tony Stone Images
Background Photo, Front Cover	Sue Cunningham/Tony Stone Images
Back Cover	Jed Wilcox/Tony Stone Images
INSIDE PHOTOS	Bruce Coleman, Inc., Don Klein
MAPS	Geosystems

Inquiries should be addressed to: Fielding Worldwide, Inc., 308 South Catalina Ave., Redondo Beach, California 90277 U.S.A., Telephone (310) 372-4474, Facsimile (310) 376-8064, 8:30 a.m.–5:30 p.m. Pacific Standard Time.

ISBN 1-56952-000-3

Library of Congress Catalog Card Number

94-068358

Printed in the United States of America

Dedication

To the spirits of the rain forest:

May they teach us how to cherish each other and the planet
Pamela Bloom, author

Letter from the Publisher

In 1946, Temple Fielding began a remarkable series of well-written, highly-personalized guidebooks for independent travelers. Temple's opinionated, witty, and oft-imitated books have now guided travelers for almost a half-century. More important to some was Fielding's humorous and direct method of steering travelers away from the dull and the insipid. Today, Fielding travel guides are still written by experienced travelers for experienced travelers. Our authors carry on Fielding's reputation for creating travel experiences that deliver insight with a sense of discovery and style.

Pamela Bloom has created a unique travel guide to one of the world's most mysterious and unexplored regions. Fielding's *Amazon* is a thoroughly intriguing book that penetrates the depths of today's most controversial ecosystem. Globe-trotting journalist Bloom takes the adventurous traveler beyond eco-tourism to discover the true nature of Amazônia by tramping through the jungle, cruising down the Amazon tributaries and more.

Today the concept of independent travel has never been bigger. Our policy of *brutal honesty* and a highly personal point of view has never changed; it just seems the travel world has caught up with us.

Enjoy your Amazon adventure with Pamela Bloom and Fielding.

RYP

Robert Young Pelton
Publisher and C.E.O.
Fielding Worldwide, Inc.

Fielding Rating Icons

The Fielding Rating Icons are highly personal and awarded to help the besieged traveler choose from among the dizzying array of activities, attractions, hotels, restaurants and sights. The awarding of an icon denotes unusual or exceptional qualities in the relevant category.

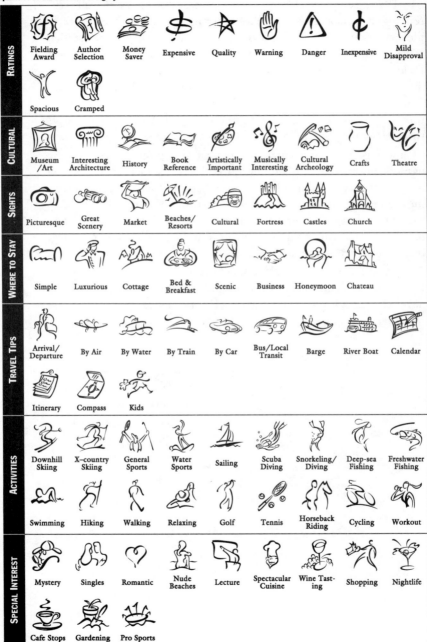

RATINGS: Fielding Award, Author Selection, Money Saver, Expensive, Quality, Warning, Danger, Inexpensive, Mild Disapproval, Spacious, Cramped

CULTURAL: Museum/Art, Interesting Architecture, History, Book Reference, Artistically Important, Musically Interesting, Cultural Archeology, Crafts, Theatre

SIGHTS: Picturesque, Great Scenery, Market, Beaches/Resorts, Cultural, Fortress, Castles, Church

WHERE TO STAY: Simple, Luxurious, Cottage, Bed & Breakfast, Scenic, Business, Honeymoon, Chateau

TRAVEL TIPS: Arrival/Departure, By Air, By Water, By Train, By Car, Bus/Local Transit, Barge, River Boat, Calendar, Itinerary, Compass, Kids

ACTIVITIES: Downhill Skiing, X-country Skiing, General Sports, Water Sports, Sailing, Scuba Diving, Snorkeling/Diving, Deep-sea Fishing, Freshwater Fishing, Swimming, Hiking, Walking, Relaxing, Golf, Tennis, Horseback Riding, Cycling, Workout

SPECIAL INTEREST: Mystery, Singles, Romantic, Nude Beaches, Lecture, Spectacular Cuisine, Wine Tasting, Shopping, Nightlife, Cafe Stops, Gardening, Pro Sports

IMPORTANT!

NEW CURRENCY

Brazil has had a crazy history of enormous inflation and instable prices, but on July 1, 1994, a new currency called the *real* (pronounced *ray-ow*) was instigated to be more or less equivalent to the American dollar. It is yet to be seen whether this tactic will keep inflation at bay, but at the very least it should make calculating costs easier for Americans. However, because nothing is predictable in Brazil, prices quoted in this book should be considered only a fair estimate and are most likely off at least $15–20 (in the case of hotels).

DISCLAIMER

While every effort has been made to assure the accuracy of facts mentioned in this guide, human mistakes are inevitable, not to mention the ever-changing landscape of the Brazilian tourist industry. All opinions expressed in this book stem from the author's personal experience only; consequently, neither she nor the publisher can be held accountable for a reader's personal experience while traveling. Any comments, suggestions and ideas for future editions may be addressed to the author, Pamela Bloom, c/o Fielding Worldwide, 308 S. Catalina Ave., Redondo Beach, CA 90277.

Pamela Bloom

ABOUT THE AUTHOR

Pamela Bloom is a travel writer, music and arts critic, and fiction writer whose work has appeared in such publications as the *New York Times, Chicago Tribune* and *Los Angeles Times,* as well as *High Fidelity, Musician, Downbeat, Seven Days, Connoisseur* and *Elle* magazines, among others. She received a B.A. in comparative literature from Trinity College (Hartford, Connecticut), attended Dartmouth College, and also studied opera at Indiana University and the Juilliard School of Music. A lively lecturer, she has taught the history of Brazilian jazz at the New School for Social Research in New York City and also presented a multimedia lecture series on Brazilian music and culture at the Ballroom Club in Manhattan, in conjunction with their annual Brazilian jazz series. As a world traveler, Pamela Bloom has pursued writing assignments in China, Spain, Greece, France, the Caribbean and throughout the United States. As a dedicated Brazilophile, she has danced in Rio's Carnaval with the Portela Samba School, interviewed many of the country's top musicians and traveled extensively throughout the country. A native of Houston, Texas, she presently resides in New York City.

ACKNOWLEDGMENTS

As part of the research I completed both for this book and my other guide, *Fielding's Brazil*, I owe much gratitude to literally hundreds of angels who guided me through this wonderful, exasperating and yet unforgettable country.

Especially in the Amazon, I would like to thank the tourist boards of the state of Pará and Amazonas, as well as those of the cities of Belém and Manaus for supporting my work. Special thanks goes to Andre von Thuranyi of Expeditours, whose passionate commitment to ecology and the soul of the forest kept me inspired through some rough and rugged adventures.

Deep gratitude is extended to Maureen Callanan of Varig Airlines, whose calm and steady spirit kept me on track.

Cheers to Beatrice Imbiriba, and her new position as Secretary of Tourism in Santarém, a true Amazon warrior in the best tradition of valor. May you succeed in all your dreams for the forest and its peoples.

Special gratitude is extended to Professor M. C. Meyer for his invaluable contribution to this book and for his own commitment to revision the resources of the rain forest for interplanetary purposes.

A lifetime of prosperity and love to Carlos Alberto Saldanha de Leite for a friendship that will never die.

To Shiva for his long-distance love and energy.

And to my mother Mitzie Bloom, my late father Dr. Manuel G. Bloom, and my brothers Kim and Kerry and their families for always supporting me through my wildest ideas.

TO MY READERS

Picture this: I'm ten years old, a definite noncamper stuck in the backwoods of Texas, and I'm facing what was for me then the epitome of horror: *an outdoor latrine*. No amount of soothing from my Scout leader could console me, so I spent the entire weekend whining and about to throw up. Little did my troop leader realize, that some umpteen year later, I would grow up to eat, sleep and tramp *joyously* through the Amazon forest.

Why the Amazon? My love affair started with Brazil itself, an irresistibly beautiful, exotic, exasperating country that seeped into the core of my being from the moment I stepped onto its soil. A country that's perpetually about to fall apart, but will never do so until it first throws an unforgettable party. A country born to sing and dance, to love, to fight, to lie on the beach, to do everything to avoid going to work—a country where it's *simple* to find a lover who will inspire in you a thousand moments of *saudade*, or unrequited longing. All that inspired me to write my first guidebook *Fielding's Brazil*, and considering the positive feedback, I think I can safely say my guide inspired a lot of other people to give themselves over fully to that wild and wooly "Brazilian experience."

The truth is, however, you can't truly know Brazil without knowing its environmental core—the Amazon and the Pantanal. As most people know by now, these two ecological systems and their delicate balance support not only Brazil but the entire planet. The Amazon forest and the Pantanal are two of the greatest natural patrimonies on this earth, and the opportunity to meet them face to face is an unsually precious privilege of living in this modern, Concordized era. Sadly, and this is the very *real* state of our planet at present, if you don't take up this privilege NOW, there may not be time in the future to do so, so delicate is their preservation and so fast is their destruction.

A critic once wrote that *Fielding's Brazil* was "idiosyncratic" (was she being complimentary?!), but the fact is, I love to write idiosyncratic books. In my opinion, whenever you actually commit yourself to leaving home and traveling abroad, you should absolutely surrender and throw yourself in hook, line and sinker. That means you need to learn everything you can, like who's fighting whom, who's destroying what, and who's banding together and struggling to survive. When you travel, I believe, you *have* to engage yourself in the life-and-death dramas that create environments on every level—physical, social and spiritual. And in that way, you will return from your trip a different person, a *transformed* person, and you will be able to contribute that much more to the community you return to.

That's what *Fielding's Amazon* is all about. In this first edition you will find a plethora of interesting facts, analyses and personal opinions that should help you begin to see the forest *for* the trees—facts revealing what the Amazon basin looked like before it split off from Africa billions of years ago, how the early explorers and scientists traipsed through the forest smeared with crocodile grease, how the early native population fought for centuries to stave off the inevitable invasion. You'll discover what is really happening behind the closed doors on Indian reservations and what *you* can do to support the political struggles of native peoples, rubber tappers and nut gatherers. For the more technically oriented, there are guides to the fauna and flora of both the Pantanal and the Amazon, and there's also a fine contribution by a leading international scientist that puts forth a fresh attitude toward forest intervention and the untapped potential of medicinal plants. There is also a look at the folklore, legends and crafts of the regions, and of course, there's *in-depth* travel information that tells you where to go, what to do and how to safely get home in one healthy piece. Researched especially for travel to Brazil, the "Health Guide for the Tropics" in the back of the book should be read *months* before planning any travel.

What can you do with this book, you might ask? If you sit on it, squeeze it to death and stomp on it a few times, it will easily fit into your knapsack. You can burn it for firewood when you find out your jungle guide has left his kerosene behind. You can pull it out on those long, soporific barge rides down the Amazon when you realize you've forgotten that fat, juicy novel. You can even shred it and feed it to piranha when you've mistakenly jumped into a bloody river full of just-gutted fish. Or you can simply sit back and enjoy it (and never go to the Amazon!) because there are several travel-adventure narratives that might keep you enthralled for days. (Some readers of *Fielding's Brazil* actually called me to say they had gotten into *bed* and read parts of it *out loud* to each other!) Well, I can't claim that *Fielding's Amazon* is as *sexy* as *Fielding's Brazil*, but I *can* guarantee you will feel a certain *frisson* when you read about the peculiar mating habits of culex mosquitoes.

In the final analysis, I have come to believe that *anybody* can go to the Amazon jungle. I wouldn't have thought so before I actually did, but there exists, in these regions, an adventure and mode of travel for every level of physical ability. Before you go, of course, you should take my "Should I Go to the Amazon Quiz", but if you fail it, don't worry—you still have an interesting book. If you *do* decide to go, make a promise to me right now that you will become the best *eco-conscious* traveler ever: that means traveling light, not unduly disturbing fauna and flora above or under the sea, and disposing of garbage properly. In other words, as they say in Brazil, "*Preserva A Natureza*" (Preserve Nature) and by doing so, we'll preserve the planet.

Not much else to say at this point, so for now, just go get out your hammock, your hiking boots and the strongest insect repellant you can find, and join me in an adventure you will *never* forget. As they say in Brazil, "*Vai com Deus*" (Go with God) and as I like to add, "Don't let the bed bugs bite."

PAMELA BLOOM

TABLE OF CONTENTS

LIST OF MAPS

FIELDING SURVEY

The author and publisher of Fielding's *Amazon* would like to hear your opinion of hotels, lodges, hostels, campsites and tour organizations. Please be as candid as you like and feel free to send your expanded comments on the reverse. If your comments are used you will receive a free Fielding Guide of your choice. Be concise, creative and opinionated.

Fielding Survey

Name:

Address:

City, State, Zip:

Phone Number:

Profession:

Date of visit to the Amazon:

Please tell us your opinion of your tour operator:

Tour Operator:

Please tell us the restaurants, hotels, lodges, hostels or campsites you chose and your opinion on them:

Location:

Location:

Fielding Survey

Location:

_____
_____
_____
_____
_____
_____
_____

Location:

_____
_____
_____
_____
_____
_____
_____

Location:

_____
_____
_____
_____
_____
_____
_____

Location:

_____
_____
_____
_____
_____
_____

"Should I Go to the Amazon?" Test

Take the following quiz to determine if you are a good candidate for an Amazon adventure. Don't cheat or it will come back to haunt you. If you rate more than six "Trues," sign up immediately; you'll probably actually enjoy yourself.

1. You are in good physical shape (heart and lungs), though you needn't be able to jog five miles.

2. You are able to withstand intense heat and humidity while trekking through a rugged forest on relatively flat land.

3. You do not flinch in the face of flying bugs, ticks, gnats, ants, or spiders and will not faint at the sight of a dead snake (screaming in the face of a live snake is permitted, but not encouraged).

4. You can endure less than haute cuisine for a few days, and, if you're traveling on a boat, severely cramped quarters.

5. Seasickness is not a problem for you, nor are you scared of small canoes with bad motors.

6. You are not overly allergic to bees or bug bites.

7. You are prepared to come home with arms and legs eaten up by mosquitoes.

8. You like mud.

9. You can handle intense, frequent rain.

10. You know how to psyche yourself to withstand "green overload," fear of the unknown, and that kind of squishy, moldy feeling that comes from being rained on and not able to change your clothes immediately.

AMAZÔNIA

Traveling through the Amazon is a rewarding challenge.

"How do I convey the scent of the wet forest, as ineffable as a mixture of crushed herbs?"

Loren McIntyre, photojournalist

"The Amazon is the last unwritten page of Genesis."

Euclides da Cunha, geographer and novelist

"Imagine if all the people in Amazônia decided in the next decade that they didn't want to treat the places they lived in as a commodity but as a sacred place."

Ailton Krenak, Krenak Indian

To travel through the great Amazon River region is a nature experience you will never forget. The innate wisdom of the forest—its voluptuous beauty, the life-and-death dramas of millions of species—are realities that will literally enter your bones as you tramp through the rain forest, cruise down the tributaries, or raft over rapids. The Amazon is about challenge, and ever since the first explorers stepped forth on the banks of the newly discovered continent, the dark, mysterious rain forest has inspired countless numbers to sacrifice life and limb for a little excitement and the promise of treasure.

These days, of course, travel through the Amazon need not be life-threatening, though it's still exciting, unpredictable and full of challenge. Despite all the recent political controversy, there's still a lot of poetry left in the rain forest: the liquid rustle of treetops, the elusive shadows of animals, the cries of unseen birds. But for most travelers, the most memorable part of a jungle adventure is the people—the locals who toil day by day in the jungle; *caboclo* fishermen who live like Indians along the river shores; old ladies who have fled to the jungle to escape city violence; little girls who paddle to school every morning and brush their teeth in the river. There are also Indians, those living on protected reservations, as well as those trying to survive halfway between "civilization" and tribal security. Add to that botanists and biologists and scientific photographers who are trying to capture the miracle of the ecosystem. And finally, there are the goldminers, rubber tappers, ranchers and industrialists—all, in their own way, attempting to bend the will of nature to their own commercial desires. A circus of cross-purposes, yes, but no matter what one's political allegiance is, each "jungle" person you meet will only add to your understanding of what the Amazon rain forest is and why it has become such a fragile paradise.

Traveling through the Amazon is not for couch potatoes, and you may have to do some solid soul-searching to see if you'll make a good candidate. (The "Should I Go to the Amazon?" quiz will separate the gnats from the gnus.) The best way to indoctrinate yourself is rent a few videos *(The Emerald Forest, Arachnophobia, At Play in the Fields of the Lord, Medicine Man)* or dive into travel-adventure narratives and novels that will let you feel the thrills without the thorns. Some of the best books are *Running the Amazon* by Joe Kane, *The Cloud Forest* by Peter Matthiessen, *Amazon Beaming* by Petru Popescu, *Amazônia* by Loren McIntyre, and (for laughs!) *Holidays in Hell* by P.J. O'Rourke.

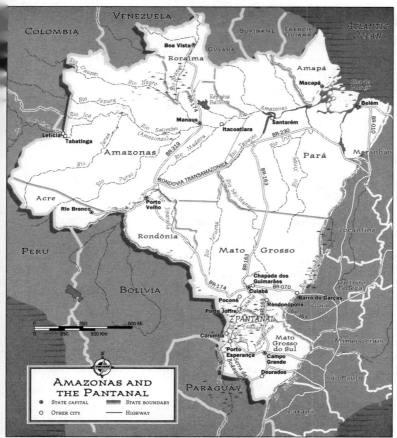

Amazonas and the Pantanal

A BIRD'S EYE VIEW

Maybe it was all those Tarzan movies, but to most people the phrase **The Amazon** has come to suggest a vast, humid jungle. Technically, the phrase "The Amazon" refers only to the river itself, including more than 1000 tributaries that stretch some 4000 nautical miles from the Atlantic Ocean to its source, Lago Lauricocha, high in the Peruvian Andes. Resembling a large funnel, the Amazon flows in a Y-shaped system into which its headwaters, the Negro-Branco, from the northwest, and the Madeira, from the southwest, converge. When the main trunk reaches the Brazilian border, it turns into the **Solimões**, a so-called "white river," dense with silt and microorganisms, until it meets the darker and clearer **Rio Negro**. Long a point of fascination among visitors, the "dark" and "light" rivers run parallel for several miles without mixing until they finally blend, forming the pale-brownish Amazon, as it is called until it empties into the Atlantic. The term Amazonas refers to Brazil's largest state (of which Manaus is the capital), which is part of Amazônia, a vast basin of forests and wetlands occupying about half of the South American continent (75 percent of Brazil, as well as parts of Venezuela, Ecuador, Peru, Suriname, Guyanas and Colombia). Within Brazil itself, Amazônia embodies the states of Amazonas, Acre, Rondônia, parts of Pará, Mato Grosso and Maranhão, and the territories of Roraima and Amapá.

AMAZONIAN FACTS

- Amazônia is the world's largest rain forest, covering 2.5 million square miles in countries.

- The Amazon River system is the planet's largest body of fresh water.

- The Amazon Basin, with 6 million square kilometers of river and jungle, is the world's largest in terms of volume and drainage. The basin holds two-thirds of all the flowing water in the world.

- Besides the Amazon River, there are 1100 tributaries (17 of which are more than 1000 miles long). All totaled, there are 48,000 miles of navigable rivers.

- The Amazon River is at times so wide (up to seven miles) that you can't see the other side of the shore.

- The flow of the Amazon River is 12 times that of the Mississippi.

- There are 15,000 known animal species, 1800 species of butterflies, 1200–2000 species of fish, four types of big cats and 200 mosquitoes. One-quarter of the world's 8600 bird species live in the Amazon.

AMAZONIAN MYTHS

Myth 1: Western fast-food chains like McDonald's are responsible for the destruction of the forest because of their use of cheap tropical beef.

Forests in Brazil are primarily cleared for pasture. Amazonian cattle ranching has no connection to the Western penchant for hamburgers. In the Amazon, cattle are used primarily as an excuse for claiming land that often has little to do with the profitability of ranching. In fact, the Amazon is net beef importer.

Myth 2: The Amazon's worst destroyers are small settlers and peasants who set fire to the forest for small-scale agriculture.

In truth, large-scale landowners and corporations are the biggest destroyers of the forest who often set massive forest on fire to clear land for ranching and mining.

Myth 3: If cultivated properly, the Amazon forest could feed the world.

This is a myth left over from the 19th century. In actuality, Amazon soil, due to its monocultural system, is most often poor and requires vast sums of fertilizers and insecticides to yield suitable crops. According to present-day scientists, if a vast array of agricultural techniques are utilized, including agroforestry and the exploitation of areas of fertile soil, it is conceivable that a large population could actually survive by living off the forest.

Myth 4: The Amazon basin is full of plants, not minerals.

The Amazon basin is loaded with mineral reserves: 97 percent of Brazil's bauxite reserves, 48 percent of manganese, 77 percent of its atanho, and 60 percent of its kaolin. The Amazon has the largest iron ore deposit in the world, and also produces gold and oil.

Myth 5: Nobody lives in the forest.

As late as a Census Bureau report in 1985, it was generally believed by the Brazilian public that there were no people in the Amazon forest. In truth, there are over two million people, including Indians, rubber tappers, river dwellers, nut gatherers and herb collectors.

AMAZONIAN LEGENDS

Legends and superstitions seem to lurk behind every plant or animal in the Amazon jungle; don't hesitate to ask locals about their folk beliefs. Among the most "enchanted" of jungle beings are *botos*, or dolphins, who are thought to transform themselves at night into white-suited cads and seduce young virgins. It's even said that *botos* are particularly attracted to the scent of menstrual blood—a folk belief so powerful that girls often refuse to bathe in the river during their periods.

The *japiim*, an Amazonian bird, also enjoys a notorious reputation. Legend has it that in the early days of the jungle, the *japiim* had a very beautiful voice, which secured him a place in Heaven right next to God. One day he came to earth and tried imitating the songs of the other male birds. When he started attracting all the females, their enraged spouses told him to get lost or reap the punishment. Desperate, the *japiim* turned to the bees for help, who allowed him to make his nest right next to theirs. As such, you can always find a bee hive near the nest of a *japiim*, whose song is often mistaken for that of other birds.

The mystical origin of the **lily pad** is particularly evocative. Once a beautiful but ambitious girl named Arari wanted to be just like the moon. She tried climbing a great mountain to reach it, but finally jumped to her death from despair, falling into a glimmering lake. The moon, who had a bigger heart than most imagined, took pity on the girl and decided to transform her into a part of the forest. Hence was born the lily pad, which is formed from a blossom that sinks to the bottom of the river, then resurfaces.

HISTORY OF THE AMAZON

THE CONQUEST

"With eyes wide open, the conquistadors lived in a lucid and endless delirium."

Jean Desola

A billion years ago there was no South America, not even an Amazon jungle. Over one single planetary landmass called **Pangea**, seas simply advanced and retreated; the only life forms were bacteria and algae. What would eventually become known as Amazônia (today called the Brazilian and Guianian shields) were merely the two highest points of land—massifs of ancient gneissic and granitic rock that formed a V-shaped flank. About 280 million years ago, as Pangea broke into north and south sectors, Amazônia became a vast inland sea opening to the Pacific. Some 150 million years later, the area called South America began to disconnect from Africa and drift westward, giving birth to the Atlantic Ocean. Then, a mere two to four million years ago, the Andes heaved themselves skyward, breaking through the soft hills of the two "shields" and initiating a flow to the Atlantic. Sediment and sand from the weathering massifs created a diverse basin floor, creating what is today termed *terra firme* (the solid floor of the forest). By the time the Pleistocene Era entered, some 1.6 million years ago, the forest itself, with its tall slender trunks, tangled canopy, and leaf-littered soil, finally emerged into being.

Scientists conjecture that the first humans arrived in the Amazon some thirty thousand years ago, over the Bering land bridge, as they fled the advancing ice cap. At that time Amazônia must have seemed a warm inviting refuge in contrast to the cold and empty highlands that offered little sustenance. Most assuredly, the first Amazonian inhabitants encountered luxuriant plant life, copious fish, manatees and giant turtles—all which they heartily consumed. Most likely, these early native tribes were also hunter-gatherers, living off the fruits of the jungle and practicing the slash-burn technique of shifting agriculture that is still used today. By the time the first Europeans arrived in the late 15th century, there were probably around six million native people scattered all over Brazil.

Since the moment the New World was sighted, however, the Old World marched in mercilessly to conquer, subjugate and exploit; neither human nor animal nor plant life were spared. Christopher

Columbus' 1942 discovery of the Americas opened Pandora's box, and in 1493, a papal decree was already divvying up the world between the two major powers; Portugal received control of all territory east of the longitude line running through Cape Verde Island, while Spain retained the western half. No less than a year later, the **Treaty of Tordesillas** moved this division 370 leagues to the west, giving Portugal even more control of a vast space that at the time seemed to do nothing more than protect the Crown's claims in the South Atlantic. Once word of a new continent had been spread, hungry adventurers—from Spain, Britain, France, Holland and the Holy Roman Empire—all stood poised to raise forts and missions along the confluences of rivers and significant tributaries.

What first inspired the early European explorers to traipse wearily through a hot, humid forest, was myth, pure and simple. Four centuries ago, the most prevailing one was that of **El Dorado**, a tribal chieftain whose wealth was so vast that he supposedly tattooed his body daily with gold dust. In 1540 **Gonzalo Pizarro**, the brother of the conqueror of Peru, launched an expedition with Ecuadorian general **Francisco Orellana** to conquer the lands of El Dorado and his "Cinnamon Forests"—a vast country so magical that it was rumored to be carpeted with the aromatic spice so beloved back home. The trip itself proved disastrous, but the threat of disease and imminent starvation finally compelled Orellana to break from the main troops and scavenge the jungle with his own party, eventually discovering the mouth of the Amazon.

It's from Orellana's own journal that we first hear reports of a fierce tribe of women warriors who once a year invited male adults to participate in their mating rituals. In fact Orellana even used the fact of sighting them as the primary excuse for never returning to Pizarro's troops. Whether Orellana's sighting was real or merely a mirage born of jungle fever has never been determined, but the tale, soon bloated from retelling, came to inspire thousands of booty-seekers called *bandeirantes* to follow in his footsteps. Later, Spanish scholars dubbed the region and its massive river "the Amazon" in honor of the women warriors in Greek mythology who removed their right breast so they could more skillfully use a bow and arrow.

From the earliest expeditions, Jesuit priests made their way across the ocean to subjugate the so-called native "heathens" and establish the sovereignty of the Church under the Crown's blessing. With little or no sensitivity to the integrity of native customs and spiritual traditions, the missionaries systematically stripped the subjugated tribes of their life-styles, indoctrinating them, however feebly, in Christian mores, and sometimes even dressing them up as Europeans. Jesuit priests could often be astute observers, however, as was one **Father Cristobal de Acuña**, whose eight-month sojourn from Quito to Belém with the Portuguese explorer **Captain Pedro Teixeira** in 1638-9 provided a wealth of insights. In his journal published under the title of *A New Discovery of the Great River of the Amazons*, Father Acuña wrote glowingly of ten-feet jungle giants, dwarfs no bigger than tender babies, and humans with their feet turned backwards (the latter is still accepted as belief by forest people). As was the tradition at the time, Acunã even had his own female warrior sighting, claiming the fierce ttribe of women he had glimpsed had not released their arms until they were confident of their male visitors' peaceful intentions. More importantly, Acuña recorded the fishing and hunting customs of various tribes and neatly identified the principal resources of the region, which remain to this day its most viable products.

Jungle travel, however, was not limited to men. One of the greatest tales of grit and courage was that of the 18th-century **Madame Godin**, who faithfully waited in Quito for over 15 years for her husband to return from a French scientific expedition. Finally hearing reports of a rescue party on the upper Marañon, she staunchly set off over the Andes with her two children, brother and several servants in tow. When she finally arrived at a village, expecting to find her husband, she discovered it had long been decimated by smallpox, thus forcing her to continue down the river without maps, food or guides. After her canoe was lost in the rapids, her bedraggled party was forced to continue on foot, but soon everyone, except Madame Godin, died from starvation or exhaustion. After nine days struggling alone in the jungle, Madame Godin was found by Indians who took her to the mission village. Finally, after a nineteen-year separation, this valorous lady, who had been to "green hell" and back, was finally reunited with her husband in Belém.

By the end of the 17th century the Amazonian pie had been carved and served—Spain and Portugal being the only real contenders. By the mid-1700s, scientists had caught up with adventurers, and in one of the most memorable expeditions, a team of botanists, astronomers, and respected intellectuals descended down the Amazon River with **Charles Marie de la Condamine**, a brilliant, young French mathematician who was determined to prove whether the earth bulged at the equator and flattened out at the poles, or vice versa. Regarding Amazonian lore, La Condamine's insights were invaluable: he found Indians (the **Omaguas** on the Solimões River) who pierced their ears, used *cahuchu* (a form of rubber) to make unbreakable vessels, and partook enthusiastically of a hallucinogenic powder made from the *curupá* plant. More fantastical, however, were his claims that the famed women warriors of the region had finally moved and settled in the heart of Guiana.

As new discoveries of land and sea were made, navigational maps began to shed some of their mystical references, to be replaced by freshly drawn demarcations and boundaries. Perhaps the most momentous geographical discovery was that made by **Alexander von Humboldt** in 1800 of the Casquiare River, following the flow from its confluence with the Rio Negro to its starting point on the Orinocco. That this waterway was truly navigable was earth-shattering news in the Industrial Age, since it provided the access to expand trade on both sides of the Atlantic.

The 19th-century travelers who visited Amazônia were a different breed from the elegant noblemen and the rough-and-ready *bandeirantes* who preceded them. Spurred by public enthusiasm, crowned heads of various European countries organized scientific expeditions led by some of the greatest minds of the century. In a hotbed of novelty like the tropical forest, botanical discoveries could often seem like magic. For example, in the 1840s Robert Schomburgh stumbled upon a gigantic water lily, some six feet across, that looked like an enormous pie plate. It was a testimony to his political loyalties that he christened the flamboyant green, pink and red flower *Victoria regis*, in honor of the British sovereign, **Queen Victoria**.

Two of the most dedicated Amazonian scientists were **Henry Walter Bates** and **Alfred Russel Wallace**. When they first met to share their jungle fever, one was an apprentice to a hosiery manufacturer and part-time bug collector, and the other was a schoolteacher. The British Museum commissioned the pair to compile a collection of insects and plants—three pence for every specimen received in "salable condition"—and in 1848 they arrived in Belém eager but penniless. The entomologist Bates, who would become the founder of protective mimicry, walked through the forest looking like a human pincushion, collecting over 14,712 species (eight thousand which were new to science). Wallace, determined to solve the problem of the origin of the species, spent four years on the Rio Negro, later contributing significantly to Darwin's resolution of the matter before the Linnaean Society in London. And yet as analytical as he was, Wallace could also wax poetical about Amazonian wonders, as his journal attests: *"The beauty and brilliance of this insect are indescribable, and none but a naturalist can understand the intense excite-*

ment I experienced when I at last captured it. On taking it out of my net and opening the glorious wings, my heart began to beat violently, the blood rushed to my head, and I felt more like fainting than I have done when in apprehension of immediate death. I had a headache the rest of the day..."

Scientific glee, however, didn't succeed in warding off the massive threat of jungle life. Humboldt's own adventure became a living hell when the crocodile grease he daily smeared on his body failed to work. Bates was attacked by innumerable insects and blood-sucking bats, almost overcome by malaria, and was even robbed by an Indian assistant who left him shoeless for an entire year. He even reported being deeply unnerved by the screeching of howler monkeys and other mysterious jungle sounds, like the clanging of iron, that woke him in the middle of the night. Perhaps the most poignant description of frustration came from the English botanist **Richard Spruce**, who wrote in his diary: *"Save willing Indians to run like cats or monkeys up the tree for me...the only way to obtain the wildflowers and fruits was to cut down the tree, but it was long before I could overcome a feeling of compunction at having to destroy a magnificent tree, perhaps centuries old, just for the sake of gathering flowers."*

It was rubber, not gold, that transformed the face of Amazônia. Contrary to popular belief, the rubber trade in Amazônia started long before Charles Goodyear accidentally discovered rubber in 1839. As early as 1750, Dom José, King of Portugal, was sending his boots to be waterproofed in Pará, and by 1800 Belém was exporting rubber shoes to New England The famous Amazonian rubber boom, however, was actually fueled by the debt peonage of isolated *serengueiros* (rubber tappers) and *caboclos* (backwoodsmen) who sold their balls of latex to the trading post for mere pittance. It's been estimated that in 1850 there were 5200 rubber workers; by 1912 when the boom peaked, no less than 190,000 Brazilians were tapping 88 percent of the world's rubber. During these giddy years, **Manaus** became a boom city, its wealth concentrated in the hands of about 100 men—so-called "rubber barons" who drank Hennessey brandy, dined on Irish linen, and built palatial homes. Soon, electricity was installed and the first tramway in South America initiated. The crowning glory in Manaus was a massive customs building modeled on that of New Delhi, prefabricated in England, and shipped to Brazil piece by piece.

In 1870, a young Englishman named **Henry Wickham**, in cahoots with the Royal Botanical Gardens at Kew, conspired a scam that would totally puncture the rubber future of Brazil. Working with the

Tapiu Indians, a detribalized tribe, Wickham raced to gather hevea seeds at their prime, smuggled them past customs with a large dose of charm, then nursed them across the Atlantic to Le Havre, where a special chartered train delivered them to Kew. From there, the seedlings were rushed to Ceylon, where in the swampy fields of Sri Lanka, the few that survived came to form the basis of the great rubber plantations of Malaysia. In a mere 24 years, the trees matured, outstripping the Amazonian market, which burst totally in 1923. With frightening speed, tycoons, speculators, traders and prostitutes departed from the tropics, leaving behind decayed palaces, a boarded-up opera house, and cobblestones full of weeds. The only beneficiaries were the native people, who would be left in peace for another half-century.

It was only a natural extension of the modern pulse that the 20th century would witness the veritable "pushing back of the jungle" or at least, determined attempts to tame it. In 1912 one of the region's most illustrious visitors was **Theodore Roosevelt**, who made an indefatigable voyage down the basin's southern tributaries. A river discovered on that mission, first called River of Doubt, was later renamed Rio Roosevelt.) Traveling intimately with local tribespeople, Roosevelt developed a greater respect for native intelligence than some of his predecessors, but his attitude toward wildlife, alligators in particular, was hardly allied to conservation: *"The ugly brutes lay on the sand flats,"* he wrote, *"...like logs...it is good to shoot them. I killed half a dozen and missed nearly as many—a throbbing boat does not improve one's aim."*

Even as late as the 20th century, tall tales were still coming out of the Amazon, and the tallest came from **Percy Fawcett**, a retired English army colonel sent to the upper Amazon in 1906 to resolve the overlapping claims of Bolivia and Peru arising from the rubber boom. Fawcett reported rumors of anacondas swallowing cattle whole and picking men right out of canoes at night, and he even claimed he once smelled a penetrating fetid odor emanating from one, *"probably its breath,"* he wrote, *"which is known to have a stupendous effect."* Fawcett also complained about the anacondas' melancholy wails at night—a phenomenon never proven by scientists. Certainly, a colorful figure, Fawcett carried no radio during his expedition, which didn't seem to matter since several spiritualists, including his wife, claimed to be in psychic contact with him. Ever in search of the lost city supposedly discovered by the Portuguese explorer Francisco Raposo in 1754, Fawcett was eventually found dead near the mouth of Xingú River, most probably murdered by Kalapa-lo tribesmen.

Only a few years later, in 1927, another world-famous American would also leave his mark in the Amazon. A most curious jungle saga began when automobile mogul **Henry Ford**, after researching sites around the world, decided that the Tapajós Valley was the best region in which to cultivate rubber trees on an international scale. (Curiously, no Brazilian had ever given it much thought.) Capitalizing on a contract that awarded him 110,000 kilometers of forest for 50 years, Ford actually transported an entire prefabricated city into the jungle, complete with all the modern facilities. The community, appropriately named **Fordilândia**, was light years ahead of other cities in the Amazon basin. Workers reaped the benefit of free housing, electric light, running water, telephones, schools, theater, nurseries, orchards and the best equipped hospital in the state of Pará.

What Ford didn't anticipate was an explosion between the social classes, including an outbreak (known as the "saucepan-breaking incident") when the native workers demanded back their old food—beans, manioc flour and cachaça—instead of the protein-enriched American rations. The real downfall of the enterprise, however, was attributed to a fungus known as "leaf blight" that devastated the plantation. In 1934, the same venture was attempted in another tract of land 60 kilometers south of Santarém (called **Belterra**), but it, too, was attacked by the same fungus as well as caterpillar blight. Today ecologists understand that the root of the disasters was monoculture—the lack of any other species that could balance the delicate ecosystem of the jungle. After 17 years the Ford company finally gave up the enterprise and "presented" the government of Brazil with the remains of the two communities for $250,000 (a loss of more than $20 million). Today, Fordilândia, though still inhabited, resembles a ghost town, with its deserted shed and picket-fence houses—a mere shadow of the imposing structures erected during the '20s and '30s.

From the time the hunting-gathering natives of ancient history first followed the massive prehistoric mammals into the lowlands to the bitter end of the rubber boom, the commercial attitude toward the Amazon's resources was almost exclusively extractive. The concept of making an investment was entirely foreign—the modus operandi was simply to take, pick up, or dig out what was there. Henry Ford was actually the first major investor to encounter serious nationalist opposition, culminating in the 1940s when **Gétulio Vargas** seized power of the federal government and urged the nation away from Atlantic shores and toward occupying—even exploiting—their own vast, and as it seemed then, unlimited space. The military coup of March 31, 1964, which threw the country into a right-wing dictatorship for more than 20 years, stabilized sentiments of the Brazilian army that were deeply rooted in nationalistic tendencies. Although conflicting attitudes about Amazônia did surface at this time, the prevailing notion continued to favor the notion of occupation as a principle of national security.

In the face of threatening foreign domination, especially from North America, the government initiated the building of the **Carretera Marginal**, a Trans-Andean highway that opened rich new lands on the eastern slopes of the Peruvian Andes. In 1965 **President Castello Branco** effected Operation Amazônia that included the issuance of several laws that would inspire development. Although Brazilian leaders in the late '60s more or less ignored the idea of small-farmer colonization in Amazônia, **President Juscelino Kubitschek**, as part of his 50 years-in-five progress program, began a road to serve as the east-west counterpart of the Belém-Brasília Highway, linking the town of Cuiabá in Mato Grosso with Porto Velho. It was down this road, often overgrown with jungle the moment it was completed, that pioneers valiantly trod, jumping off their trucks to clear jungle with their own hands and building primitive shacks along the highway. As a result, when a mineral rush of cassiterite and tin ore was discovered in 1952, Porto Velho became an overnight boom town, creating the kind of rough-and-ready frontier that made the jungle itself seem an "oasis of tame." A sign on the classic Porto Velho Hotel said something about the usual clientele: "Spit neither on the floor, nor on the walls, nor beside the bed."

Highways have been the bulldozers of primitive culture, and in 1970 President **Emilio Garrastazu Médici**, shocked by the poverty in the Northeast, decided to build a road that would provide refuge into the fertile Amazônia. The Trans-Amazon highway ran east to west from the town of Marabá on the Tocatins River, due south of Belém, clear across to Benjamin Constant on the Solimões at the border with Columbia. An additional plan was to settle one million families at selected spots along the highway, where it was felt there was good farming. Despite promises of easy credit, health, education and technical assistance, substantial obstacles arose: malaria epidemics, poor soil and lack of social integration. Soon larger commercial enterprises superceded concern for the individual migrant, and by the mid-1970s cash development for large-scale Brazilian and foreign enterprises pushed the rate of Amazonian deforestation sharply up as virgin forests were cleared for cattle-grazing.

In 1979, the owner of a two-bit cattle ranch, **Gensio Ferreira de Silva**, discovered that his scrubby grasses and skinny cows were astride the most important gold strike in Amazonian history. By 1985, over 500,000 prospectors were toiling up and down the vast pits dug into the mountainside—a frightening tableau of human mudmen right out of a Breughel painting. The federal government, worrying about the potential danger of so many unruly men near Carajás, the largest iron development in the world, finally sent in troops. In May, 1984, the military occupied the **Serra Pelada**, led by **Major Cúrio**, who, descending from his helicopter, flashed his Magnum and cried, "The gun that shouts loudest is mine." Though the military occupation brought a much needed health center, bank, post office, telephone line and wholesale government store, the *garimpeiros* (goldminers) staged a rebellion down the Belém-Brasília Highway, eventually forcing the government to retreat.

The last two decades of Amazonian history have erupted in an openly bloody conflict between all the inhabitants of the forest as goals, life-styles and environmental concerns have collided in cross-purposes. As international environmental organizations, backed by the warnings of eminent international scientists, have protested to preserve the rain forest in the face of irrevocable planetary destruction, those who live and work in the forest have struggled to maintain their own individual lives. At least in the Brazilian segment of the Amazon forest, this socioeconomic dilemma must be understood against the backdrop of the enormous financial crisis threatening the entire country (not only overweening inflation, but ongoing natural disasters such as severe droughts in the Northeast), which force Brazilians to eke out livings in any way they can. Consequently, many who become gold miners (the life of which is difficult, dirty and often without pay-off), are forced to do so because of even worse circumstances back home. Nevertheless, their merciless invasion of government-sanctioned Indian reserves have increasingly erupted in violent clashes with tribespeople; their pollution of rivers and streams with mercury continues to devastate not only wildlife but human life as well.

The most prominent name in recent Amazonian activism was that of **Chico Mendes**, a poor rubber tapper born in Seringal, Cachoeira. Illiterate until the age of 18, he gained most of his worldly education from listening to Radio Moscow, Voice of America and the BBC Portuguese Service; when he finally learned to read, he discovered the price of rubber was being outrageously exploited by the *seringalistas*. As ranchers and settlers came to clear the rain forest, the rubber tappers were forced to leave, but Chico refused, urging his fellow workers to unionize. With no knowledge of Gandhi or Martin Luther King, Mendes naturally hit upon the idea of nonviolent resistance, and in 1976 organized a series of human stand-offs that prevented work crews from using their chainsaws. In 1989, Indians joined the lobby in favor of extractive reserves set aside for use by rubber tappers and gatherers of nuts, fruits and fibers; today over a million acres of forest have been preserved. In December 1988, after returning home from a labor-organizing trip, Mendes stepped into his backyard and was fatally blasted by a shotgun at close range. The 31-year-old son of a rancher who hated Mendes finally confessed to the murder, but general opinion conceded that his father, **Darli Alves**, was to blame. In 1993, father and son escaped from a loosely secured prison in Rio Branco, Acre, and have not been found. Following the murder of Mendes, Hollywood descended on his family and his wife, Ilzamar, who was reported to have received a million dollars for the right to his life story.

The 1990s will be decisive for Amazônia. Before the dawning of the third millennium, planners and policy-makers must decide whether the world's largest remaining area of tropical rain forest will follow much of Africa and Asia down the path of irreversible destruction, or whether the resources for this vast region will be harnessed for the benefit of Brazilian society and the world as a whole. The Brazilian portion of the Amazon Basin occupies two-thirds of the entire region's 4.2 million square kilometers. By the end of 1988, it was estimated that 12,000 square miles of forest, the size of Belgium, had already disappeared from the face of Amazônia, that is to say, 12 percent of the total forested area.

For more information on the history of the Indians in Brazil, see the following chapter.

THE INDIAN ISSUE

The real history of the Amazon region belongs to its native peoples—a subject that deserves not a few paragraphs but tomes (among the best of which are *Red Gold* and *Amazon Frontier: The Defeat of the Brazilian Indians* by John Hemming). When the first explorers arrived in 1500, there were 6-9 million Indians in the Amazon basin; today they are less than 200,000. Like all North American Indians, those of the Amazon Valley had descended from **Paleo-Mongoloids**, somewhere between 30,000-70,000 years ago, having crossed from

Siberia to Alaska on a temporary land bridge over the frozen Bering strait. Their features, still apparent today, were clearly mongoloid, with high cheekbones, black eyes and an epicarthic fold of the eye; characteristically, they had no beard, eyebrows or eyelashes. Indeed, so strong was their connection to the East that many of their arti-facts—blowgun, penis sheath, panpipe and the chewing of lime or ashes with a narcotic—can be found in indigenous Asian cultures. The Indian peoples who entered the New World were already ac-complished hunters, used to stalking game, mastodons, mammoths, ground sloths, giant cats and even camels. As they moved slowly (one kilometer a year), it took these tribal people 40,000 years to reach the rain forest, gradually evolving from nomadic hunters to farmers. As they fanned out and became isolated, four major linguis-tic groups developed—**Tupi Guarani**, **Jê**, **Karib** and **Aruak**. A few of the most remote tribes like the Trumai and Yanomami invented lan-guages that have no relation to others spoken in the Amazon basin, or, indeed, anywhere else in the world.

When **Pedro Alvares Cabral**, the Portuguese explorer credited with "discovering" Brazil in 1500, first set foot on soil in what is now the state of Bahia, the native people who shyly met his boat were friendly enough, even generous in their innocence. They were Tupi-Guarani, who were short and bronze-colored, with long straight black hair. Though the Tupis tended toward cannibalism (they ate the first bishop to arrive in Bahia), they were true masters of tropical survival—cleaning and pruning just enough land for their crops, wearing no clothes and indulging in intricate body designs made from the juice stains of plants. Although they were not equal in culture to the sophisticated Aztecs of Central Mexico, the Mayas of Yucatan and Guatemala, and the Incas of Peru, they had developed a strong tradition of spirituality, in which the *pajé* or medicineman, communed with nature spirits and prescribed herbal medicines culled from the forest. Though these pajés were known to be deeply visionary, the one thing they did not foresee was their own imminent destruction.

What today makes up the characteristic multiethnicity of the Bra-zilian people—a mixture of Portuguese, African and Indian roots—owes its origin to those early white colonists who mixed freely with the Indian population. Among the first white men the Indians en-countered were often *degredados*—exiled criminals ordered to live among the Indians and learn their language. Since Portuguese women were excluded from the first colonies, the conquerors, who were already accustomed to the dark-skinned beauty of the Moorish,

African and Asian females, soon discovered a veritable paradise. Some men, like **Diogo Alvares** (renamed **Caramuru**) actually sired an entire village of miscegenational offspring with Indian women. As a result, a new race quickly appeared—the *mameluco* or *caboclo*—a blend of European and Indian blood well adapted to the physical demands of living in the tropics. In return, the Indian taught the white man the best methods for farming and hunting, introduced him to new crops like manioc, and showed him the best way to pass the night in the tropical heat—in a hammock.

As ship captains bartered with Indians, exchanging trinkets for brazilwood, a temporary truce between them was enjoyed. But soon enough, Jesuit missionaries set out to convert the "heathens." At the same time the arriving colonists, supported by daring explorers, were rounding up conquered Indians as candidates for enforced labor. In time, the Jesuits would severely antagonize the Court with their viewpoint that the enslavement of Indians was contrary to Christian intent, but the fathers themselves managed to violate their subjects' basic human dignity. Institutionalized in missions called Reductions, the Indians were forced to adapt to a spartan routine of work and worship. (One Amazonian historian suggested that the transition to the rigid discipline of the Reductions was made easier for the Indians by the fact that, long before the Jesuits' appearance, flagellation had played an important part in their religious and erotic lives.) Nevertheless, though some Indians became acculturized, most either rebelled or ran away, or, more frequently, succumbed to death when their immune systems proved too weak to fight even the slightest Western cold germ. Fortuitously, in 1769, under pressure from business interests, the King of Portugal threw the Jesuits out of the Amazon. (In the 20th century, the Salesians, who are Roman Catholic, are still making converts, as well as the nondenominational Summer Institute of Linguistics, begun in the 1930s, to teach indigenous populations to read and write in their own tongue, with the ultimate goal of translating the New Testament. In 1977 FUNAI, the federal Indian-protection agency, canceled their permit under suspicions they were a CIA front.)

The Jesuit missionaries were only one form of unnatural control. What truly undermined the Indian was *cachaça*, happily provided by the *bandeirantes* (rough-and-hardy pioneers), who soon discovered that liquor was the only way to press-gang the natives into submission. The tribes that escaped such ignominy, including the rape of their women, the theft of their children, and a legacy of incurable alcoholism, retreated deeper and deeper inside the forest.

Some of the journals of the early scientists often revealed the depth of the western prejudice toward meeting "uncivilized" tribes. In 1854 **Alfred Wallace Bates**, the entomologist, discovered an unspoiled village in Matari, what he called "a miserable little settlement of Mura Indians." As he inspected the twenty slightly built "mud hovels," he discovered several women who were employed cooking a meal. As he wrote in his journal: "Portions of a large fish were roasting over a fire made in the middle of the low chamber and the entrails were scattered about the floor, on which the women with their children were squatted. They offered us no civilities; they did not even pass the ordinary salutes, which all the semi-civilized and savage Indians offer on a first meeting. The men persecuted Penna for *cachaça* (sugarcane liquor), which they seemed to consider the only good thing the white man brings with him."

Although many scientists held a similar disdain, one group of 19th-century Portuguese explorers, armed with awe, talent and respect, did make a momentous journey through the Amazon, compiling an invaluable collection of illustrations documenting the life of Indians and fauna. A doctor of natural philosophy, **Alexandre Rodrigues Freire** and his companions who were artists from the Royal Natural History Collection in Lisbon, covered over 24,800 miles in nine years, painting and drawing a variety of Indian tribes with such magnificence that their work became true journalistic art.

By depicting the everyday tools and weapons of the Indian, Freire and his team came to deeply respect the ingenuity of the tropical Indian who had learned how to extract the best potential from the plant world. Through trial and error, the natives had learned that reeds could be used for arrows, that toxic vines beaten in the water could daze fish; that the seeds of the Beixa orellana smeared on the skin could give it a bright red color; and that resins or infused leaves, when ingested, could produce hallucinogenic symptoms.

A typical story of native development and demise is that of the **Xavantes**, once one of the proudest tribes in Amazônia. At the turn of the 18th century, two thousand *bandeirantes* led by Captain de Moto, settled on the Rio das Mortes, in the heart of Xavante country, winning confidence by giving gifts. One day, however, a *bandeirante* killed a Xavante, and the next day the entire settlement of pioneers was wiped out. In 1765, the governor of the state of Goiás sent a man named Tristão de Cunha to reestablish friendly relations; he eventually persuaded a few thousand Indians to settle closer to the city of Goiás. But when the Indians managed to eat all the food in the city, the order was given to Portuguese troops to drive them away. Half the Xavante community was killed, the rest retreated behind the Rio das Mortes and killed every white man in sight. Until 1842, when they allowed an anthropologist to study them, they remained an isolated and feared tribe.

Of the 260 Amazon tribes that were identified by studies in 1900, only 143 remain today, totaling about 250,000 individuals. In western Amazônia, several villages of **Amahuaca**, **Machiguenga**, and the head-hunting **Jivaros** live well back from the main river. In Acre, along the Peruvian frontier are the **Mayoluno** and some of the more remote **Mayarunas**; in Amazonas the **Macu** and several other small groups. In Rondônia live the **Caheça-Secas**, some of the **Surui**, and some of the **Cintas-Largas**. In the northeastern state of Pará, there are three **Kayapo** and one **Kreen-Akroare** villages and several in Mato Grosso. (This is only a partial list.)

In the second half of the 20th century, the onslaught of "progress" has continued to devastate the native population. The construction of the two highways—the Transamerica and the Cuiabá-Santarem—has dislocated over 10,000 families (50,000 originally intended) and nearly wiped out through disease the tribes of the **Araba**, **Parkana**, **Kreen Akroare** and **Txucurramai**. In 1969, three Brazilian-born brothers named **Orlando**, **Claudio** and **Leonardo Villas-Boas** persuaded the government to create a national park for the Xingú tribe, whose lands during World War II had been invaded by the construction of military airstrips, connecting Rio to Manaus. Entranced by Indian life, the Villas-Boas brothers not only fought for native rights but also managed to live with various tribes for many years. (Today the Xingú National Park covers 12,000 square miles in Mato Grosso and houses 18 tribes living traditionally.) Until they succumbed to old age and malaria, the brothers fought valiantly to secure the federal government's protection of the area from rubber tappers, hunters, industrialists, journalists, missionaries and even anthropologists. In 1971, however, builders overrode public sentiment and drove Highway BR-080 right through the park.

Today Brazilian Indians are championed by FUNAI, the successor of the Indian Protection Service founded in 1910 by **Colonel Candîdo Mariano da Silva Rondon**, who himself was part Indian. The organization tries to mediate conflicts between Indians and *civilizados*, rubber tappers and nut gatherers, skin hunters, *caboclos*, gold miners and ranchers. They also contact remote tribes, explaining they are citizens of a country named Brazil and set up posts from which medicine, tools, clothing, fishing lines and other products are distributed. A controversial agency who is always dodging fire from all sides,

FUNAI itself was implicated several years back in the wholesale slaughter of Indians by dynamite, machine guns and sugar laced with arsenic.

In the late '50s and '60s, contact with some native tribes proved to be exceedingly tragic. A telling example is that of the **Kreen-Ak-roare**, a primitive, semi-nomadic group on a territory of 5000 square kilometers southwest of the Air Force base at Cachimbo in the state of Pará. The Kreens are mostly hunters who until lately couldn't even make pots or manioc bread and had never seen a gun. In 1957 their traditional enemies, the Menkranoti, armed with shotguns, attacked one of their villages; by the time the Kreens could flee, totally defenseless, fifteen of their tribesmen were dead. In 1961 the Kreens killed Richard Mason, an English botanist working near the Air Force. Six years later, a two-engine Air Force plane flew over another village. Kreens took aim and brought the plane down, killing twenty. In 1968 they were again attacked by Menkranoti, who killed 35 of them; when the Kreens approached the air base with corpses in hand, the commander panicked, fired shots in the air, and sent them running back into the forest. A year later, as two highways were being built through their count, the Villas-Boas brothers, who had been nominated for the Nobel Prize for setting up the Xingú National Park spotted some Kreens from the other side of the river. Since the brothers had other natives with them, they shouted to the Kreens in 14 different tongues, but the latter disappeared from sight.

In 1970 **Claudio Villas-Boas** returned bearing gifts, waiting for one year in the clearing without moving. Finally in February 1971, three Kreen appeared to Claudio and Orlando, who threw down their gun, paddled over and embraced. One tribesman gave a speech for an hour, but nobody understood him. Later, after being showered with gifts, 40 more Kreen showed up with women to dance. Claudio, knowing full well that the highways would kill the Indians, didn't finish the "contract" by entering their village, but later, another *sertanista* did. By 1972, 40 Kreen had died of pneumonia contracted from road crews building the Cuiabá-Santarem highway, now only two kilometers from their village. Soon the tribe was reduced to eating urucum seeds, from which their red body paint is derived; a picture in Rio's *Globo* newspaper, showed the devastatingly sad photo of several starving Indians on their knees begging for food.

In December 1974 only 70 Kreen were left, three-quarters killed by pneumonia, flu and malaria. The Villas-Boas brothers arranged for them to move to Xingú National Park, where the Kyabi agreed to give them their village of Prepuri along with some plantations. The Kreen had much to learn, however, like learning to fish with hook and line instead of arrows, and to cook manioc, instead of eating it in its poisonous raw state of toxic prussic acid. Eventually they had to move in with the Txucurramai because other Xinguano tribes would visit and eat their food, trying to intermarry and dominate them. They finally moved to a third village. In January 1976, only 64 remained at a time when only ten women could bear socially acceptable children.

In the last decade, Indian activism and international press coverage has reached record highs. During the 1980s Indians began to display political self-determination when a group of **Txurramai** from the Xingú National Park held the director of the Xingú Park hostage to demand demarcation of their land, severed from the rest of the park by Highway BR-080. For a short term, a Xavante Indian chief even enjoyed his own seat in Congress. In February 1989, in the town of Altamira, over 500 Indians from Amazon tribes gathered together with international environmentalists to protest the Brazilian Eletronorte's Xingú Dam Scheme. Few who were present (or saw the documentary film) will ever forget the sight of a Kayapo women brandishing a machete at Eletronorte's CEO and fervently crying: "Do you think we are so stupid that we don't know what your plans are for us, for this forest?"

In the last few years, a Kayapó Indian chief—**Paulinho Paiakan**—has emerged as a worldwide icon of native power. Touted as Brazil's wealthiest Indians, the 5000 Kayapo Indians earn millions of dollars a year in royalties from gold and mahogany reserves in central Brazil. In recent years, the chief solicited the support of the rock star Sting, who founded the Brazilian Rainforest Foundation and he even managed to sell brazil-nut oil to The Body Shop, an international cosmetic chain. But on the eve of a $40 million movie to be made of his life (not to mention numerous international awards), Chief Paiakan was abruptly arrested when the 19-year-old white Portuguese-language tutor of his children accused him of rape. In Brazil, a national furor erupted, turning environmentalists against feminists (the latter enraged that rapists rarely go punished in Brazil, and raising the ire of the Indian rights movement). The results of the case were still pending at press time.

Among the most tragic native situations at the present moment is that of the **Guarani-Kaiowá** of Jaquapiré, Mato Grosso, whose legally demarcated lands are being invaded by ranchers. As such, finding themselves without land, and without forest, the center of their religion, the 250 Guarani of this tribe have pledged to commit collective suicide if they are expelled from their homeland. In 1992 the area they occupy was declared their permanent possession by an act of the Minister of Justice, but ranchers persist at ever-increasing rates to clear forest for pasture. As a result, many have already committed suicide, and in the summer of 1994, their chief passionately addressed a conference sponsored in New York by the Amanaka'a Network, where she pleaded for international assistance.

Perhaps the most highly publicized tribe in the last few years has been the **Yanomami** tribe. The largest indigenous tribe in the Amazon, the Yanomami people, until the 1980s, was one of the most isolated tribes in the Amazon. Today approximately 9000 Yanomami live in the northern state of Roraima and another 12,000 across the border in Venezuela.

The name Yanomami means "human being." They live in small villages, grouped by family and kin in one large communal dwelling called a *shaboono*; this disc-shaped structure with an open-air central plaza, is an earthy version of their gods' abode. They hunt and fish over a wide range and tend large gardens, cultivating the forest.

A deep-seated animism lies behind the Yanomami's sacred traditions, a belief that the natural and spiritual world are a unified whole; nature is the source of all, and therefore sacred. They believe that their fate, and the fate of all people, is inescapably linked to the fate of the planet. Destroying the environment is, to the Yanomami, tantamount to suicide.

In the 1980s, the isolated lands of the Yanomamis were mercilessly invaded by miners in search of gold, diamonds and tin. In 1989, President **Sarney** brought national attention to the plight of the Yanomami Indians when their 9000-sq. kilometer reserve on the border between Brazil and Venezuela was overrun by 40,000 goldminers bringing sickness and disease. Military troopers were sent in, but in the end the army simply refused to subdue 45,000 burly *garimpeiros* (goldminers), even though they were poisoning the Yanomami River with mercury and attracting new strains of malaria. Today, some 70 percent of the Yanomami reservation has already been confiscated by mining concerns, but even more tragic has been the physical devastation brought on by constant contact with the outside world. The first case of AIDS has already been reported.

In recent years a devastating massacre of a Yanomami community brought international attention to their plight, but the government failed to act in retaliation and attempts were made to discredit first-hand reports. Tribesmen who escaped the massacre were loathe to testify for fear of reprisal. Today international organizations have started to galvanize support, one of the most active being the New York-based **Amanaka'a**, who raises money for the Yanomami Health Project (also supported by Oxfam and Medicine Sans Frontiers). Presently, the leader of the Yanomami, Chief Davi Kopenawa Ya-nomami has emerged not only as an international spokesman for his people, but as a spiritual voice for the planet. In 1988 he received the Global 500 Award from the United Nations for his efforts in pre-serving the environment.

At the present moment, however, the fate of the Amazonian Indi-an is trapped between a rock and a hard place. Despite valiant efforts by activist groups (including the Rainforest Action Network, the Rainforest Alliance, and others), the future of Indian tribes will more than likely depend on how well they can self-empower themselves and span thousands of years to step into the twenty-first century. Eternal protection in this age of the ubiquitous bulldozer will most likely prove itself to be a pale fantasy. Perhaps the only future is one of studied cooperation, a possible program which is put forth in a subsequent chapter called "A Scientist Speaks Out." Beyond threat of disease and loss of cultural identity, what the native population of the rain forest truly stands to lose in the inexorable forward-push of "progress" can hardly be grasped by dimmed western eyes. Perhaps the best answer was given by a Waura chief named Taxapuh who, when asked how he could return to his village after having been ex-posed to the wonders of São Paulo (he had been flown there for an emergency hernia operation), replied with stunning conviction:

"How can you breathe this foul air or sleep with these noises (of traf-fic)? How can you eat this food made to have tastes not its own? Why would men want to have intercourse with these women who are afraid to be women and hide themselves and cover their eyes? Who are these men with guns who stand in the paths of the village?"

A QUICK RAIN FOREST TOUR

To the uninitiated, the jungle looks like so much green mess, but actually the terrain that runs through the Amazon river system is extremely diverse. Some soils are deeply fertile, others approach bleached sand; along the Negro River, the vegetation is stunted, whereas in southeastern Pará, the forest, with its purplish-red soil, abounds with wildlife. There are also huge areas of wetlands and large expanses of savannah.

The rain forest itself grows in distinct layers, a natural hierarchy formed by the access (or lack of access) to the sun. Most of the activity takes place in the luxuriant canopy, 100–130 ft. above the forest floor, where plants compete for sunshine and where the majority of animals and birds live. Above the canopy poke the trees that form the skyline of the forest. A poorly defined middle layer of understory merges with the canopy, hosting a variety of epiphytes—plants that derive moisture and nutrients from the air and rain but live on the surface of other plants. About 50 to 80 feet above ground spreads a tangle of seedlings, saplings, bushes and shrubs. On the forest floor, plant life is limited because the thick vegetation of the canopy blocks out all but one to two percent of available sunlight. Ants and termites live here among the scattering of leaves and decaying plant matter.

TYPES OF FOREST • There are three types of Amazon forest: *várzea,* or floodplain, regularly flooded by the rivers; the *igapós,* which are occasionally flooded; and the *terra firme,* generally unflooded land that forms the majority of the surface area. Much of the terra firme is high forest where animal life exists as much in the canopy as on the ground. When the forest is destroyed, the land turns to scrub since its fertility is bleached out.

WHY PRESERVE THE FOREST? • Rain forests are intimately tied to global weather conditions, and their preservation helps prevent the global warming trend known as the Greenhouse Effect. Deforestation causes up to 30 percent of all human-produced carbon dioxide to the atmosphere, as well as unknown amounts of methane and nitrous oxide—gases that exacerbate global warming and threaten the quality of life worldwide. Rain forests also provide a natural defense against hurricanes, cyclones and typhoons, absorbing the punch of howling winds and preventing storm tides from eroding beaches.

The products that come from the rain forest are part and parcel of our daily lives. As a fantastic natural pharmacy, the forest is home to thousands of medicinal plants that can be turned into antibiotics, painkillers, heart drugs and hormones. The National Cancer Center in the U.S. has identified 3090 plants as having anti-cancer properties—70 percent of which come from the rain forest. Other products that can be taken from the forest without destroying it range from cosmetics to automobile tires.

Tropical forests also provide the planet with much of its biological diversity. Every species that lives there is a living repository of genetic information, i.e., the building blocks of life. If the food chain that binds them together in a complex web of relationships is disturbed, it is not clear that humankind itself could survive. At the very least, we'd be facing the future with a shrunken world, a hostile climate, and a genetic base vulnerable to mutations.

Last but not least, the forest is home to millions of indigenous people, who have known no other way of life for thousands of years. Within their memory banks is a trove of natural wisdom, including how to use plants medicinally, that can never be reduplicated once they pass from the earth. With very few exceptions, the forced relocation of indigenous forest people in the face of the bulldozer has invariably spelled disease, despair and death.

IS ECO-TOURISM KOSHER? Many eco-conscious travelers ponder whether joining the rank and file of tourists tramping through the rain forest will ultimately endanger it. Truly in Brazil, the phrase eco-tourism has become the buzz word for the 1990s, though in many cases it's merely a marketing device referring to any outdoor adventure, be it beach, mountain or forest. There are a select number of travel agencies and operators, however, who are deeply dedicated to preserving not only the forest but also its native peoples. Among these are **Expeditours** in Rio, **Lago Verde Turismo** in Santarém, and **Ariaú Jungle Tower** outside Manaus. A prevailing philosophy in Brazil these days is that eco-tourism actually serves to preserve the forest by giving its residents another way of making a living besides cutting down trees. Of course, one need only imagine the trash and debris that could clog the mighty Amazon and its tributaries when gum-chewing, smoking, beer-drinking tourists hit its banks. The nightmare needn't happen, however, if each traveler takes responsibility for his or her actions.

Eco Alert

The best way to preserve a rain forest is to travel with a conscience. Here are some Do's and Don'ts for visiting national reserves:

1. *Don't give food to the local animals.*

2. *Don't hunt.*

3 *Don't destroy trees or break branches.*

4. *Don't throw litter.*

5. *Don't kill turtles, fish, birds, or other animals except in self-defense.**

6. *Don't mistreat animals.*

7. *Don't make a fire.*

8. *Always have a reliable guide.*

9. *Do not cross into Indian reserves without special permission from FUNAI (nearly impossible to get). This law protects native people from unwanted diseases and cultural disturbance.*

*Federal law prohibits the killing of dolphins, turtles, alligators, peixe boi (cowfish), tortoises, birds, and capybaras. Any animal that lives in the forest belongs to the state. Anyone caught red-handed by IBAMA agents is sent to prison from three months to 1 year.

WHO'S WHO IN THE FOREST: A GUIDE TO FAUNA AND FLORA

Macaw

When you first set foot in the forest, you may be sorely disappointed. The only animals you may see are ants, mosquitoes, and a few transparent butterflies, surrounded by the sounds of crickets and cicadas, which create a kind of permanent background buzz. Unlike the zoo, animals don't exist in the forest to be seen—many are extremely well camouflaged. To really make write-home-about sightings, you should be prepared to stay for weeks and months crouched silently behind a bush. Simply, camouflage is the art of jungle survival, developed through millions of years. Bits of bark, green leaves, dead leaves, all sorts of leaf fragments with holes in them, small ticks, broken twigs, even pendant drops of water have been imitated by nature.

And forget looking for an elephant, rhinoceros, hippopotamus, zebra or giraffe in the Amazon. They don't exist. The largest animals, which are all actively hunted, include tapirs, peccaries (both the collared and white-lipped species), brockets (about the size of the European roe deer), and the larger marsh deer in the southern border regions. Raccoons, coatis, American potto, and the less well-known olingos belong to a family completely native to the Americas. Armadillos, anteaters and tree sloths are the last survivors of the *edentates*, a very ancient South American order of mammals. Cats like the jaguar, puma and ocelot have become rare. Scientists still ponder why there were many species of large animals throughout the Neotropical region during the Tertiary period, the last representatives which died out during the Pleistocene era. One theory is that the advent of the first humans led to their extinction when they were not able to defend themselves.

Eco-safari

To experience the Amazonian animal world firsthand, it's best to hire a boat for a day trip and be paddled or pooled down one of the numerous tributaries by a reliable and knowledgeable guide. It's best to choose a river that not only flows through the forest but also has side streams of its own and areas of still water covered with floating plant life.

If you are lucky, one of the first visitors to trail behind your canoe may very well be a sweetwater dolphin, of which there are two species in the Amazon. One of them, the Amazonian dolphin, grows to a length of 2.5-3 meters. The species is nearly blind and has to find its way through echo-sounding. There are also in the Amazon river and its tributaries a number of other creatures that originated in the ocean, among them the sweetwater ray, whose sting is greatly feared as well as herrings, garfish, croakers, and even sole—all of which have their sweetwater equivalents.

One of the great icons of the river region is the black vulture. Whenever a dead creature is washed ashore, you will inevitably see these large black birds, the size of hens, gathering about to scavenge. Often hanging about such kills will be another bird, whitish with dark wings, called the yellow-headed caracarás, which belongs to the family of vulture falcons. Turkey vultures, which are also prominent, are among the very few birds that have an excellent sense of smell.

It is usually at the confluence of a small tributary with a larger one that animal life becomes more varied. Birdlife also increases. Since South America is the richest region in the world, not only in fish species, but also in birds (out of some 8600 bird species in the whole world, about 3000 occur in the Neotropical regions). Unfortunately, you will see few of the larger birds since they have been decimated by hunters. Among those prized by hunters are the orinocco goose, the muscovy duck (which is the original form of the South American domestic duck), the Brazilian teal, and the whistling or tree duck. Other birds hunted enthusiastically are the larger herons and storks as well as spoonbills and squacco cranes. (Note: many of these birds are described in the chapter "Fauna in the Pantanal.")

Red Tegu lizard

The Central American jaçaná, the fin foot, and the sun bittern are all that remains of prehistoric birdlife and ought to be protected as effectively as possible. These loners stand in contrast to the huge groups of other Neotropical varieties such as hummingbirds (233 species), nuthatches (211 species), tyrant flycatchers (315 species) and tanagers (179). The Central American jaçaná, with its incredibly enlarged feet, is splendidly adapted to moving about in the perpetually swaying undergrowth of floating plants in the calmer areas of the rivers. One special bird is the fin foot, which is a very good diver, capable of swimming on the water like a small duck while it carries its young on its back. The sun bittern resembles a small heron, but with a slightly longer tail, easily recognized by its tranquil flight and the large red-brown markings on its rounded wings.

Giant Kingfisher

One favorite riverbank bird that you should search for is the kingfisher; there are many species in Amazonia. They all boast similar colorings, but are of different sizes. Swallows are omnipresent, flying around the river looking for food or perching on sticks and roots that emerge from the water. A relative of the woodpecker, called a swallow wing, looks like a black and white swallow but breeds in small holes in the earth near the riverbank. Another frequent inhabitant of the bush growth along the riverbank is the anis or cuculiform—a bird that resembles the European blackbird, but with a bigger beak. It does not steal the broods of other birds like the European cuckoo, but rather builds its own nest in which several females lay eggs that they hatch together.

A little extra luck is needed to see the hoatzin, also known as the gypsy hen—sociable birds that live in the bush and trees along the riverbank in small flocks. Before seeing them, you may hear a kind of wheezing snore or panting. They feed exclusively on leaves which they prepare for eating and store in their large crops, since their stomachs are very small. When the crop is full, they become top heavy and while sitting the breast has to be supported on the ground; hence the species has developed a special callus for that purpose. Fossil remains of the hoatzin date back to the Oligocene era about 40-50 million years ago; an astonishing discovery was made recently that it was related to the cuckoo.

In the woods along the riverbank, you might encounter a fowl-like bird which attracts attention by a loud crackling noise. This call sounds as if it were made by one solitary bird, but in fact it is the joint call of a male and female couple. They call out separately but the sounds are so well matched that they produce a perfectly regular *u-du-aa-ra-ku* motif, incessantly repeated. This is the call of the chacala, a smaller member of the Cracidae family, a purely Neotropical family to which belong a number of large and very shy forest birds, such as the helmeted curassow and the razor-billed curassow.

Lizards abound in Amazonia; most frequently found on riverbanks are the ameivas that belong to the telid family. Among the larger ones are the red tegu which can grow to 1.4 meters and the caiman lizard that can reach up to 1.25 meters. The caiman lizard leads a largely aquatic life in flooded woodland and is able to crack open the hard-shelled water snails with its strong jaw filled with stone-like teeth. Another even more multiform family of American lizards is that of the iguanid, the most common species being the iguana, a typical denizen of the riverbanks, which can grow up to 3.2 meters. They often lounge for hours on branches overhanging the riverbanks and let their horny legs dangle.

Giant Swallowtail butterfly

Butterflies in profuse quantities are one of the great blessings of the Amazon; their appearance in swarms always seems somehow magical. They are to be found everywhere in Amazonia, both on riverbanks and in cultivated areas. Many like to light on damp sand in order to suck up the moisture, and whenever possible, they choose places where mammals have left urine. In some places, vast swarms can be seen, hovering closely together for hours in one place to which they will return if they are disturbed. Most of the butterflies are whites (Pieridae), but some are exquisitely colored flambés and swallowtails. Sometimes, near a group of white and yellow butterflies, a small group of brown-black species will collect together. During the mating season, the butterflies spread their wings and fly around each other in pairs so that the various species may be readily identified by the color patterns peculiar to them. In Amazônia, a large number of varieties take their nourishment from rotten fruit, carrion, excrement and urine traces.

Pollination in the Amazon occurs not so much through insects but through birds. The king of pollinators is the hummingbird. The largest are the size of a swallow and the smallest no bigger than a large bumble bee. All are accomplished in the art of hovering; they are capable of suddenly interrupting their whirring flight and lighting quietly on a blossom in order to extract small insects and nectar. Most hummingbirds make an identical round each day, during which they visit in exactly the same order the individual flowers they have come to know. If you are taking photos, note the time you see a hummingbird so you can catch him at the same time the next day.

Basking on the riverbanks will most likely be some crocodiles. The black caiman, which can grow to a length of almost five meters, has long since been exterminated in settled areas because of the value of its skin. Also along the banks can be spotted water tortoises.

About five o'clock in the evening, the capybara (water hog) leaves the thicket that protects him from the daytime heat. Since they are not hunted for food in Amazonia, capybaras are more frequently seen and they are not shy. The capybara is the largest rodent that has survived to date, reaching a length of 1.25 meters. Another large rodent is the paca, which is hunted everywhere for its excellent meat.

Towards evening (or at dawn), you may see parrots, particularly the Aratinga, which fly strictly in pairs, though in large groups. (A wonderful sighting of this phenomenon can be found at Ilha dos Papagaios, a little island outside Belém, where green parrots fly off at dawn squawking loudly in pairs). As nightfall approaches the croak of frogs intensifies into a bass symphony of grunts and gurgles. Included in the voicings are the croaking of the large tree frog and the bark-like hooch of the giant piping frog. The large number of piping and tree frog varieties is one of the things that gives the amphibious fauna of South America its distinctive flavor; of almost 2000 kinds of frogs in the world, nearly half live in the tropics. In Amazonia the highly colored and sometimes very poisonous Dendrobatidae, also known as the colored tree frog or tree climber, should be avoided.

Sometimes at sunset, you can hear the loud sound of the six o'clock cicada and shortly afterwards, the first bats will leave their daytime hiding places. You also might glimpse the archenemy of the bat, the bat hawk. Many bats eat insects which they catch during flights while others are fruit eaters or take nourishment from flowers. There are even fishing bats which, through an echo-sounding process, can so perfectly analyze the waves made by fish on the surface of the water that they can catch them by reaching out and seizing them with their elongated legs. South America is also the home of the vampire, medium-sized bats that feed on blood. They land at night on a sleeping mammal and approach it on all fours. With razor-sharp teeth, they make a small painless incision and then lick the blood that flows from the wounds. Cows can become greatly weakened by this nightly blood loss, and there is also the possibility of rabies transmission. Dogs usually notice bats immediately and bite them to death.

As twilight settles, swallows also awaken. The pauraque, or cacho, is particularly common on cultivated land and near rivers and makes a loud "o-ro-hu" sound. As darkness descends you may also hear a more melodious birdsong that consists of four or five descending notes on the scale almost human sounding, from the common po-too, or as the Brazilians call it, *ayamama* (mother of the dead) or *urutau*. In native folklore the melancholy song is thought to be a lament.

Waking up in the jungle at dawn is delicious. You will wish you had brought your cassette recorder to tape the symphony of wake-up calls that stir the innermost recesses of the forest. By that time, as the sun comes up, it's probably a good idea to check your hammock for any creepy-crawlers that might have snuggled in with you.

MAMMALS

Pygmy Anteater

Anteater
Tamandua tetradactyla
TAMANDUÁ-DE-COLETTE
   OR TAMANDUÁ-MIRIM

Confined to Central and South America, the anteater is aboral, with no teeth, a long snout and tubular mouth, and a tongue that can be extended for some distance. It prefers to scavenge during the night, sleeping most of the day. It feeds on wild bees, ants and termites, which it finds in hollow tree trunks or on the ground. It knows how to open hard clay mounds with its powerful claws, drawing in the ants with its sticky tongue and then swallowing them whole. The Great Anteater about eight feet in length, lives on the ground; the Lesser Anteater, about half the size, lies in trees, aided by a prehensile tail which helps it swing through branches. The anteater's biggest love is honey.

Jaguar
Pantera onca onca
ONÇA

The jaguar is the western hemisphere's biggest cat, weighing up to 250 lbs. Many Indian tribes claim they are descended from jaguars; in the Andes, the animal's pelt is still used for ritual dancing. In 1967, Brazil instigated a hunting ban which failed to save half a million felines that were slaughtered for pelts. Today the two to three kittens in each litter are more heavily protected by international controls. Up close, a jaguar in pose is exquisite, with an apparent calmness of expression. Although it seems to be a heavy animal, its suppleness and elegant bearing are easy to perceive, yet it is vicious enough to successfully attack a crocodile.

Giant Otter
(Brazilian giant) otter
Pteronura brasiliensis

This otter is a very rare species, confined to the slow-flowing rivers and streams of South America.Also called saro and margin-tailed, the otter has completely webbed feet and usually brown fur with a large whitish chest patch. Marvelous swimmers, they sleep at night in dens tunneled into the riverbanks and spend days diving beneath floating vegetation to catch fish. Giant otters may eat up to three tons of fish a year, competing with fishermen who attack them with machetes and rifles. Early explorers claimed their canoes were surrounded by barking otters. Extremely playful, they enjoy sliding down a steep bank of mud, but occasionally fall prey to jaguars, pumas, and anacondas. In 1971 they were declared protected, and are now among the 23 most endangered species in the world.

Manatee
Trichechus jagouarundi
PEIXE-BOI

Called *peixe-boi*, or cowfish, this aquatic mammal weighs up to 1300 pounds and reaches ten feet long. Since manatees are slow swimmers, they are easily caught as food by *caboclos* (backwoodsman) who harpoon them at night, then suffocate them by stuffing wooden plugs into their nostrils when they surface to breathe. Commercial exploitation started in the 16th century with the arrival of Europeans, who fried manatee meat in its blubber, then shipped them home. After an era of tanning hides, the manatee became an endangered species. Today the Brazilian conservation agency INPA employs *caboclos* to capture manatees who have been abandoned and bring them to their labs for renewal.

Maned Wolf
Guará
CHRYSOCYON BRACHYURUS

With legs like a pelican, the guará is not a wolf, but a dog so tall that locals have dubbed it "fox-on-stilts." It is usually golden brown or reddish-brown in color with black stripes on its legs. A solitary, nonthreatening creature, the guará roams at night and mainly feeds on rodents. Today, the guara is a vanishing species, since it often unconsciously courts its own demise by pausing to look back at pursuers. Its height, however, allows it to see over the tall savannah grasses that cover the expanse of the Amazon.

Puma
Felis concolor
SUÇURANA

The puma, one of seven species of smaller cats, is highly adaptable, and roams such habitats as tropical forests and the desert; it is best identified by tracing its tracks in the sand or mud. It is noted for its uniformly brown color, in contrast to the ocelot and jaguar. As a couple, the male and female stay together for about two weeks. After a gestation period of ninety days, two or three kits are born, always in a very well protected place, such as a cave or a stone cavern. The mother suckles her young for three months or more, although they begin to eat meat as well before they are six weeks old. Around the age of two, they master tracking small animals and become independent, finally leaving the mother.

Sloth
Bradypus tridactylus
PREGUIÇA

The name sloth originates from the extreme slowness of this mammal's movements, which results from a very sluggish metabolism. Although slow-moving on land, it is a very fast swimmer. It sleeps hanging from a branch by its four legs, its head between its forearms, curled like a ball. Its fur harbors an immense variety of parasites, including two kinds of ticks. The shoots and tender leaves of the trumpet tree *(cecropia)* are its favorite food. Sloths seldom descend to the ground, and because they cannot walk, they pull themselves along the ground with their claws, thus becoming easy prey for jaguars and other larger animals.

There are six living species of sloths in tropical South and Central America.

Collared Peccary
Tayassu tajacu
CAITUTU, CATETO

Few animals that live in the dense forests are as feared as peccaries, whose sharp knife-edged tusks have forced many a local up into a tree for hours. Also known as the wild pig, this mammal has a smelling gland in its tail, which it uses when irritated. It travels about in small groups led by a male elder. The litter generally consists of two suckling pigs that follow the mother a few hours after birth. Peccaries are accustomed to feeding in the morning and evening and eat various kinds of animals, such as insects, worms, snakes and frogs, as well as roots, fruits and nuts. Frequently their presence is noted by the peculiar odor emitted by a gland on its rump or by rooted-up soil.

Amazonian Skunk
Coneptus
FUINHA

A genus of skunk endemic to the Amazon forest, it belongs to the Hog-nosed skunk family, named for its characteristic long, naked snout. Its coarse fur is black with a white tail and its body length ranges from 12-20 inches. Like all skunks, it is noted for its offensive odor produced by glands on either side of the anal opening. Most species exhibit a characteristic warning behavior, such as foot stomping, and if the threat continues, the animal turns on its hindquarters toward the target and ejects a fine spray of yellow, odoriferous liquid as far as 12 feet. Primarily nocturnal, they feed on rodents, insects, eggs, birds, and plants. Their litters, gestating from 42-72 days, contain 2-10 young.

Tapir
Tapirus
ANTA

The tapir, which attains a weight of several hundred pounds, is the largest indigenous land mammal and is much sought after for its meat. Heavy-bodied and short-legged, tapirs are about 6-8 feet long. The eyes are small, the ears short and rounded, and the snout extends into a short fleshy proboscis or trunk that hangs down over the upper lip. The young of all tapirs are dark brown, streaked and spotted with yellowish white. They are shy inhabitants of the deep forest or swamps, traveling on well-worn trails, usually near water. When disturbed, they usually flee, crashing through undergrowth and often seeking refuge in water. Their main enemy is man, though in the South America it is the jaguar.

Ring-tailed Coatis
Nasua Nasua
QUATIS

Related to raccoonlike carnivores, coatis are found throughout South America. About 29-54 inches in length, they have long flexible snouts and coarse grey to reddish-brown fur with light underparts and light facial markings. Early morning or at dusk, alongside grassy marshes, or at the edge of the forest, one might glimpse groups of 7-10 females, with their tail erect, searching for food.The males are solitary and join the groups only during the short mating season. Coatis eat birds, eggs, insects and fruit, and they also root in the humus looking for worms and larvae. They tend to love sweets and when thrown some in a group, fight and squeal over the booty.

Capybara
Hydrochoerus hydrocheoris
CAPIVARA

The capybara, the largest rodent in the world, looks like a giant guinea pig, and may weigh up to 100 pounds. It lives along the Amazon and its tributaries and is an excellent swimmer and diver. Its flesh, though considered a delicacy, is used for food and is frequently dried for shipment to market; its hide is made into high-quality leather. Often as large as a real pig, it reaches a length of four feet, and weighs about 75 pounds, sporting webbed feet, small ears, coarse brown hair, and no tail. When it snoozes among water plants with just the top of its nose above water, it is not easy to find. Capybaras live on vegetation growing both in and out of water. Other common rodents found in the region are paca, agouti, spiny rat, and a species of squirrels, rats, mice and porcupines.

Deer
Mazama americana
VEADO-MATEIRO

In the Tupi language, deer are generally called *çu-assú*, which means meat, much food, or big game. These graceful deer, also called *suassupita*, belong to the genus *Simplicornis*. Instead of branched antlers, they have single horns, no more than 12 centimeters long. They live in the forest, and also like to graze at dawn and at nightfall, sleeping during the day in the dense woods. In regions where hunters seldom go, they don't always run away from visi-

tors, and may often come to peer intently at them.

PRIMATES

The darlings of the jungle, monkeys, called *macacos* in Portuguese, are mammals with an almost human appearance and social habits; if you have the chance to inspect them up close, you will be thrilled, if sometimes appalled at their human similarity. Their tails may reach twice their body length and function as an additional hand and point of support. They feed on fruits and insects, and when showered with human attention while in captivity, they can develop intense attachment.The large consumption of monkey meat and fur in the Amazon has significantly reduced the population. There are 30 species unique to the region. Among them are:

Spider monkey
Ateles paniscus
MACACO-ARANHA , CUATÁ

This monkey has a slender body with forelegs shorter than its hind legs. Its prehensile tail is longer than its body and provides mobility and support. It can mostly be found in bands high up in the forest trees. Spiders are thoroughly adapted to life in the treetops and can do more things at one time than a juggler—hold fruit in one hand, pick up more with a foot, place food in mouth with a second hand, and walk and swing from branches with the other foot and tail. They are known to break off branches and throw them at human invaders. Still, they are gentler than other species and make desirable pets if given the right care. They are the prey of eagles and other predatory animals.

Marmoset
Callithrix jacchus
SAGÜÍ

The world's smallest monkey, the marmoset is kept as a pet by Indians who wear them in their hair to remove lice. Because of their size and behavior, they often seem more like squirrels than monkeys. They live in troops, climbing in the forest trees, feeding on fruits and insects and occasionally uttering chirping noises. The white-eared marmoset is known for its thick and silky fur and white tufted ears, which make it resemble Albert Einstein. Marmosets bring forth two or three young at a time. One marmoset kept in captivity was noted never to have washed its face, hands or coat—with one exception—an almost violent obsession to groom its tail, which was twice as long as he was.

Squirrel monkey
Saimiri scicureus
MACACO

Squirrel monkeys are the most common primate in the region; they command the food supply simply because of their number. With a black snout, black upper head and white rims around the eyes, it resembles a stuffed toy; the head and short trunk are extremely rounded. Squirrel monkeys live in the same jungle as howlers, wooly monkeys, spider monkeys and capuchins. This small-sized primate boasts a yellow-grayish fur, with a black spot around the mouth.

Wooly monkey
Lagothrix
MACACO-BARRIGUDO

This primate has a strong large body and prehensile tail. To move about along the ground, it uses only its hind legs, swinging its forelegs to keep its balance. Wooly monkeys are quite large and are covered with a dense coat of woolly fur. They are grayish or reddish in color and have a prehensile tail, which helps them to swing playfully through the forest trees.

White-faced capuchin
Sapajou
MACACO-CABLUDO

This monkey has a stout body covered with rather woolly fur. The head is round and the eyes large and bright. Often it's been described as looking like a little old man as seen through the wrong end of a telescope. They usually eat insects incessantly by examining crevices in trees and withered leaves, seizing the largest beetles and munching them with great relish. It's very fond of eggs and young birds, and plays havoc with nestlings. They usually travel in troops, but scatter when one is shot by a hunter.

Owl or Night Monkey
Aotus vociferans
MACACO DA NOITE

As opposed to other monkeys who are active by day, this owl monkey hides and sleeps in a hollow tree during the day and roams at night in search of insects, small birds and other small animals and fruit. It occasionally utters "cat calls" to herald its coming. A small quadruped monkey with a long and large body and round eyes, it uses its hands and feet to propel itself along the ground. Its eyes are particularly noticeable, extremely large and yellowish in color, a condition often developed by nocturnal animals. Their senses are so developed that when a person passes by a tree in which a number are concealed, he or she may be startled by the sudden appearance of a group of little striped faces crowding into a hole in the trunk.

Howling Monkey
Alouatta caraya
GUARIBA-PRETO, CARAJÁ

The opera singer of the forest, the howling monkey emits cries of such depth and volume that they can be heard from 1-2 miles away. It has a naked face and retreating forehead, with its hair slicked back 50s style. Its body is robust, reaching up to 27 inches with a tail almost as long. Early explorers dubbed it the ugliest monkey in the forest for its protruding jaw and bulbous eyes. Some have been known to scatter urine and dung on passersby from their perches high up in the treetops. The screaming voice is produced from an enlarged windpipe. Traveling in troops of 4-35, they communicate with strong gesticulations and a variety of sounds, which includes a deep metallic cluck of the male leader, the wail of a mother, and the squeal of playing young. A howling group of monkeys can sound louder than the roar of a lion.

BIRDS

Parrots
Amazona
PAPAGAIO

There is an enormous variety of parrots in the Amazon, from the red-fronted Amazona which is predominantly green, with a red area on its beak and tail, to the blue-fronted Amazona which is predominantly green, with its upper wings colored red. Chiriri parakeets are small and green while canary-winged parakeets are green with yellow feathers at the base of the wings.

Parrots vary in length form 3-40 inches, including their tail. The short neck and sturdy body, along with the stout feet and thick bill, give them a bulky appearance. Pointed wings and a long tail are usually found in species that travel a long distance. Their predominantly green plumage is marked with other bright colors, chiefly on the upper head; the sexes look alike. They live in the rain forests and are difficult to breed. They may become aggressive as well as squawky. Parrots use their toes and hands in manners similar to humans, but their extremely powerful jaws can become quite dangerous, especially if you pet them in a way that is irritating. Most are gregarious and noisy, forming small groups. Parrots are monogamous and their courtship techniques have included vocalizations, bill-caressing, mutual preening, bowing, wing-raising, tail-spreading and feeding the mate. Of 81 genera recognized in the 1937 revision of the taxonomy of parrots, the Neotropical region (South and Central America) has 28, none of which are found elsewhere.

Toucans
Rhamphastos
TUCANO

Along with the hornbill, the toucan enjoys the distinction of having the largest bill for the size of its body of any bird. The horny sheath, however, is only about 1/30-1/50" thick and the inside is filled with air and a delicate filigree of bone. The beak is used to pick fruit from trees and capture insects. Soft fruit is cut by the serrated edges of the bill while the smaller morsels are held by the tip of the beak, tossed into the air, then gulped. One species utters a call that resembles the Brazilian word *tucano*. One peculiar characteristic is the presence of a ball and socket joint that hinges the tail to the body so that the tail can be bent up over the back. Nearly an icon of the Amazon, the white-chested toucan has a beak sometimes longer than its body and emits a sound similar to a scream, which drives people to address it as "You crazy bird!"

Curassow
Cacidae (order Galiformes)

Any number of tropical American birds belong to the above family, but the term "curassow" refers to 7-12 species in which the male is glossy black (often with white belly) and has a curled crest of feathers and brightly colored bill ornament; the female, lacking the ornament, is smaller and brownish. It is a game bird and its flesh is considered a delicacy; however, the razor-billed curassow of the Amazon is critically endangered. A noisy, terrestrial bird, the curassow makes its nest in trees, feeding on fruit and small animals.

Cock-of-the-rock
Rupicola
Galo-da-seea

The cock-of-the-rock belongs to one of two species of brilliantly colored birds, noted for the males' flattened circular crest

extending over the bill. During much of the year the males display in open glades near the forest floor, maintaining and defending communal areas. Much of the individual display consists of static posturing, interspersed with stylized eye-catching movements, especially when the female is visiting. To perform courtship dancing the male clears spaces on the forest floor. Indian trappers search for the secret little dance halls and strew them with mud and twigs, coated with resin, which stick to the birds' feet and inhibit flight, not to mention mating. The pawnbroking female builds her nest of plant materials, plastered with mud, against a rock wall.

King Vulture
Sacroramphus papa
Urubú-rei

Known as the "condor of the tropical forest," the uburú-rei sports a bizarre face and beak and its huge flapping wings can scare monkeys and humans alike. It is smaller than the Andean bird and has appeared in ancient manuscripts of the Mayan civilization as the glyph of Cip, the thirteenth day of the month. Like a true king, this vulture always presides over a carrion feast and lesser vultures wait until it is finished. Vultures are considered the garbage collectors of the jungle and their presence nearly always signifies dead carcasses.

Great White Heron
Ardea cocoi
GARÇA

This magnificent white heron lives in swamps as well as in occasionally flooded fields. At the time of reproduction, it acquires nuptial feathers and makes a ritual out of choosing its mate. Nests are built in colonies where both parents look after their young, and are generally located in rough platforms of sticks constructed in bushes or trees near water.These herons usually feed while wading quietly in the shallow waters of pools, marshes and swamps, catching frogs, fishes, and other aquatic animals. Acrobatic masters, they fly with legs loosely bent and the head held back against the body, instead of stretching the neck out front as most birds do.

Hoatzin
Opisthocomus hoazin

The strongest of Amazon birds, the hoatzin differs so much from other birds that its kinship is doubtful, but it is most closely related to the game birds. Although sporting wings, it prefers to creep among the branches of trees in which it lives, rather than fly. The flight from tree to tree is slow and labored. The adult is about the size of a mourning dove, dark olive with white streaks above and rufous streaks below, and it uses its wings like arms, climbing awkwardly about trees. In order to digest mangrove leaves, its gullet is 50 times larger than its stomach. It feeds on fruit and leaves of certain tropical trees that grow along the riverbanks. The flesh of the bird is particularly disagreeable in odor, resembling that of raw hides, leading locals to dub it a "stinking pheasant.

REPTILES

Alligators and crocodiles
Alligatoridae
JACARÉ

The alligator, also found in the Pantanal, is one of the most impressive creatures of the Amazon. They rarely attack humans, unless provoked, and instead feed on a variety of fish, mammals and birds, which are usually eaten in the water. Today, they are under great threat by poachers, who can kill up to 12 in an hour, 100 before daybreak. Flank skins are sold to dealers, with each skin going for about a dollar. Caimans leave their river habitat to lay eggs adjacent to a termite nest, who incorporate the eggs into the nets where they mature at perfect temperatures for each sex: cool for female, warm for male.

SNAKES

Bushmaster

Lachesis muta

JARARAGA

The bushmaster is the largest of all Amazonian vipers, reaching a length of 12 feet. It is rumored to be extremely aggressive, but in truth fatal bites rarely occur. The bushmaster inhabits tropical Central and South America, especially in damp, steamy forests, where it frequents holes in the ground made by armadillos and other animals. It is usually reddish-yellow with dark cross-bars, and a black stripe extends from the jaw to the eye. Bushmasters roam at night mostly, hiding under roots and logs while they hunt for mammalian prey. Following a good feeding, they will remain there during the duration of digestion, which may take up to 2-4 weeks. A bold snake, it behaves as if it were conscious of its power; indeed, because of its long fangs and large amount of poison, it is extremely dangerous. Most vipers bring forth their young alive, but the bushmaster lays eggs.

Pit Viper

Crotalus terrificus

CASCAVEL

Pit vipers are the most feared snakes in the jungle. They have large triangular shaped heads and short slender tails. Large sensory holes between the holes allow heat receptivity, which registers infrared radiation, thus helping to locate prey. All vipers have highly evolved, well-developed teeth used to inject venom into victims. The poison primarily affects the blood and initial symptoms include local pain, vomiting, sweating, headache, and swelling. When not treated, pit viper venom can cause death in about seven percent of the population, as a result of hypotension, renal failure, or intracranial hemorrhage.

Boa constrictor

Sucuri

ANACONDA

The largest snake in the world, the anaconda can grow to nearly 40 feet. It's a venomless boa constrictor that kills by wrapping around and strangling its prey. Silverish-green in color, it feeds generally on fish, birds, mammals and alligators. Underwater, it flicks its tongue constantly to attain chemical information about the environment. Also called a water boa, it often lies in the rivers of the Amazon basin with only its head above the surface waiting for a luckless bird or animal to pass by. After strangling its victim, the boa swallows it under water. The most common in Amazonia is the Rainbow Boa *(epichrates cenchria)*, which is hunted by local farmers because it preys on chickens.

RIVER TURTLES

The South American river turtle *(Podocnemis expansa)* migrates along rivers in large masses that may impede the passage of boats. The turtles gather on the sandbars of large rivers to lay their eggs. Sea turtles, on the other hand, migrate over long distances, to lay their eggs on special beaches and then disperse over a wide area. The **arrau**, or side-necked turtle, gets its name from the method of protecting the head and neck by bending them to the side, rather than withdrawing them backward into the shell as most other turtles do. It grows to a shell length of about 30 inches, and its eggs have been a source of human food. Among several turtle species in the Basin is the world's largest freshwater turtle, the **tartaruga**, which reaches 150 pounds. A bizarre turtle, the **matamata** has a distinctive nonretractable neck so it must swing its head under its carapace sideways. When prey approaches, it opens its mouth, creating suction that pulls the victim into its throat. Green turtles *(Chelonia mydas)*, which deposit their eggs on the coast of Costa Rica in Central Mexico, disperse through the Gulf of Mexico and the West Indies, and have been recovered on the coast of Brazil, 4000 miles away. Hunted by river people for their meat and eggs, Amazonia's turtle population has been badly depleted. The island of Fernando de Noronha and the resort of Praia do Forte in Bahia are leaders in their preservation. (For further information on these sites, see my other guidebook *Fielding's Brazil.*)

WATER LIFE

Pirarucu

Arapaima gigas

The king of the river, the pirarucu is the largest of all freshwater fish. There is a 100-year-old record of a pirarucu that was 15 feet long. They belong to a group of fishes having primitive characteristics and an ancient fossil record. They have a tail that appears unusually full and rounded because of the proximity of both dorsal and anal fins to the tail fin. The fish uses a primitive lung adapted from its swim bladder, which permits it limited air breathing. Dried scales are sold as fingernail files in many shops in Belém, Santarém and Manaus.

Piranha
Serrassalmineo
PIRANHA

Pira means fish and *rana* means tooth—nasty, toothy little fish found throughout the rivers and lakes of the Amazon basin. Their viciousness, though exaggerated, is not unfounded. Piranha only become dangerous when trapped in lagoons during dry season or when they smell blood. Seeing local people splash in infested waters is misleading; anyone foolish enough to wash meat or gut fish in a river ought to know that piranhas don't just take one bite but nibble continually and they seem to be insatiable. So sharp are their teeth that Indians use them as a cutting tool. Not all piranhas eat meat; some chow down on fruits and nuts of the flooded forest.

Dogfish

Rhapidon vulpinus
PEIXE CACHORRO

The dogfish is a kind of small shark of the families Squalidae, Scyliorhinidae and Triakidae. They are often a nuisance in schools, where they damage fishing nets but they are edible and sometimes sold as food. Amazon fishermen catch these efficient predators, which reach a length of two feet, as they pursue migrating fish schools upstream during the dry season.

Called *peixe cachorro* in Portuguese, this fish uses two enormous canine teeth to stab fish as large as itself, then swallow them whole, head first.

River Dolphin

Inia geoffrensis

Boto

The fresh water or long-snouted river dolphin, is light gray when young, but takes on a pinkish hue as it grows older. Its very long snout is covered with strong hairs or bristles that are sensory in function. With 25-27 teeth on each side of the jaw, the river dolphin feeds on fish, including armored forms which it chews whole. Botos, or *bufeos*, as they are called, are widespread in the Amazon and Orinocco basins, and during times of flood they even penetrate into the flooded forests, where they swim among the trees. They often turn on their backs to search for food on the river bottom, probably because their downward vision in an upright posture would be impaired by their bulbous cheeks. Because these rivers are usually filled with debris, dolphins in captivity prefer to have obstacles in their tank. Legends about dolphins turning into men and impregnating girls abound in the Amazon. Another tradition says that burning bufeo oil in lamps causes blindness, and that to carry a bufeo tooth means bad luck.

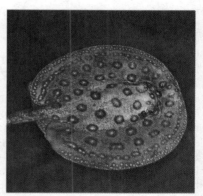

Sting ray

The sting ray is one of more than 50 species of oceanic fish in the Amazon, which also include bullsharks, herrings, anchovies, soles, toadfish, and puffers. The sting ray's flat body allows it to live on the bottom of the river, and its lateral fins expand to serve as rudders. It's a rather obnoxious fish since it lies half-buried in the sand, unnoticed, until someone steps on its tail with a bare foot and is severely injured by one of its spines. Wounds due to these spines are ragged and ugly and often subject the victim to the danger of blood poisoning; they are, however, not deadly. In many riverside medicine markets, the spines are sold for magical purposes.

Tetras

Characin

Tetras are any of numerous attractively colored freshwater fish of the characin family, *Characidae*, which are often brought back to the States for aquarium use. They are characteristically small, lively, hardy and unaggressive. They are egg-layers and breed by scattering their eggs among aquatic plants. The neon tetra is a slender fish most popular with aquarium owners, whose hind parts are a gleaming regrowth its side a neonlike blue-green stripe. The cardinal tetra *(Cheirofon axel-rodi)* is similar but with more red on its body. The glowlight tetra *(Hemigrammus erythrozonus)* is a hardy fish that grows up to 1.7 5 inches and has a shining red stripe along each side of its body. A yearly festival is held in the city of Barcelos, which attracts collectors and fishermen from all over the world (for more information, see under the city section for Manaus).

Lungfish

This species exists today only in Amazonia and Australia—the first survivors of a prehistoric fish group that was once rich in different species over millions of years ago. Now only about five species in the world remain alive. During the summer when marshes are dry, lung fishes safely rest in the mud. They burrow down to a depth of 18 inches, where they coil up in a flask-shaped chamber, with a hole in the cover through which they obtain air. As in hibernating animals, the fish live on fat stored up in the kidneys and other organs during the four or five months they remain underground. When the rainy season returns, they wriggle out of their underground cells and breathe with gills again. Specimens of lung fishes in their "cocoons" have been successfully shipped to various parts of the world where they are revived and become active as soon as they are released in water.

INSECTS

There are insects of every shape, size and color in the Amazon, from hundreds of beetle variations to flies, mosquitoes, gnats, ants, etc. They can be fascinating, irritating, or painful, depending on your attitude. As writer Alex Shoumatoff said about the culex mosquito, "all it takes is three in your room to leave you a sleepless wreck," due to the whine with which the female attracts the male, a by-product of their wings beating together 500 cycles per second. Repellant at dusk in all areas is a must.

In many Amazonian Indian groups, insects were, in the past and still today, venerated religiously, playing a central role as deities or mythic figures. In Warao cosmology, the four guardians of the cardinal points are social insects—two wasps, a bee and a termite. Rituals also incorporate insects; for example, the giant hunting ants *(Dinoponera)* in puberty ceremonies practiced by various Amazonian tribes. Similarly, among the Gorotire-Kayapó Indians, pain is endured from the stings of wasps whose nests are purposely molested as part of rites of passage. Metallic beetle parts and even gallas are used in body ornamentation by Indians in all parts of the region. Insects, especially musical species (crickets and katydids), luminescent forms (headlight beetles) and large beetles and orthopterans are kept as pets and curiosities. Many species are eaten by natives and locals, both for sustenance and as delicacies.

Spiders
Arachnida
ARANHA

Spiders abound in Amazonia, feeding on the ubiquitous insects on the ground, in the air, and among the foliage. Most are reclusive and select dark quarters as living quarters. In seasonal climate they may be most abundant on wet periods when prey is available. Sound is highly developed in many spiders and they also keep in touch by tugging and vibrating the web, through pheromones, and more rarely through vision. All spiders are obligate carnivores and possess venom used to subdue prey. Tarantulas, called *caranguejeiras* in Brazil, are usually feared for their size (a body length of 12 centimeters). While usually shy and retiring, they may become aggressive, if threatened. Some Neotropical specimens can produce a snakelike hiss by rubbing the surfaces of basal segments of the pedipalps against the opposite surface of the first legs. Some spend their days in burrows while others dwell in trees.

Ticks
Ixodoidea
CARRAPATOS

Ticks comprise an isolated and specialized group of mites. After molting, they wait on the tips of twigs or leaves, forelegs outstretched and ready to snag any passing animal. They anchor themselves onto the host's skin by a median holdfast organ with recurved teeth called the lypostome. They do not drop off until they finish feeding, and if it is forcibly removed, the hypostome (erroneously thought to be the head by most people) may remain in the wound and fester. They feed primarily on the blood of mammals, birds, reptiles and amphibians. Some remain on their single host for a lifetime. Specimens may reach the size of a grape after 5-6 days of feeding.

Centipedes
Chilopoda
CENTOPÉIAS, LACRAIAS

Centipedes are slender, very elongated, and many segmented arthropods. They are distinguished by bodies with only one pair of legs per segment, reaching from 15-81 segments. They possess a single pair of long, very flexible antennae and mandibulate, and forward-projecting mouthparts. The majority are relatively small, but some very large ones have been known to bite humans and cause pain and great inflammation. It is probably a myth that they leave a wound with each leg as they crawl over bare skin. There is no evidence that

the legs contain venom. Centipedes are most at home in warm, humid retreats, where they hide by day under stones, beneath loose bark, in rotting wood, and in caves and similar niches.

Crickets
Gryllidae
GRILOS

Although many orthopterois produce highly audible and complex sounds, it is the crickets that are best known for their musical talents. Males can make a variety of notes; most characteristic are short, pulsed chips or continuous soft trilling, more melodious and less rasping than the katydids. The sound is produced by the vibration of membranous areas of the forewings. Most crickets are small but have enlarged, muscled hind femora, making them good jumpers. In Caraguatatuba, Brazil, a black cricket is a signal of sickness, a gray one is a sign of money, and a green one, hope. In Rio Grande do Sul, Brazil, killing a cricket is thought to bring rain.

Cockroaches
Blattodea
CUCARACHAS

Cockroaches are among the most primitive and ancient of winged insects, dating back 250 million years. Ecological niches occupied by tropical American cockroaches are extremely varied. They are associated casually with vegetation, usually seen sitting on the upper surfaces of leaves, or are disposed to feed on the fruit, leaves, bark, roots and other parts of living plants of particular species; others consume the wood of rotting logs. A number live symbiotically with ants. Numerous cockroaches are capable of sound production, by rubbing the abdomen against the wings. Of the 3500 known species in the world, about 30 percent are found in Latin America.

Termites

Isoptera

CUPINS

Termites are the analogues in tropical soil of earthworms in temperate regions. Their physical burrowing to construct nests and digestion of plant structural material (cellulose) add significantly to soil fertility and earn termites a place in nature as highly beneficial. They live in nests of their own making, either wholly subterranean or above ground, and form conspicuous edifices in the landscape. The materials may be clay, soil, excrement or plant fragments mixed with saliva. Nests provide an inviting abode for other animals, including nesting birds. In the forest, away from sunlit river banks, crocodiles find termite nests a convenient incubator for their eggs. Like bees, they are organized into a social caste, with a queen, attendant male, sterile workers and soldiers. The queen can grow to enormous proportions over a lifetime. In times past in Brazil, large, hard, termitaria have been hollowed out and used for ovens. The same nests were pulverized and used as a kind of cement to make concrete floors for the early settlers.

Giant hunting Ants

Formicidae

TOCANDIRAS

The two best known and largest of the gigantic forest ants are the smaller Paraponera and the larger Dinoponera. The smaller version is fiercer and can subdue a healthy adult with a venomous stab that is often described as "like a blow from a hammer or bullet." Serious symptoms that may follow a sting and last a day or longer are prolonged, aching pain that rapidly spreads from the site of the wound, sometimes labored breathing, cardiac palpitations and fever. Death is rare. The larger ants are gentler, less apt to sting. Because of their ferocity, these ants are employed in male initiation rites by Amazonian tribes. Large numbers are caught and tied to contrived wickerwork panels and applied to the initiate's bare skin. The maddened mass of ants sting repeatedly and only youths who can endure the excruciating experience silently are deemed worthy of passage to manhood.

**FIRE ANTS:
Tell me it's not true**

Texans know this quarter-inch nasty as the fire ant, scientifically labeled Solenopsis saevissima. In the fall of 1993, the United States Department of Agriculture experts were called into save Envira, a town of 7000, located on the River Tarauca, twelve days by river from Manaus. So many thousands were attacking the residents that they couldn't even eat in their houses, and had to retreat to the concrete streets to sleep. One woman reported that she was bitten at least once every hour. People became so desperate that they were spreading diesel oil on the flood stilts of their rickety wooden houses and setting them on fire to bar the ant's entry. Even with house stilts on fire, the ants found ways to drop down on people from the ceiling, especially, it seemed, when they were sleeping. The only way out of town is by small plane or boat, but since the average salary is less than $1000, most people can't leave. The USDA's Agricultural Research Service, deterred by the residents' aversion to using DDT, which inflicts harm indiscriminately on any animal it comes into contact with, tried using Logic, which acted as a natural birth control, but the problem has not been entirely solved. Traveler's warning: During the rainy season, these clusters of ants in infected areas can float downstream unscathed and burst into a swarm at the very moment they hit something hard–like a canoe.

**BULL SHARK:
And he didn't even use a
credit card.**

A 7-foot bull shark, whose normal habitat is the sea, made a winding 1860-mile journey up Brazil's Amazon River, where groggy and weakened by hunger, it was finally hooked by a startled fisherman in January, 1994. He sold it for $20 to a local fish merchant, who donated it to a research institute. This was the second case in ten years.

A FISH YOU WOULDN'T WISH ON YOUR WORST ENEMY

The candirú açu, a minute catfish found in the waterways of the Amazon, is one of the most feared animals by locals. Almost invisible, it swims with great energy against the stream and is known to force its way into the urethra of the bather, spreading its thorny spines outward, thus making it difficult and excruciatingly painful to extract. It is said they can cause death if the fish are not removed by surgery. As such, be cautious about swimming in unknown waters, avoid urinating in the river, and jump in only after your guide has done so.

TRAVELER'S WARNING:

Do be aware that some animals mimic rain forest plants in order to hide from predators or sneak up on prey (as explained above). Snakes, in particular, love to look like vines. For protection, wear ankle-high boots and tuck them into your pants.

FLORA

For the early explorers, Alfred Wallace Bates, and modern researchers like M.C.Meyer (see his article in this guide), the Amazon jungle has yielded hundreds of thousands of plants for examination. Among the most beautiful are the orchids, which perch like parasites on host trees. About 500 species of orchids can be found in the Amazon Basin, showing an impressive range of inflorescence, from minute single petals to profuse blooms.

Pollination of orchid flowers by insects is a highly specialized art, often involving bizarre ecological behavior. Most orchid seeds are distributed by the wind, but a certain species of bees, called orchid bees (family *Euglissinae*) are attracted to orchids which mimic the scent of female bees. Among the many varieties are *Catasetum macrocarpum*, *Oleanesia amazonica*, *Rodriguezia lancelata*, and *Acacallis firmbriata* and *Gongora quinquenervis*.

The largest water lilies are those of the tropical South American genus *Victoria*, comprising two species of water lilies. The leaf margins of both the Amazon, or royal, water lily (*V. amazonica*, formerly *V. regia*) and the Santa Cruz water lily (*V. cruziana*) have upturned edges, giving each thickly veined leaf the appearance of a large, shallow pan 2-6 feet across and accounting for its common name "water platter." The fragrant flowers of Victoria have 50 or more petals and are 7-18 inches wide. They open white toward evening and shade to pink or reddish two days before they wither, to be replaced by a large berrylike fruit. They provide food for fish and wildlife but sometimes cause drainage problems because of their rapid growth. Many varieties have been developed for ornamental use in garden pools and conservation.

Cipó d'água, or water vine, is extremely important to be able to identify since it often provides drinking water for jungle travelers. Common to high, nonflooded ground, it is a large liana. To retrieve the water, hold a piece of the stem up and cut; a substantial quantity of clear, fresh water should run out. Water can also be drunk from the surface of a species of the Cecropia, a common tree in Amazonia.

The water hyacinth, called *aguapé-purua*, sports a beautiful blossom which lasts only a day, wilting after sunset. It grows profusely, branching out in all directions and sprouting plants on barely new tips. Within a few months, an entire tangled network of plants is established, which often proves hazardous to waterways, except in Amazonia, where the ecological balance keeps it under control.

Among one of the most important crops grown in the Amazon is guaraná *(Paulinia cupana var sorbilis)*, from the Sapindaceae family. It was first discovered in 1800 by the scientists Humboldt and Bonpland along the upper Rio Negro. When it remains in open ground, it grows as shrub; in the shade, it grows like a liana. It is used in the production of a popular soft drink by the same name and for various medicinal uses.

(For more information on the healing qualities of plants, see the article "A Scientist Speaks Out" in this guide.)

TREES

There are thousands of tree varieties in the Amazon region. Here is a just a sampling that your guide might point out to you.

Sumaúma/Kapok Ceiba

Ceiba pentandra (L.) Gaertn.

BOMBACACEAE

As one of the forest giants, the famous kapok ceiba stands branches above most other trees in the canopy, reaching well over 50 meters in height. It casts enormous tabular roots called *sapopomebas*, since it grows on humid, unstable soils along waterways. These roots are used as huts by Indians and other forest dwellers. It's thick and irregular with an aculeate trunk and branches, a feature also found in adult trees. The trees bloom at the end of the fall season, and the digitate leaves are replaced each year. The capsule-like fruits appear soon after flowering and when mature, break open to reveal numerous black seeds enveloped by white cotton. This cotton is used as mattress, pillow, and cushion stuffing and is used industrially in the manufacture of life jackets. The kapok ceiba wood is pinkish white and opaque, and is used to make rafts.

Pau-de-Tucano

Vochysia tucanorum Mart.

VOCHYSIACEAE

The pau-de-tucano is one of the most brilliant trees of the rain forest, for its yellow inflorescences which, from a distance, resemble the beak of an exotic toucan bird. The taller trees reach six meters in height. In general, the verticillate leaves are grouped by fours on each node and have a highly coriaceous texture and bright green color. The bright yellow flowers emerge between December and March and stand erect, displaying the characteristic spores of their corollas. The small, dark fruit appears from September-November. The wood is light and used for making crates, boards, and paneling.

Rubber Tree
Hevea brasiliensis Muell. Arg.
SEREINGUEIRA

The first Portuguese who arrived in Brazil noticed the Indians playing with black heavy balls made of the latex extracted from a local rubber tree. Native to the Amazon, the tree produces a yellowish latex with a strong odor, which provides the raw material for its first-class rubber. The tree has a rough, pale green, slightly wrinkled bark and can reach up to 40 meters in height. Due to the tree's longevity (over 200 years), the latex can be extracted for a significant period of time. Leaves are formed by green folioles, which turn reddish or brown before they fall. Its yellowish white flowers bloom from the beginning of July and the fruits appear in October. The seed itself produces a yellow thick drying oil, adequate for the production of paint and varnish. Its light wood serves as raw material in the production of crates.

Sapucaia
Lecythispisonis Camb.
LECYTHIDACEAE

The Sapucaia tree attracts attention due to its enormous stature. Its natural habitat is the Amazon jungle and the Atlantic forests between the states of Ceará and Rio de Janeiro. It can reach up to 50 meters in height. In the wintertime it loses all its leaves that sprout again shortly before the flowers appear in the spring. The pale-purple aromatic flowers attract bees, thus playing an essential role in the pollination process. Various Amazonian tribes consume the fruit, a large pyxidium containing 11-30 oily seeds. The tree's brownish-red, uniform wood has a smooth resistant and somewhat opaque surface and is used in the housing and naval industries. Young monkeys, eager for the fruit, have been known to stick their hands into the urn-like fruit and become stuck, unable to pull their hands out afterward.

Mogno/Brazilian Mahogany
Swietenia macrophylla King
MELLIACEAE

The Brazilian mahogany tree, also known as *aguano*, is one of the most well known hardwood species in the world. The tree was discovered in 1923 in South America, but is now widespread throughout the Amazon jungle. It has a tall, upright trunk with a narrow crown covered by dense, bright green foliage. It reaches 30-50 meters in height, forming tabular roots at the base of the trunk. The tree blooms soon after the leaves are renewed, between August and September. The flowers are small, creamy-colored, and aromatic. The fruit is a dark brown capsule with woody valves. Its seeds are winged and easily dispersed. The color of the wood deepens over time from a reddish-yellowish brown to a uniform reddish-brown shade with fine stripes. With its shiny and golden surface, it is used to make luxury furnishings, light sailing vessels and rulers, among others.

Copaíba/Balsam Copal tree
Copaifera langsdorfii Desf.
LEGUMINOSAE

A native of the "cerrado" and of tropical and subtropical forests, the long-living balsam copal tree is an exuberant specimen, easily recognized by the red coloring of its bark. Its branches spread out in different directions forming a wide and attractive crown. The leaves are characteristically compound, generally formed by six small folioles. In the summer its delicate pink flowers emanate an aroma very attractive to bees, which extract their nectar. In the fall its fruit becomes mature and releases dark seeds. The balsam copal tree oil is popularly used in small doses as an anti-blennorrhagic, a stimulant and as an anti-bronchitis medicine. The wood has a pale red duramen with dark grooves and is widely used in the naval industry and in luxury cabinet-making.

Chichá
Sterculia chica St. Hil.
STERCULIACEAE

Parrots and apes can often be seen eating the fruits of the chicá tree. It grows along the ciliar forests and rain forest, in the Northeast and in the states of Minas Gerais, Mato Grosso, São Paulo and Espirito Santo. In the forest, it reaches about 30 meters in height, with a trunk covered by smooth gray bark, featuring irregular grooves. It's supported by tabular roots called *sapopembas*, which provide a stable base. The large, duck-shaped leaves fall in the winter, leaving scars on the thick branches. The small flowers have no petals, but usually bloom from February-April, and sometimes continuously until June. Its capsule-like fruit is red and emerges between July and August , with a velvety texture and containing 7-8 black, oily, and edible seeds, similar to peanuts. Quite tasty, these seeds can be roasted or cooked for consumption.

Castaneira-do-Pará/Brazilian Nut Tree
Bertholletia excelsa Humb. & Bonpl.
LECYTHIDACEAE

This exuberant tree reaches up to 50 meters, way above the general canopy of the forest. Due to its rich nut, it is considered one of the main food resources of the forest. Its trunk is smooth and very long, with a wide spread-out crown, covered with simple, alternate leaves. Its white or white-ocra flowers have a rare and exotic beauty and emanate a pleasant aroma. This attracts bees, which extract their nectar, helping the pollination process. Generally the nuts are ripe from December-March. The wood is used in housing and naval industries.

VOICES FROM THE FOREST

Open Letter from a Yanomami Indian

The chief spokesman of the Yanomami tribe, Davi Kopenawa Yanomami was born in the 1950s, in the Yanomami region of Toototobi, in the state of Roraima, in the northern Amazon rain forest. His father-in-law initiated him into the training of a shabori, or shaman. He first became active in the western world as an interpreter for FUNAI. In 1974 he helped form the Commission for the Creation of the Yanomami Park (CCPY), an independent organization which has been instrumental in fighting for the demarcation of Yanomami territory. Currently CCPY, with Davi, are constructing The Demini Health Outpost, a clinic that will serve the 1000 Yanomami in Davi's home region, and campaigning for a second outpost in Balawau village.

Dear Friends,

I am Yanomami. We Yanomami used to think that Whites were good to us. Now I am seeing that it is the last invasion of indigenous land, all land. Foreigners are teaching Brazilians to destroy our place. The same thing happened to our Indian brothers and sisters in America.

The government is not respecting us. It thinks of us as animals. We have the right to speak out. Foreign people help us, but if we ourselves don't do anything, they cannot help. If we send them letters, they will put pressure on our government to change something.

The government knows that we are the oldest Brazilians, that we are born here. Our name is known to the world. We know nothing about money, shoes, clothes, and few Yanomami understand what is happening. The government got us by surprise.

The government does not know our customs, our thoughts. We too do not understand the government. All it understands is money. Our thought is the Earth. Our interest is to preserve the earth, or there will be sickness for all the people of Brazil, not only the Indians.

The rivers, fishes, and the forest are asking for help, but the government doesn't know how to listen. It says we all die of hunger if mining is closed off. But, if they stop mining, we will plant macacheira (manioc), banana, cara, taioba, papaya, sugar cane, pupunha, and no one will die of hunger any more. We Yanomami want our land. We do not want our customs to die. Until today, we have not lost our tongue and the Earth. That is why we fight.

We Yanomami are dying of diseases that Indians don't know, brought by miners from the outside. Pajé (medicine men) can cure Indian illnesses, but white people's sicknesses, we cannot cure.

In our land there are many mountain ranges. In the mountains live the Xapori and Hekura, the spirits of nature. Between the mountains are the Xapori's paths, but no one sees them, only the pajé knows about these connections. The mountain ranges are sacred places, where the first Yanomami were born, where their ashes are buried. Our elders left their spirits in these places. We've been using these spirits for years, they never end. We call on the Hekura to cure our ills. Omam left these spirits to defend the Yanomami people. Omam gave their origin to everyone, to the whole world. This is why it's important to preserve the mountains where his spirit lives. We want to preserve these places in order not to finish with our history. I'd like white people to understand this ancient story, so they respect it.

—**Davi Yanomami**

The letter is reprinted with permission from Amanaka'a Amazon Network Newsletter, Update #1, Summer 1993.

TRAVEL ALERT:

In general, travel to Indian reserves is expressly prohibited by the federal government, except for special projects which must receive permission from FUNAI and other agencies. Isolated tribes have no resistance to flu, pneumonia, measles, tuberculosis, or even the common cold. A sneeze from a tourist could wipe out a whole tribe. Furthermore, when a village is seized with an epidemic, the food-gathering system itself breaks down and more actually die of starvation than the original disease. Please take caution.

A Scientist Speaks Out

By Professor M.C. Meyer

A passionate spokesman for the potential of Amazonian pharmacology, Professor Mario Christian Meyer provides a privileged look into the future potential of Amazonian plant life. Trained as a neuropsychiatrist at Université Paris VII, he is presently a guest professor at the University of Paris as well as Deputy Governor and senior adviser to the Governor of Amazonas for international business development. He is also a senior expert of scientific, technological and industrial cooperation in biotechnology and environmental sciences to leading industrial groups around the world. As a liaison between medicine, science and business, the Brazilian-born Meyer represents a new kind of Amazo-

nian advocate—dedicated to utilizing the resources of the planet in a life-supporting, Earth-supporting capacity for all involved.

The Amazon possesses nearly two-thirds of the world's living plant and animal species, and, by consequence, two-thirds of our planet's genetic heritage. For thousands of years Amazonian Indians have been well aware of the active therapeutic properties found in the colossal arsenal of jungle plants. Even prehistoric man used medicinal plants. Researchers have detected pollen in medicinal levels of usage in bones dating as far back as 50,000 B.C. What we have come to discover is that prehistoric usage of medicinal plants had been related mainly to stimulants, diuretics and astringents. Aspirin, today one of the widest known and most consumed medicines in the world, was initially an extract of willow bark, from which the active principle "salicine" was isolated along with vitamins, glycosides, etc.

Since the beginning of the century, teams of the "Institut Pasteur" have traveled to Amazônia in order to extract natural substances from plants; these studies have becoming increasingly important today in the face of AIDS and other immunological catastrophes that are affecting our modern-day population. It was nearly ninety years ago that Professor **Charles Richet**, a French scientist, discovered in Amazônia a new vegetal toxin, the crepitine, an extract from the plant *assaku*, that allowed him to understand the basic functioning of the immunological mechanism of humans. Today crepitine appears to be an important antivirus compound. In 1908 Richet brought back from Rio Purus (a tributary of the Amazon) the latex of this plant that the Indians used to "poison" the river water in order to facilitate the capture of fish.

BIOTECH AND BIO-INDUSTRY

Plant-based medicines, once reserved mainly for shamans, folk medicinemen, and herbalists, and at the beginning of the century, for artisanal biological-chemistry scientists (discoverers of aspirin, for example) were later harnassed by pure chemists who often replaced the plant-based molecules with synthetic molecules. Today plant-based medicine moves away from pure chemists and synthetic transformation and onward to an original universe of high-tech production, based again upon biological models. From this movement has arisen the present-day advent of the **BIO-industry**, that is to say, any technology-oriented industry that uses biological systems, living organisms or derivatives to make or modify products or processes for specific use.

Given the vertiginous evolution in biotech research, one could conjecture that by the end of the century pharmaceutical labs will have even more performant techniques of isolation, chromatography, spectroscopy, ultracentrifugation and nuclear magnetic resonance. This advanced technology would permit, on one hand, the identification and selection of new natural molecules of Amazonian origin, and on the other hand, verification of the active principle in a considerable number of plants prescribed in the treatment of three-fourths of the illnesses of the planet—diseases treated even today, in many cases, by an artisanal plant-based therapy (traditional natural folk medicine, over-the-counter herbistry, etc.).

TECHNOLOGICAL, ECONOMIC AND ENVIRONMENTAL CHALLENGES

Due to high research and development costs, pharmaceutical giants find themselves today confronted with a significant slowdown in the number of chemical innovations in pharmacology, reducing the discovery, on average, to only one new and profitable molecule per year among 10,000 synthetic molecules tested. In contrast, twenty years ago, twenty new molecules were being discovered per year.

Pharmaceutical companies are now particularly interested in research alternatives that traditional medicine and its "living" molecules can offer. For example, a leading U.S. pharmaceutical company, interested in identification and selection of plants having new therapeutic properties, recently passed special agreements with **INBIO**, a Costa Rican Institute and the government of Costa Rica. In return for a $ 1 million investment for technical assistance on the part of the American company, the Costa Rican side agreed to furnish 100 plant extracts and microorganisms, together with an exclusivity on the pharmacological analysis for a period of two years.

As a result of our anthropological and biotechnological work on the rational exploitation of Amazonian natural resources, major French pharmaceutical laboratories have committed themselves along the same lines for plant research in the Amazon, precipitating a landmark Franco-Amazonian government commitment without precedent. This cooperation has great potential for the establishment of joint-ventures as well as significant positive social-economic repercussions for the Amazon region. This kind of rational exploitation of the Amazonian biodiversity, through BIO-tech, is, in my opinion, the only pragmatic and realistic way to deal with delicate and crucial environmental problems. Indeed, it could be said that natural molecules from Amazonian flora and fauna have, in themselves, a direct and indirect economic value. In fact, they serve as a direct raw-materials source for medicines as well as indirect models for new synthetic molecules even more active, more specific, and provoking fewer side effects than classical chemical medicines.

HIGH-TECH VS. SAVAGE MIND

The contribution of natural molecules raises a crucial question as the century comes to an end. It concerns access to genetic resources and the "royalties for Nature's know-how." This was a key point in the Convention of Bio-Diversity at the Summit of Rio 1992, attended by 160 heads of state as well as numerous scientists, ecologists and activists.

In my own opinion, the utilization of Amazonian Indian knowledge by First-World pharmaceutical companies requires some fundamental reflection. In fact, I have come to believe that there is an inherent cultural conflict between the Amerindian and Western scientists in their perceptions of their psychocultural identities.

In my own project called the "Franco-Amazonian Project for Scientific Technological and Industrial Cooperation," the cooperation between the Amerindians and high-tech scientists has demonstrated that we must give important consideration to the means and limits of their interaction in order to avoid potential perverse consequences of the "power struggle" between Indians and Western-thinking scientists. Indians who today come into contact with urban Amazonian centers, often enticed by money or too embarrassed to return to the tribe because of a failure at urbanization, are exploited as prostitutes, or fall under the influence of drug dealers or garimpeiros (goldminers) as well as being adversely affected by the polluting effects of mercury used to mine gold. Moreover, isolated native tribes that come into unsupervised conflict with outside influences are also at great psychological risk, and have been known to suffer deeply from loss of roots, emotional orientation, intellectual dynamism, and even brain functions, resulting in a psycho-social form of schizophrenia. If those in the so-called "civilized" sector continue to invade and exploit the forest as they have done for many centuries, without forethought to social, psychological and environmental consequences, tribal peoples, the true kings of the richest forest in the world, may easily become the "rubbish" of this cross-cultural conflict.

In the final analysis, the only way to safeguard tribal peoples from acculturation or even extermination is to respect their knowledge in a practical way by integrating their traditional technology and their "science of nature" into the development of modern society. The Indians, in fact, as "scientists of nature," could be integrated into the labor force at a level where their skills and thousand-year-old traditions would be respected and passed on to advanced technological and industrial projects, human and environmentally friendly, in a fairly balanced cooperation. Otherwise, the Amazonian Indian will become what they themselves fear most: just an insignificant piece of a fossilized "ecological Sanctuary" or a "Wax Museum zoo."

SACRED AND SECRET "NEW" MOLECULES

The ancient botanical knowledge of Indians, often times characterized as sacred and secret, has from its initiation been associated with myths of longevity and youth through invoking the "gods of Nature" or by cultivating the "magical" (and even pharmacodynamic) virtues of plants.

It is therefore not surprising that our analytical and structural chemical studies of these plants have shown the presence of powerful antioxydants and anti-free radicals in high concentration (such as various flavonoides of the rutaceaes family). Responsible for equalizing cellular metabolism, these plants contain important protective and regenerating properties for tissue: external tissue in the field of dermatology, by improving the quality of collagen and elastine, thereby acting against skin aging, as well as internal tissue, in the field of cardiology, where they have proven effective against rigidity of the arteries as well as being highly beneficial to the vascular system. In the same Amazonian plant family, we have identified numerous plants, particularly rich in saponines, glycosides and terpenes—often associated with rare metals such as germanium, which according to nonpublished Brazilian and Japanese studies, have strong pharmacodynamic reactions against cancerous tumors. Such is the case with a recently discovered molecule, *hexacyclique nortriterpene*, unknown until the present, which is reported to inhibit the growth of cancerous cells in vitro, according to 1986 research at Tokushima Bunri University in Japan.

Through the efforts of my collaboration with many Brazilian and French scientists, a large arsenal of **vegetal hormones** has recently been identified, which has proven effective in regulating the human metabolism, notably diminishing the cholesterol level in the blood and increasing the coronary circulation. Stigmasterol and sitosterol are principally responsible; the latter has the power, among others, to increase the level of estrogen in the organism in a balanced manner, as well as playing an essential role in the regulation of the cellular aging process.

As scientists delve deeper into the hidden aspects of forest potential, they are finding that native legends often provide "sacred" clues into the vast potential of a species. For instance, according to legend, the well-known Amazonian plant guaraná was given to the Indians as a gift by the Thunder god Tupan to help them fight against the evils of the bad spirit Juruparo. The plant was rediscovered by Europeans in 1669 as a result of the mission work of Superior Betendorf, a Jesuit priest, among two Amazonian tribespeople, the Andiras, and the Sateres-Mawes. Throughout centuries guaraná has been used by jungle inhabitants as a psychostimulant tonic, appetite suppressant, and as an anti-cramping compound, as well as an aphrodisiac when associated with an energetic neuromuscular tonic (family olacaceae). Today, all strata of the population continues to consume guaraná in many forms (bark, powder, and as an additive to a popular Brazilian soft drink, among others). In the future, untapped usage of guaraná may include weight control as well as anti-cellulite combat, but at the present the research results remain industrial secrets.

The entities involved in this research include the Universidade do Amazonas, Fundação Oswaldo Cruz, INPA (Instituto Nacional de Pesquisa da Amazônia), EMBRAPA (Empresa Brasileira de Pesquisa Agropecuária), UTAM (Universidade Technologica do Amazonas, among others.

AN EXOTIC PHARMACY
by Professor M. Christian Meyer

The richness of Amazonian biodiversity constitutes a double treasure for specialists of "natural medicine;" first, the large variety of plants with therapeutic properties and second, the great diversity of mammals naturally extracting healing substances from these plants.

In response to the pressing need to discover new superior medicines in plant life in the face of growing epidemics like AIDS and other social and environmental illnesses, a new, exotic specialist has thus been inspired to arise within the scientific arena—the zoopharmacologist. These specialists study plants which animals use to treat their own illnessess (such as antibiotics) or to regulate certain vital biological functions, such as contraception.

For instance, among the uncountable varieties of monkeys in the southern regions of the Amazonian forest, we find the muriqui, the biggest monkey of the Americas, measuring about 70 centimeter in body) with a tail just as long. Apparent masters at controlling their own population, the females manage to reduce their fertility, thanks to the ingestion of certain leaves rich in isoflavonoides, which have a physiological effect similar to that of estrogen. Inversely, the same females have been found to ingest "orelha de macaco" (monkey's ear), a vegetable rich in a steroid that facilitates fertility. Scientists have discovered that these females often tend to chew on this plant during times of ovulation, suggesting that they may have the firm intention to be fertilized.

OTHER MEDICINAL PLANTS

Copaiba: The copaiba tree can be found in copious amounts in the Amazon's *terra firme* regions. Rich in beta-caryophylene and copaene, its therapeutic property is antivirus and antipsoriasis. Its oil is anti-inflammatory, antirheumatic, and has other numerous healing properties. It's also used in cases of chronic varicose ulcerations and pharyngitis.

Crajiru: This is a type of creeping plant used as an anti-inflammatory. The dry leaves contain tannins, quinonas and alkaloids. The plant, often served as a tea, is used to counteract intestinal colic and uterine inflammation. Other therapeutic properties are used as an astringent and as a powerful anticheloid (to heal rough scar tissue). In Amazonas, silkworms fed crajiru leaves (rich in flavonoid pigment) produce red thread.

Urucum: The seeds of this plant, which contain carotenoidlike beta carotene (pro-vitamin A), have properties capable of increasing the pigmentation of fatty tissue and thus making the skin resistant with natural coloration (it contains an excellent UVB filter which acts as sunscreen). It is also a bioinsecticide, a cure and protection against insect bites. It can either be ingested as capsules or by cooking with it in powder form similar to that of paprika. For thousands of years Amerindians have used urucum for their body-painting rituals because of its bright color. They also mix the pulp which surrounds the seeds with the oil of the Amazonian fish to make a cream which protects against the sun and insect bites.

AMAZONIAN CULTURE

CUISINE

Since Brazil was a country populated primarily through immigration, its various delicious cuisines reflect an enormous variety of ethnic influences. From the German delicacies in the South to the Portuguese fare in the interior, Brazilian cuisine at its best has incorporated old-world traditions of cooking along with native products to create a heady blend of taste and textures. By necessity, cuisine in the Amazon is highly original and regional—combining tropical fruits, vegetables and fish with cooking techniques that often come straight from jungle practices.

The state of Pará, which includes the cities of Belém and Santarém (both covered in the "Where to Go" section) has over generations developed specific dishes that are not to be missed.

Pato no Tucupi (Duck in Tucupi Sauce)
This is one of the most tantalizing dishes in the Amazon. The *tucupi*, a yellow liquid extracted from the manioc or cassava root, contributes the intense flavor. Long hours of cooking and blending are required, primarily because the manioc root is poisonous in its raw form. After the duck is roasted, it is cut into pieces and left to simmer in the tucupi sauce, to which has been added garlic, basil and chicory. *Jambu*, a sharp-tasting plant, is boiled in salt water, drained, then placed over the tucupi-basted duck. The dish is best served with fluffy white rice, *farinha d'agua* (a starchy flour made of fermented manioc that is eaten as habitually as bread), and *pimenta-de-cheiro* (hot pepper).

Desfiado de Pirarucu (Shredded Pirarucu Fish)
Dried slices of pirarucu are soaked to remove the excess salt, then boiled and shredded. The mixture is then sauteed with a common Brazilian seasoning of crushed garlic, olive oil, onion, cheiro-verde (green herbs and tomatoes. A more substantial dish called *mexido* is made by adding eggs. (For more information on the fish *pirarucu*, see the chapter on "Animals in the Amazon."

Pirarucu Grelhado or "na brasa" (Grilled Pirarucu Fish)
After soaking to eliminate excess salt, pieces of dried, salted pirarucu are grilled or cooked over a brazier until golden. The traditional sidedish is *farinha-d'água* (manioc flour), which is eaten often with *feijão manteiguinha-de-Santarém* (butter bean) salad. A delicious variation is to serve the sliced fish sprinkled with olive oil and topped with onion rings.

Pirarucu no Leite de Coco (Pirarucu Fish in Coconut Milk)
The dried, salted fish is first soaked overnight, then simmered in a delicious tropical coconut milk, which is not coconut water, but juice extracted from

the coconut meat through an ardurous process of grating and pressing. At times, a tantalizing substitute is the milk of the *castanha-do-Pará* (Brazil nut).

Pirarucu na Chapa Quente (Pirarucu on Hot Plate)

This is a huge freshwater crayfish served sizzled over a hot plate.

Peixada (Fish Stew)

This steamy broth is usually made with only one type of fish, preferably filhote, pescada amarela or tucunaré. The fish steaks or slices are first marinated with lemon, salt and garlic. Separately, a stock is made with fish head and seasoned with *cheiro verde* (green herbs such as parsley, coriander, onion along with salt and crushed garlic). When the heads are cooked, they are removed and potato halves and fish slices are added to the stock and simmered. The accompaniments include hard-boiled eggs, *farinha seca* (dry manioc flour which tastes a little like provocative sawdust) and *pirão de farinha d'água*, a flawlessly smooth, gelatinous gravy of manioc flour, using the same fish stock. *Pimenta de cheiro* (hot pepper) puts a tang to the flavor.

Caldeirada (Caldron of Fish Stew or Chowder)

The huge kettle in which fishermen cook their freshly caught fish is called a *caldeirada*. Similar to peixada in style of cooking and seasoning, the dish "caldeirada" involves a potpourri of fish and vegetables. It's excellent as a light, nutritious meal. Served alongside are usually boiled eggs and *farinha seca* (dry manioc flour) or *farinha d'água* (manioc flour mixed with the same stew liquid.)

Vatapá paraense (Shrimp dish)

This glutinous shrimp entree, with the texture of a thick gravy or mush, requires two days for preparation. It's delicious, though not visually appealing. Dried salted shrimps are soaked in cold water, then sauteed with palm oil ((*dendé*) with onions, tomatoes and chives. Coconut milk is added and the mixture is left to simmer. Rice flour, cornstarch, or bread crumbs are used to thicken it. Garnish with cooked jambu leaves (sharp-tasting) and shrimp.

Tamuatá no Tucupi (Tamuatá Fish in Tucupi Sauce)

This typical Amazonian fish, also known as "*cascudo*," has a hard shell and yellowish meat. Seasoned with salt and lemon, it is cooked in tucupi sauce, spiked with chicory or endive and basil. The topping is the ubiquitous *jambu*, a plant with a sharp tang.

Maniçoba (Stew of Maniva and Meats)

Appreciate this dish since it takes one week to make. Shoots of the maniva species of manioc are ground, then cooked no less than four days. Then an array of products reminiscent of the Brazilian feiojoada is added: jerked beef, calves' feet, bacon, smoked pork, blood sausages, pigs feet and ears. The difference is that maniva shoots are used instead of black beans.

Caranguejo Toc-Toc (Whole Crabs)

Toc-toc is the noise made when cracking open crustaceans. Freshly caught crabs are boiled in water spiced with salt, lemon and garlic. Diners are given a little wooden mallot to break the shell and are expected to eat the crab meat without the use of a fork.

Unha de Caranguejo (Crab Claws)

After the crab claws are boiled in salt, garlic and lemon, the part with meat is wrapped in a mixture of potatoes, shredded crab meat, egg, and corn meal, then deep fried. *Pimenta-de-cheiro* (hot pepper) is sometimes added for spike.

Casquinho de Caranguejo (Stuffed Crabs)

After the crabs are boiled in water and salt, the meat is removed and sauteed with olive oil, various herbs, and the little yellow pepper indigenous to Pará. The mixture is served in the crab shell and covered with *farinha d'água* (manioc flour toasted in butter or olive oil and sometimes mixed with eggs).

Caruru Paraense (Shrimp Dish)

Shelled dry shrimp is the staple of this dish, sauteed with palm oil, onion garlic, scallions, green peppers and black pepper. Everything is boiled in water, then thickened with sifted *farinha seca* (manioc flour). Okra cut crosswise to resemble little wheels (amount subject to the chef's whim) is added while the mixture boils. The finished dish is often garnished with cooked jambu leaves and dry shrimp

Tacacá (Shrimp Soup in a Gourd)

You'll find lots of urban Amazonians sipping this soup on the street. Traditionally it's drunk from a small bowl made from a gourd, called a *cuia*. It is sold by *tacacazeiras*, generally in the late afternoon on the principal street corners in such cities as Belém. Various ingredients are mixed into the cuia after you order one, such as tucupi (a preparation of manioc liquid spiced with onions, jambu leaves, etc.), cooked tapioca and dried shrimps. If you want added spice, ask for pimenta.

Farinha d'água (Flour sidedish)

One of the numerous varieties of farinhas (flours) that are made from manioc, this dish is a ubiquitous companion to most Paraense dishes. The finest quality comes from the colonies (small truck farmers). The flour itself can be purchased in the local outdoor markets, but it must always be toasted. Other types of flour made from manioc include tapioca and seca.

Jambu (A Condiment)

This sharp-tasting narcotic plant is an inseparable companion of the tucupi sauce, and is also essential to other dishes native to Pará, like *tacacá* and *pato no tucupi*. If you chew the leaves, you will experience a small quivering of the lips; as such, it is sometimes referred to as an aphrodisiac. It must be boiled rapidly in water with a little salt before it can be added to dishes.

Pimenta-de-Cheiro (Fragrant Hot Pepper)

Among the enormous varieties of regional plants, this little round hot pepper, an indelible mark of Paraense cooking, is remarkable for its unusual and aromatic perfume as well as its brilliant yellow or red color.

Tucupi (Manioc sauce)

As explained above, tucupi sauce is the yellow liquid extracted from the manioc root. Its preparation has never wavered from the original Indian technique, which incorporated an elongated woven straw called espremedor as a squeezer. Since it is poisonous the juice must be cooked for a very long time before it can be added to dishes. Its addition to dishes like tacacá, leitão (suckling pig), and all forms of game and fish is indispensable

SPECIALITIES FROM AMAZONAS

Many of the dishes above can be found in the state of Amazonas as well, with some local variations in cooking style and spices. As in Pará, local fish remains a mainstay of the Amazonas diet, which is cooked with some Portuguese, African and French influences. Among the principle fish that are eaten in this region is the *tambaqui*, which is typically served baked or in a chowder. The pirarucu, known as the codfish of the region, is preserved for eating through a salt process. *Tucunaré*, with its milder taste, is often used in chowders. The *jaraqui*, a local favorite in Amazonas, is served with manioc flour and hot sauce.

AMAZONIAN FRUITS

Do not even think about leaving the Amazon without tasting at least one (a few score) of the literally hundreds of tropical fruits. Freely found along the riverbanks and on terra firme are hundreds of edible regional fruits. They come in all shapes and sizes, and are made into a variety of forms—from the raw fruit itself, to fruit juices and unbelievably delicious ice creams. Among some of the most favored are:

Açai

A staple of the Amazonian diet, the açai fruit is made into a popular local drink, taken cold and mixed with sugar or with farinha made from manioc. It comes from the small fruit of the açaizeiro palm. Tupi Indians called the palm *yasa'i*, or "the tree that cries." Ropelike tassels of fruit (dark, almost black round seeds the size of the end of human finger) hang from the thin palm, which reaches up to 30 meters high. To make *açai*, the berries are soaked in water to soften the fine covering, then squashed in a clay vessel (or modern equipment) and strained. The condensed purple liquid has a flavor similar to grape juice, aromatic and substantial. It comes as ice cream, mousses, liqueurs and strong red wine.

Bacaba

The Tupi Indians discovered this palm fruit, giving it the name of wa'kawwa, meaning "it produces soil." The tall, 12-meter palm has crinkled leaves that resemble fans. Its fruit is similar to the *açai* and is often described as a horse's tail, hanging with dozens of seed kernels. The process by which the dark-graying liquid is obtained is the same as that of açai. It's a refreshing drink for the hot tropical clime. It's also served with sugar or manioc flour, farinha de tapioca or farinha d'água. It's extremely popular as ice cream.

Cupuaçu

One of the most popular of the Amazon, the sour-tasting cupuaçu is an elliptical-shape fruit, about 20 centimeters long, 13 centimeters in diameter, rounded on the ends, and weighing about 2 kilos. It has a strong smell and a brown egg-shaped shell with a velvet aspect. Inside the shell are 50 seeds surrounded by a thick, white pulp with a strong roselike perfume. Honey from the cupuaçu flowers is considered an aphrodisiac (like many other related tropical fruits). Related to the coca plant, a chocolate is made from the toasted seeds. A beverage known as cupuaçu wine is made from the pulp and is quite popular in Pará. Omnipresent are jellies, puddings, pies, creams, candy, liqueurs, fruit preserves, fillings, mousses and innumerable desserts made from cupuaçu. The ice cream is particularly delicious.

Castanha do Pará (Brazil Nut)

Pará's principal export, the tasty Brazil nut comes from an impressive tree 50 meters high. Equally impressive are the large globular capsules 8-15 centimeters (about the size of a man's head) and weighing between 700 and 1500 grams. This hard shell shelters about 11-22 tightly packed, triangular oily nuts which are themselves covered with fine shells. The flavorful nuts are rich in protein and can be eaten raw or roasted. They are excellent for making sweetmeats, fillings, pies, cake icings and various other desserts. Also, a variety of indigenous fish recipes makes use of this nut

Bacuri

The fruit of the *bacurizeiro*, a magnificent leafy tree 20-35 meters high with rose-colored flowers, is a little larger than an orange. Its thick yellow rind must be removed with caution as the resin it secretes can irritate the skin. Inside are two or three large seeds, covered by a salty, white, perfumed pulp with a bittersweet taste. Between the seeds are *filhos*, which are pieces of pulp with no kernel that are used for making beverages, ice creams, liqueurs, jellies, marmalades, pies, creams, cakes, mousse, candies and other delicacies.

Pupunha

Rich in vitamin A and oil, the pupunha is harvested from a tall palm whose trunk is completely covered with thorns. This makes collecting the fruit, which gathers in red and orange clusters, difficult. About the size of a plum, the oval fruit is flat in the upper part where it is attached to the cluster. Before eating, pupunha must be cooked in salt and water to remove the skin. The yellow pulp is fibrous, mealy-like and delicious. In the middle is a small coconut (*coquinho*), which is in fact the pip. It can be eaten as is, or with syrup or butter; it makes an excellent complement to coffee or tea. It's also quite tasty when caramelized or made into fruit preserve.

Tucumã

The *tucumanzeiro*, a palm tree about ten feet tall, produces numerous greenish yellow, egg-shaped fruits in bunches. The yellow fibrous pulp is edible.

Muruci

Muruci is the fruit of a small tree of the same name that bears yellow flowers. Similar to plums, the fruit is generally round, flat on the bottoms, and approximately 1.5 centimeters in diameter. Inside the yellow skin is a yellow pulp which envelopes a small round seed. The pulp, considered the sweetest in northern Brazil, literally melts in one's mouth. It has an agreeable perfume unlike any other fruit. The sour-sweet muruci makes an excellent beverage as well as ice cream and an infinite number of other desserts.

Piquiá

This round fruit about the size of an orange comes from the tree of the same name. It has a grayish-brown coloring, with a thick and fleshy outer covering which protects four kidney-shaped segments of yellow pulp surrounding one woody stone. The stone itself contains a wonderfully flavored kernel. The pulp must be cooked in water and salt before it's edible.

Taperebá

The enormous *taperebazeiro* tree bears a cylindrical fruit, rounded on the ends, about the size of a small plum. Inside the thick skin is three millimeters of dense pulp clinging to a pit, which is the major part of the fruit. Taperebá is a dark yellow, perfumed fruit, tart but of a sweetish flavor. It is quite popular as a beverage, ice cream and liqueur.

Graviola

Extremely strong tasting, graviola has a sweeter aroma than cupuaçu. Its pulp is used to make juice, custard and ice cream.

Buriti

The buriti is one of the largest palms in the Amazon and its fruit is rich in oil. It's often consumed as a yellow wine marked by a very strong taste.

Other fruits native to the Amazon are mango, buriti, graviola (custard apple), abricó (apricot), taperebá-do-sertão, goiaba (guava), jaca (jackfruit), tamarindo, sapoti, sappodilla, carambolo (Chinese gooseberry), mari-mari, bacaxi [a]pineapple), and biribá.

DAINTY MORSELS AND SWEETS

Besides the above-mentioned ice creams, beverages, puddings, pies, creams, liqueurs, fruit preserves, mousses and candies, you will also encounter homemade confections such as *beijo-de-moça* (literally "girl's kiss), *munguzá* or *mingau de milho* (corn kernels cooked in syrup and sometimes in milk or coconut milk).

Author's Note:

For further descriptions of Amazon fish, see chapter "Who's Who in the Amazon: Fauna."

HANDICRAFTS

The rich mixture of Portuguese and Northeastern Brazilian culture, which itself is a study in multiple ethnic groups, have produced a remarkably colorful and even indigenous Amazonian folklore. A deep-rooted mysticism and a profound connection to nature runs through all the traditions. Through the year popular folklore celebrations, from the spiritual to the secular, occur in Manaus as well as in other cities in the interior. In June in Manaus and Paratins, a huge festival celebrating the legend of the legendary *bumbas* (bulls) takes place, with open-air markets of typical foods, processions, and impressive dance performances. (In Manaus, performances at the Amazonas Cultural Center accommodate up to thousands of people.)

In the city of Paratins, the last three days of June draw over 35,000 people to cheer the two great **bumbas** "Garantido" and "Caprichoso." This highly competitive folklore festival called **bumba-meu-boi** tells the legends and indigenous mythology of the Lower Amazonas regions. You can recognize the bull Garantido by its red and white colors, and Caprichoso by its blue and white. During this celebration, Paratins is petitioned off with colorful banners. In a rivalry almost tantamout to that of soccer, family members sometimes fight over the loyalties they feel to their chosen bull; participants in the festivities actually dress up as bulls. Animating the festival is the music of the *toada* (folk song), which gives the beat to a variety of dances with ancient Indian roots. Hot-beating drums propel the odd assortment of characters who fill the streets as cowboys, Indian chiefs, medicine men, ghosts of the forest, wild animals and satirical characters such as "Pai Francisco" and" Mae Catirina."

As with the festivals, the local handicrafts emerge out of a strong connection to roots, utilizing the natural resources drawn from the forest. Handicrafts produced by riverside dwellers most always use Indian techniques, even if the artists are not Indians. **Pottery** is particularly fine, especially in the city of Belém, where there are two major traditions. (For more information, see the section under "Belém.") **Artisan products** made from the paste of the guaraná plant are an explosion of Mauense ingenuity, but many feel that these handicrafts stem from the **Sateré-Maué** tribal culture. One of the most characteristic objets d'art are miniatures of typical Amazonian riverboats filled with regional products such as fish, manioc flour or fruit.

Fine basketware from the Upper Negro Region is made by the **Tucano**, **Baniwa** and **Dessana** tribes, among others. In the Upper

Solimões region, the **Tikuna** are recognized as the only specialized sculptors in the state, specializing in wood carvings representing human and animal figures; they also are inventive with masks and clothing made from tree bark. The **Hixkaryana** are masters of the art of feather adornment. Among the peoples of the Javari Valley, a region on the Brazil-Peru frontier, the **Marubo** tribe craft adornments from shells (freshwater mollusks); the **Matis** are known for their fine seed necklaces, shell earrings and nasal ornaments made from wild boar teeth.

(For more information on local products, see "Shopping" in the various city guides.

OPTIONS FOR TRAVEL

In all honesty, it takes a certain kind of traveler to enjoy a jungle adventure. Sometimes, however, human beings can vastly surprise themselves. I, who was nearly sent home in tears from Girl Scout camp, immensely enjoyed my Amazonian treks, but they were not always easy, nor was I left with an overriding desire to return for the *unbeaten* tracks. (The beaten tracks were plenty exciting.) On your first trip to the jungle, I would not suggest braving it alone or with unreliable guides; believe me, you will want to feel there is someone looking after your welfare. Good guides (usually those officially trained) know the trails where you are least likely to meet poisonous snakes, voracious ants, man-eating piranha, and malaria-infested pools, not to mention mudslides and other debacles of nature. As for travel options, there is such a variety of possibilities that anyone from senior citizens to responsible children (nine and older) can make the grade. My suggestion is to plan a number of different treks that will give you a multidimensional perspective of Amazonian life. Among the possibilities:

- **Packaged boat tours** (or special charters) through the *igarapés* (streams) shooting off from the Amazon, near Belém, Manaus, or Santarém.
  Advantage: Good for those with limited schedules; trips usually last between four and 48 hours. Can include fishing, jungle walks and overnight stays in the forest. Best trip is out of Belém, with Amazon Star Turismo. Travelers seeking air-conditioned cabins should investigate the 22-passenger "Tuna" or the eight-passenger "Hawk," which conduct three-day and six-day cruises out of Manaus. For more information contact **Brazil Nuts** at ☎ *(203) 259-7900* in the U.S.

- **Two or three day stays at lodges built inside the jungle**, mostly accessible by boat from Manaus.
  Advantage: Secure accommodations with adequate to good food, bath and organized excursions day and night.

- **Two or three day trips down the Amazon on public river boats** (the region's buses), like the *Cisne Branco*, which goes between Santarém and Manaus.

Advantage: Slow, relaxing, requires no effort and gives you a chance to hobnob with locals. Best for those who speak Portuguese.

- **Sidetrip excursions to river beach sites** such as Alter de Chão near Santarém, and Marajó Island near Belém.
Advantage: Change of greenery, cooling beaches and exotic culture.

- **Luxury resorts**, like the Floresta Amazônica in Alta Floresta, Mato Grosso where you can sleep in comfort and take expeditions into the forest, down the river, to neighboring farms and even to gold mines.
Advantage: Offers the greatest options of adventures and the largest perspective of Amazonian lifestyles.

THE AMAZON SURVIVAL KIT

MOSQUITOES AND BUGS

Almost all lodges near Manaus were chosen for their mosquito-free locations. Even so, independent-party mosquitoes always managed to find me, especially on my boat cruise from Santarém to Manaus. Off-the-beaten trekkers must be careful; some areas of the Amazon are so ridden with mosquitoes that few human beings venture there. In his book *The Amazon* (Time-Life), Tom Sterling recalls how he had to wear a bathing cap to protect his bald head in the notorious Jari River region.

Yellow fever, transmitted by mosquitoes, is considered endemic in Brazil, except around the coastal shores.

Health authorities advise that the most infected areas are Acre, Amazonas, Goiás, Maranhão, Mato Grosso, Mato Grosso do Sul, Pará, Rondônia, and the territories of Amapá and Roraima. Vaccinations are good for 10 years and are essential if you are traveling either to the Amazon or the Pantanal. You may be required to show proof of vaccination when entering the country from Venezuela, Colombia, Ecuador, or Bolivia; it's best to always travel with it. (For more information, see the *Health Kit* in the back of the book.

WHAT TO PACK

Swiss Army knife, canteen or plastic water bottle, thermos (with cup big enough to eat from), compass, binoculars, journal, pens, small backpack, and collapsible fishing gear. Pack water purification pills (but use in emergencies only; it's better to drink bottled water). If you plan to take river trips on the public boats, a hammock is advisable, even if you secure a private cabin. Mosquito nets are not generally needed, unless you venture out into the jungle on your own. Take plenty of bug repellant (see *Health Kit* in the back of the book) and reapply especially at dusk and before going to sleep. A fellow traveler in the Pantanal swore by Avon Skin-So-Soft bath oil as a natural repellant (available through Avon Products). Suntan lotion with a high SPF is an absolute must; the sun at the equator is the hottest in the world, and the river water will reflect it even more intensely. You should wear sun-block even in the tree-shaded jungle. Pack extras of all personal medicines, contact lenses, and glasses, etc. If you're taking a two or three day cruise down the Amazon, a juicy paperback will be deeply appreciated after two hours.

THE AMAZON SURVIVAL KIT

IN PREPARATION

Be in good physical shape; even though the terrain is more or less flat, hiking through a humidity-intense jungle can be exhausting. (In contrast, river trips border on the soporific.) Time your vaccinations over the month before you leave because you can't take them all at the same time. To ward off mosquitoes, many people swear by taking daily doses of Vitamin B two weeks to a month before the trip (and during) to ward off critters. Some professionals even believe that foregoing sugar helps. If you are particularly allergic to bees, make sure you travel with your own remedies (emergency medical assistance will probably be miles away). And above all, break in your new boots before leaving.

MALARIA

To take malaria pills or not to take—that is the question that doctors, north and south of the equator, are still debating. On the con side: Prophylactics tend to mask symptoms; once the illness is diagnosed, they make it more difficult to treat. Also, new species of mosquitoes (from which malaria is contracted) are always developing and the latest medicines are not usually up-to-date. On the pro side: Pills give you some peace of mind. What's best is to wear strong repellant and avoid areas commonly known as breeding grounds, particularly stagnant water. Personally, I took every form of vaccination possible before leaving for Brazil including yellow fever (required), tetanus, and gammaglobulin (for Hepatitis B) as well as a complete round of malaria pills before, during, and after my trip to the jungle. For the latest official advisories, contact the Centers for Disease Control, Atlanta, GA 30333 (Parasitic Division, Center for Infectious Diseases). (Also see *Health Kit* in the back of the book.)

PHOTOGRAPHIC EQUIPMENT

I went down the Amazon River with a professional German photographer who didn't give a whit about humidity-rot, bugs, or human carelessness—until I nearly knocked his equipment overboard. Truth is, bugs and infinitesimal-sized tics are rampant on these boats and fungus abounds; the spray from the river alone is enough to render delicate mechanisms inactive. To avoid ruined film, keep rolls tightly secured in waterproof baggies and store all equipment with a small packet of silica gel. At least once a week expose lenses and camera to direct sunlight (minus the film!). Also, remember to develop film promptly (Manaus has some good 24-hr. processing shops), and if your camera allows for exposure adjustments, underexpose a 1/4 F-stop.

WHAT TO WEAR

Light cotton clothing. Although native people walk through the rain forest barefoot and in shorts, I don't suggest it for foreigners, whose immune systems are unaccustomed to jungle life. Wearing jeans (tucked into boots) and light cotton long-sleeved shirts (with roll-up sleeves) will cut down on scratches and snake and bug bites. In both wet and dry seasons you'll need sturdy tennis shoes and/or waterproof hiking boots (I loved my lightweight, waterproof Merrell boots made of Goretex). Heavy-treaded soles are needed to help you balance on tree logs. On any river trips you'll need a sunhat and good sunglasses with a strap to keep them from falling off. Kerchiefs are excellent for wiping sweaty brows. In rainy season, take a lightweight hooded rain poncho and an extra pair of clothes for when you get soaking wet. A swimsuit will come in handy, but pack a coverup. Some agencies supply rain gear (rubber boots and ponchos) when necessary.

WHERE TO GO IN AMAZONIA

SANTARÉM

Located near the western border of the state of Pará, **Santarém** is the major city in the **Tapajós River Basin**—an enchanting, near magical region distinct from other Amazon terrains. Also called the **Lower Amazon**, this area is a verdant, almost continuous plain, rarely exceeding 300 meters high and overlaid with lakes, tributaries, island rivers, and narrow streams called *igarapés*. During low tide (July–December), vast stretches of fine white sand and green water graced by pink porpoises turn the Tapajós into an Amazonian resort. Though there are roads in the region, they are torturous to traverse during rainy season, so most people travel by way of the *estradas líquidas* (liquid highways). Travelers can pick from every kind of water transport imaginable—from flat-bottom barges to diesel-powered canoes to *barcos de linha* ("water buses") where everyone, from teens to salesmen to old ladies with grandchildren hang up their hammocks and settle in for the two to three day journeys.

Santarém is situated on the exact point where the Tapajós River pours its greenish waters into the brown waters of the Amazon. Ecologically, Santarém is fascinating because it represents an unusual microcosm of the Amazon, where all three types of jungle systems can be fully experienced: *várzea* (flooded plain), *terra firme* (flat forest ground), and *igapó* (stream). Because of this privileged location, numerous cruise lines use Santarém as a stopover, not only because of the varied ecosystem, but because the city itself is a lovely Amazonian port to visit. Along the **Avenida Tapajós**, you'll see hundreds of boats loaded with goods that are sold to villagers within moments of arrival. There's also a colorful wharfside market, a few imposing colonial houses and several sleepy baroque plazas. Although you can browse through this Rip Van Winkle town easily on foot, the best way to see it is to hire a cow-drawn cart and go rambling down the dusty, cobblestone streets.

Cruiseliners also tend to stop at the nearby primitive community **Alter de Chão**, known for its folklore and its "illusory" lakeside beach (some cruises leave their passengers off in Santarém and pick them up in Alter de Chão). Extra excursions can be made to **Alenquer**, a former Indian village, where an impressive assembly of hieroglyphics point to the remains of an ancient civilization. Also, a few hours away by boat is the community of **Monte Alegre**, a region ripe with rock paintings as well as amethyst mines and an unusual ecosystem: its meadows, part of the Great Lake, boast semi-submerged forests and an enormous variety of fish.

Insider Tip

Typical of the region are enormous water lilies that look like saucers right out of Alice in Wonderland. Called Vitória Régia, this lily has bright green leaves that measure almost two meters in diameter and a flower of 30 centimeters, making it the largest in the Americas.

HISTORY

Prior to the European discovery, the Lower Amazon was inhabited by several indigenous groups, including the **Tupaius**, from which the Tapajós River got its name. In 1661, an Indian mission was founded, and in 1758 the name of the burgeoning settlement was changed to Santarém, after the town in Portugal. If you come across a few locals with last names like Vaughon, Jennings, Hennington, Wallace and Riker, that's because two years after the American Civil War, 100 **Confederates** immigrated to the region straight from the southern United States. (Sadly, practically none of their descendants speak English today.) Between 1821 and 1912, nearly half a million people from the Northeast migrated to the region in a desperate bid to flee a ravaging drought, helping the region become the world's prime producer of natural rubber. In 1927, American ingenuity entered the Amazon when auto mogul Henry Ford, after researching sites around the world, decided to recreate an urban city in the middle of the jungle, called Fordilândia (for more information, see the "History" chapter in the front of the book). Despite the nearly inhuman efforts to import every single element, the enterprise failed because the delicate ecological balance was not taken into consideration. In 1958, the Lower Amazon was shaken by another explosion: an enormous vein of gold discovered in the upper Tapajós river valley, from Itaituba northwards. In 1969 the Santarém-Cuiabá highway was opened, enabling makeshift towns and villages to multiply as thousands hurried to the river and its tributaries to "*bamburrar*," or "get-rich-quick." Unfortunately, little money from the gold rush returned to Santarém, and many rivers were contaminated with mercury as a result of the rampant prospecting.

In the last two years, however, Santarém has made a tremendous comeback that should be well noted. A new local government has stimulated substantial growth in tourism and agriculture, adding to the industrial economy based on extraction of gold, wood, Brazil nuts, rubber and jute, as well as textile, cattle farming and fishing industries. Qualification progams for hotel and restaurant employees, guides, and taxi and bus drivers have been developed, and school children are being educated about the historical and cultural aspects of the region. Impressed by the potential of the mineral-rich *várzea*, the World Bank is now investing time and research into extensive harvesting without insecticides or fertilizers. Even the Japanese government is investing in a recuperation program of the most devastated ecological regions.

A BIRD'S EYE VIEW

To get a pleasant picturesque view of Santarém, walk down **Av. Tapajós**—past the riverboats, chicken coops and floating gas station to where you can view the meeting of the Amazon and Tapajós River. From July to January, the beach in front of the avenue is full of sand and lined with mango trees. A night tour to scope out alligators can be taken to Ilha de Ponta Negra, an area known for its cattle and huge water lily lake. Early morning trips are best for bird-watchers. Beaches near Santarém are exquisite. Located about three hours by boat, the **Arapiuns River** is reputed to be the most beautiful beach in the area, with 40 meters of white sand and dark rocks and excellent resources for fishing in unpolluted waters. Three or four kilometers into the forest, you'll discover a stunning waterfall. Four kilometers from Santarém is **Maracanã Beach**, which local people frequent. Among the chic beaches is **Pajussara**, about 30 minutes by boat from the city, full of lovely summer homes and palm-lined white sands. You must take your own food.

SIGHTS

ON FOOT

Santarém is a cinch to see on foot; just be careful about the heat, or the rain (during the rainy season).

Markets

Start at the marketplace along the wharf near **Praça do Relógio**, where 6–10 a.m. you'll find the perfect picture-postcard version of an outdoor third-world marketplace. Nearby is the indoor **Mercado Modelo**; between the two you'll find everything from live chickens to tropical fruits to hammocks, which run about $16–$17.

Nossa Senhora da Conceição

Walk up **Rua Siqueira Campos** to the cathedral,, whose original structure was built in 1711 by French architects, but had to be rebuilt 20 years later when it collapsed. The fully clothed model of Jesus holding the Cross in the

front right vestibule is paraded during the Círio festival (for more explana-
tion, see "Belém"). In front of the church is the **Praça da Matriz**, where
about 60 years ago, a band used to perform.

Rua Siqueira Campos

Walking down the main shopping avenue you'll pass two record stores with
good discount bins as well as recordings by regional musicians like Ray
Brito and Tinho. Even if you're not heading out on a river trip, an interesting stop is the supermarket on this street called **Formigão** (Big Ant). You
can stock up on beer, cookies, crackers and especially Tang™ (the American
orange drink mix, good for dehydration).

Varig

On the next block you'll find the Varig office *(Rua Siqueira Campos, 277.
Daily 7:00–11:30 a.m., 2:00–5:30 p.m., closed Sun.)*.

Pastelândia

Across the street is this clean and airy snack bar specializing in *pastéis*
(baked dough pastries filled with meat or cheese), cooked right under your
eyes. Camera and film stores are next door. Along Siqueira Campos are also
several drugstores that may exchange dollars; talk to the owner.

Turn left on **Rua Senador Lameira Beittencourt**, also called **Rua 15 de Novembro** past more shops, then right on **Rua do Comércio**, a pedestrian mall full
of sportwear stores.

Mascote Bar

On the right is this spot, a good stop for lunch. Nearby, at Rua Sen. Lam
Bittencourt, 31 (the street running into Rua Comércio) is one of the best
artisan stores (for more information, see under "Shopping").

Rua Francisco Correa

Turning left from Rua do Comércio onto Rua Francisco Correa, walk up
the steep hill for a wonderful view of the *meeting of the waters;* you'll see
the blue of the Tapajós River and the brown of the Amazon. Fortunately,
there's also a cool breeze here, perhaps the only one in the city. The odd
illusion is that you'll feel as if you are looking out onto the ocean; the water
is so clear because the river is full of plankton (plants) and, therefore, does
not allow for the penetration of light. Walk back to Siqueira Campos and
turn left, passing the only banana stand in the city.

Centro Cultural João Fona

Rua do Imperador. Also called the Museuo de Santarém, this fine museum
was formerly the city hall, parliament, court and prison. Today it holds a
famous collection of Tupaiu Indian crafts (there's also a good view of the
Meeting of the Waters from here). Anthropologists and archaeologists have
been studying the Tupaius' pottery, called *ceramica tapajônica*, and have
discovered that they were the most culturally advanced Indians in the Amazon; some of their pieces date back 8000–10,000 years. Ana Roosevelt,
granddaughter of the American president, has led research teams in the area

and may be producing a book soon about this tribe—considered to be the most ancient civilization in South America.

To end this walking tour, walk back along the wharf, where the best place to watch the sun set is at **Mascotinho**, an open-air café where you can indulge in pizza and cold beer. You'll also find an ice cream parlor where you can stock up on sweets and pastries, especially great if you're planning a boat trip. Along the wharf you'll see cows tied to carts, still used for transporting goods and people. If you would like a tour through the city on a cow, contact **Lago Verde Tourism** at ☎ *522-7577* and they'll round one up.

BY CAR

Aparecida Hammock Factory

Av. Borges Leal, 2561; ☎ *522-1187. Daily 7:30–11:30 a.m., 1:30–6 p.m.* Thousands of *redes* (or hammocks) are handmade daily at this factory where you can watch artisans work (until 3 p.m.) on looms imported from Southern England. Excellent quality is assured here, and you're sure to find all varieties and colors (if you're looking for cheap, better go to the Mercado Modelo). At Aparecida, you can pick up a single hammock for $11, a double for $20 (good for one large person) and a child's for about $7; all profits go to support social-welfare programs. If you're making any jungle trips—by land or water—a hammock helps beat the heat. Do practice slowly getting in and out; many a gringo has fallen flat on his or her face, to the enormous amusement of locals, who do it so gracefully. (One hint: The safest way is to lie down diagonally.) Before you invest, note that a hammock takes up considerable bulk in a suitcase but will fit nicely in a backpack.

Herb Farm

For the past 15 years, **Farmácia Viva**, a dirt-road community of 3000, has supported this herb cooperative famous for its medicinal remedies. The village, about 10 minutes from the Tropical Hotel, is full of ethereal-looking children with curly, bright-golden hair that no one can explain, but the old ladies who tend the garden seem like the salt of the earth. They'll love to show you their patches of patchouli, *capim santo*, and other herbs whose tart aromas fill the air. And they'll be even more delighted if you buy some of their homemade tonics (usually under $1). The *banho capilar* is reported to grow hair on a bald head, and there's even a plant called "Vick" that's good for headaches. Stomach ailments, colds, cysts—just name the ailment and you'll get an herbal cure. Since the way to the plantation often confuses even locals, you'll probably have to go with a guide, but be careful about getting stuck in the mud (though, if you do, the whole community will turn out to help). To get there, take the road to Cuiabá, turn left on Av. Moaçara, right on Trav. Rouxinol and Rua Maravilha. And keep asking.

National Forest

Sixty-two kilometers by good road from Santarém is the **Floresta Nacional de Tapajós**, a virgin forest where you can see a variety of animals, including gangs of wild pigs, monkeys and tropical birds. Ornithologists often come to research South American landbirds, which appear in volumes in the early mornings. To visit the park, call **IBAMA**, ☎ *522-3032,* and speak to Rion-aldo Almeida, director of the the National Forest. You must provide your own transportation (boat, plane, or jeep) and translator, but you are also required to be officially accompanied by one of their guides. Lago Verde Turismo travel agency also provides a five-hour walking tour of this forest (see "Travel Agency" in Hands-On Santarém).

WHERE TO STAY

In Santarém, there is the Tropical Hotel, and then there are the others— a gap of about three stars. If you're rugged enough to spend a few days in the jungle, you may be perfectly happy with lower-class accommodations in the city, but there's nothing like coming back to clean sheets, civilized service and reliable air conditioning.

Expensive--- **Over $50**

Inexpensive -- **Under $20**

Tropical Hotel Santarém

Av. Mendonça Furtado, 4120, ☎ *522-1533, FAX 522-2631.* Not as elegant as the Tropical in Manaus, but it is the best hotel here. It's also owned by Varig, so you'll find an airline office in the lobby. Rooms are tiled to accommodate jungle trekkers, and every effort is made to maintain high standards of cleanliness. (122 apts.)   *Expensive. All cards.*

Santarém Palace Hotel

Av. Rui Barbosa, 726; ☎ *522-5688; 522-5993.* The best of the budgets offers rooms that are spacious to a fault, with painted corridors and carpeted floors. All rooms are air-conditioned and come with color TV, telephone and minibar; even the lobby is air-conditioned. Local tours are offered in the lobby. Singles run $14, doubles $16. (47 apts.)

Inexpensive. No Cards.

Brasil Grande Hotel

Trav. 15 de Agosto, 213; ☎ *522-5660.* Nearly a "dive," but at least it's clean and efficiently run. In fact, it was chosen the cleanest hotel downtown, according to quality control in 1994. A favorite among locals, the fan-cooled restaurant with MTV serves regional fish for $5. Across the street is the Mascote Ice Cream Parlor, with exotic Popsicles. Standards with fan, color TV and minibar run $12 for one person, $15 for two; suites with air conditioning, color TV, and minibar run $14–$16. Rooms with only fan and collective bathroom run $7. (20 apts.)

Inexpensive. No Cards.

City Hotel

Trav. Francisco Corrés, 200/212; ☎ *522-4719.* Funky on the verge of sleazy. What's called a suite has a double and single bed in one air-conditioned room, with a color TV and minibar. Since rooms vary in size, check out what's available when you arrive. The lobby is dominated by a color TV, dirty plastic plants and a grungy aquarium. Laundry service available.

Suites run $15, double deluxes $14, standards $11. The simplest rooms,
with fan and minibar, run $8–$10.   *Inexpensive. No cards.*

WHERE TO EAT

Moderate --- **$5–$10**

Inexpensive --- **Under $5**

Mascote Restaurante

Praça do Pescador, 10; ☎ *522-5997. Daily 11 a.m.–midnight.* Santarém is
not the culinary king of the Amazon, but a good meal can be had here for
under $5. Pizzas are good, as is the *Peixada de Tucunaré,* a fish similar to
black bass that arrives in a light soup. The service is not fast, but you can
spend the wait gazing out the window at the *gaiolas* loading up.
Inexpensive. All Cards.

Canto do Sabiá

*Est. Santarém/Curuá-Una, 6 kilometers; Daily 10 a.m.–2 p.m., 5 p.m.–1
a.m.* Set outdoors in the middle of a forest about 10 kilometers from the
city, this is a great place to see the Amazon moon and stars. During the day,
you can swim in a natural pool made from an *igarapé* or cool off at the big
canopied tables. Local families crowd in on the weekend to feast on great
barbecued chicken and beef. Plates run about $3, no desserts.
Inexpensive. No Cards.

Mascotinho

Riverside. The "little" version of Mascote, perched on the bank, perfect for
pizza, sandwiches and dock-watching. Sunsets are spectacular here.
Inexpensive. No Cards.

Lumi

Av. Cuiabá, 1683, ☎ *522-2174. Daily: 11 a.m.–2 p.m., 6 p.m.–11 p.m.*
Authentic Japanese cuisine made by the descendants of immigrants who
arrived during the rubber boom.   *Moderate. No cards.*

Peixaria Canta Galo

Trav Silva Jardim, 820; ☎ *522-1174. Daily, noon–5:00 p.m. and 6:00
p.m.–1:00 a.m.* Specialty is regional fish cooked Paraense-style. Browse
through the aqaurium of local species.

Tupaiu (Tropical Hotel)

Av. Mendonça Furtado, 44120; ☎ *522-1533. Daily, noon–3:00 p.m., and
7:00 p.m.–10:00 p.m.* Air-conditioning is high on the list of assets here,
with a decent array of international cuisine.

Storil

Rua Turiano Meira, 115; ☎ *522-3159. Daily: 11 a.m.–3 p.m., 6 p.m.–
midnight, closed Monday.* Regional food in an air-conditioned setting.
Moderate. No Cards.

Insider Tip

Bolo de Macacheira (Macacheira cake) is a delicious sweet heavy cake made of shredded macacheira root (the non-poisonous variety of cassava root), sugar, eggs, coconut and butter. You're not likely to find this on any menu, so stop by Dona Antônia's Lanchonete Quero Mais Av. Rui Barbosa, 23.

NIGHTLIFE

A few years back, locals liked to confess that Santarém was no stranger to boredom at nights. But with the recent influx of capital, there are now several cafés offering regional and Brazilian music, as well as nightclubs for dancing. Ask someone in the know for details on who's playing where. Live music can also be found at the Mascote Restaurant during dinner on Fridays and the Mascotinho (café) on Friday and Saturday (see "Where To Eat").

Denis Bar
Av. Mendonça Furtado (corner with Irv. Barjonas de Miranda). Live music on Fridays and foods typical from the Northeast of Brazil.

Babilônia
Av. Menonça Furtado, 2940; ☎ 522-7122. Open daily 5 p.m.–last customer. Shows are held in this 3000-seat theater on Saturdays, Sundays, and holidays featuring top Brazilian musicians. Check the newspaper.

Bom Paladar
Av. São Sebastião, 309; ☎ 522-3891. Live music Tuesday–Sunday, with a capacity of 600.

Signus Club
Av. Borges Leal, 2712. Live music on Saturday and Sunday only.

Boite Tropical (Tropical Hotel)
Av. Menonça Furtado, 4120; ☎ 522-1533. The nightclub at the city's nicest hotel features live music only on Friday.

Boite Ancora
(at the Yacht Club) Av. 24 de Outobro. This nightclub for 500 features live music on Friday.

Insider Tip

Ask about Sebastião Tapajós, a fantastic local guitarist who's become well known in France and Switzerland for regional Amazon folk music.

SHOPPING

Santarém is just finding its sea legs touristically speaking, so the likelihood of finding serviceable souvenirs at the marketplace is negligible. Normal goods, such as sandals, can run outlandishly high here (what costs $20 in Manaus goes for $60 here). The following stores offer some unique crafts made by isolated artisans. Also, check record stores on **Rua Siqueira Campos** for regional music.

Cerâmica Art Sousa

Av. Gonçalves Dias, 747. Pottery specialists José Aniceto and his son Joel sell mainly to arts and crafts shops throughout the Amazon Region, but they welcome visitors. Joel was an exchange student/professor at the University of Missouri-Rolla in 1981.

Loja Regional Muiraquitã

Rua Senador Lameira Bittencourt, 131; ☎ *522-7164.* João Mileo's store has the most complete assortment of regional handicrafts and souvenirs in town, including Indian arts. Take the time to browse.

All cards accepted.

Artisanato Dica Frazão

Rua Floriano Peixoto, 281. The most famous industry in town, Dona Dica has been creating her own cottage industry since 1949, crafting natural bark, root and vine fibers gathered by Indians on the upper Tapajós River into dresses, tunics, purses, and fans. Some of her handmade arts are in the Vatican at the Pope's table and Queen Beatrice of Belgium bought one of her dresses.

Galeria dos Artistas Rock Lima

Av. Alvaro Adolfo, 492. This father and his sons produce the most famous wood-carved furniture in town.

Artesanato e Souvenirs

Rua Senador Lameira Bittencourt, 69-B. You'll find a wide assortment of arts and crafts from the region here.

Livraria e Papelaria Ática

Trav. 15 de Novembro, 193; ☎ *522-2745.* Stationary, fine gifts and books by regional authors such as Benedito Monteiro, João Santos and Wilde da Fonseca.

Prönatus

Rua Galdino Veloso, 278. Mon.–Sat. 8 a.m.–noon, 2–6 p.m. Across the street from the Brasil Grande Hotel, this store sells natural products from the Amazon, such as herb soap, shampoo and various herb capsules for impotency, urinary problems, etc.

Cabana

Travessa 15 de Agosto, 211. Mon.–Fri. 8 a.m.–noon, 2–6 p.m., Sat. 8 a.m.–noon. An endlessly fascinating store that sells *umbanda* and *candomblé* paraphernalia, including statues of Christian and African saints, incense, candles and all types of potions. (I once spied a very serious middle-aged man buying a potion to attract love.)

Manipulação

Trav. Francisco Correa, 168, ☎ *522-1303.* A homeopathic store selling brown rice, homeopathic medicines and antidiabetic teas.

EXCURSIONS

ALTER DE CHÃO

Thirty kilometers from Santarém is Alter de Chão, Santarém's weekend resort. It's an outgrowth of a village of the Borari Indians, a place of magical leisure because of the still-native community and unusual beaches that spread over the bay of the Tapajós River.

Muiraquitãs Lake

Alongside the village, this lake's clear water changes daily from deep blue to green. The area's folklore survives in the region, especially the celebration of the **Festa da Sairé** in the beginning of July. Slowly the village has been surrendering to modernism. Today, most of the locals, who used to fish and hunt, live mainly off tourism and their clay homes are now being squeezed in between more modern summer homes. During high season the city is so crowded you can barely walk through the dusty streets; at other times it looks deserted. One concession to modernity is that the beachside avenue is now paved. The city's "garbage collectors" can be seen flying over the city—huge black vultures called *urubus*. (They're also called turkey vultures because their heads look like turkeys.)

Praça de Nossa Senhora da Saude

The main square is fronted by a native church and shaded by big-leafy *jambeiro* trees, whose fruits are quite tasty. Here, you'll also find native women selling *tacacá*, a native dish usually served in coconut shells. On the far side of the plaza, down **Travessa dos Mártires** (a side street from the beach), is an area of rubber trees, where at 4 p.m. every day, the seeds blow up and explode, sounding just like a revolution breaking out.

Between January and June, **an island in the bay** appears out of nowhere with 40 meters of sand, becoming the makeshift summer residence for about 1000 *caboclos*. For about a dollar each way, little boys will ferry you in rickety canoes across to the island; there you'll find *barracas* for drinks, snacks, and barbecue fish and chicken.

It's best to avoid swimming on the river side (south); instead head for the north side of the island, where trees are growing out of the lake and the water is cooler and cleaner. Windsurfing is excellent (though you must have your own equipment) and kayaking is superb (rentals available). A very healthy hike can be taken up **Morro do Cruzeiro**, the mountain with a cross on top (about 45 min. one way). At the peak, you'll get an impressive view of Piranha Lake, Tapajós River and Green Lake.

Center for the Preservation of the Indigenous Art and Culture

Rua Dom Macedo Costa. This beautiful museum in Alter de Chão has one of the finest collections of Indian tribes in the Amazon River (over 75 represented). Visitors say there is no other place like this in the Amazon. Fee is $3 per person.

Instituto de Pesquisa Amazônica

Buffalo fanatics can head for the fazenda of**Wil Ernesto Leal,** whose 1000-

hectare farm also houses the most famous research institute in the area. The land is primarily savanna, a vegetation uncommon to the Amazon, comprised of thin tall trees around which scamper monkeys, capybaras and exotic birds. For more information contact **Lago Verde Tourism** ☎ *(91) 522-1645.*

If you stay overnight in Alter de Chão during high season, you'll have to reserve a hotel in advance. Only primitive pousadas are available.

Pousada Alter do Chão
Av. Lauro Sodré; ☎ *101, ramal 2.* This is the best spot for location and food. Under Tia Deney's care you can find a room for $7 per person, including breakfast, bathroom, but no air conditioning. (12 apts.)
                                                      Inexpensive. All cards.

Lago Verde
Daily 7 a.m.–6 p.m., weekends, open at 6 a.m. This is another good restaurant lakeside. Try the regional *tucunaré* (a family of black bass) or the *bolinho de pirarucú,* (an extremely tender fish wrapped in a crispy fried crust).

Arte Grupo Lago Verde

This handicraft store features an interesting snack called *beijo de moço* (kisses of a young girl), a kind of tapioca flour baked into crispy crackers. Also stock up on jars of *doce de cupuaçu* or *licor de cajú,* sweets and liquers made out of regional fruits. Native crafts include hand-painted logs and twigs found in the forest—a little kitschy for my taste since the local style is to paint over the natural bark with artificial colors.

Getting There • Some cruises that anchor in Santarém often leave passengers at port, where they can take a bus to Alter de Chão (the ship, via regional boats, retrieves them later in the day). Some cruises drop anchor directly at Alter de Chão, requiring passengers to reach shore through tenders. The trip to Alter de Chão from Santarém by car was once rough and rugged, but the road is now paved.

A favorite stop for cruises is about three hours by vessel from Santarém—the point where the Amazon River meets the Cruá-Una River. This tributary of the Amazon's right side is singular in that its banks host the greatest amount of native wildlife to be found in the entire Amazon's terra firme (primary forest that never floods). Upriver is **Pacoval**, an original village settled by fleeing black slaves and native Indians.

MONTE ALEGRE

Heading down the Amazonas River between Santarém and Belém is the town of Monte Alegre. Etched into the Ererê and Paituna mountain ranges are caves, rock formations and primitive designs and paintings belonging to prehistoric Amazônia. Two hundred meters from the port is one of the largest egret rookeries in the region. At dawn and dusk, millions of birds can be seen flapping their wings in a magnificent display. Another attraction is the thermal springs, where pools of sulfurous water are used to treat skin diseases. For more information contact the **Secretaria da Cultura e Turismo/Prefeitura Municipal de Monte Alegre** at *Av. Presidente Vargas;* ☎ *(91) 533-1147, Santarém, PA.*

ALENQUER

Nicknamed the "City of the Gods," Alenquer can be found upstream on the Amazon River between Santarém and the border of Pará. About an hour from the town are lakes and streams with giant water lilies. A family of rock pedestals with smaller stones in identifiable shapes can be found in Morada dos Deuses. There is also a tall cliff in a valley that forms a canyon with a waterfall. The folklore event **Festa do Marambiré** is held every June.

LODGES

Tapajós-Amazon Lodge Hotel Ecológico

Av. Alavaro Adolfo, 1232; ☎ *(91) 52202330, FAX 522-5866.* Tucked on the left bank of the Tapajós River (two hours by boat from Santarém), this new and extraordinary lodge is the only one in the Amazon to offer a beach of white sand and crystal water for swimming. Built into 150 hectares of natural wildlife (130 of which is untouched tropical forest), the palm-roofed lodge's 18 wood bungalows (with bathrooms) actually sit on stilts inside a lake, offering terrific views. A footbridge links the rooms to the restaurant, known for its fresh fish. Two day/one night packages run $80 per person, including transfer, jungle walk, fishing and cruise down the river. Contact directly or through Lago Verde Turismo in Santarém ☎ *(91) 522-7577; FAX 522-2118.*

EXCURSION PACKAGES

Lago Verde Turismo

A few good tour operators can be found in Santarém, but this is the most reliable, whose various options can be tailored to your time, budget, and interest. (Also see "Travel Agencies" under *Hands-On Santarém.*)

River Curuana

An excellent three-day/two-night package that could serve as an exotic honeymoon starts from the airport, where you transfer to a 10-person boat and head up the river. Here, a canoe with outboard motor will be awaiting you for navigation through the numerous *igarapés* full of water lilies, pink dolphins, alligators and birds. The region is known for having more native trees than any other, and as the river meets the Amazon, *varzea* appears, which is good for piranha fishing.

After lunch you return to the regional boat and go up river to visit **Vila Pacoval**, a village founded by runaway black slaves originally from Guyana. At dusk (5:30–6:30 p.m.), small canoes are taken out for alligator hunting. Afterwards, a special candlelit dinner is served in the middle of the forest. The next morning you visit the outdoor and indoor labs of **SUDAM**, a research center for reforesting projects.

Then you cruise down river to **Alter de Chão**, arrive at dawn and breakfast on the island. After breakfast, you are invited to climb the mountain; successful trekkers are feted with ice cream and champagne. The rest of the day is spent at Alter de Chão (at the beach or in canoes); then you may either head for the airport in the evening or spend the night in a hotel. Groups of 8 to 10 people run $300 per person. A private package for two people runs about $1900.

Lago Verde Turismo also offers excursions to both Monte Alegre and Alenquer on a three-day package. (For address and telephone, see under "Travel Agencies" in *Hands-On.*)

HANDS-ON SANTARÉM
ARRIVALS

Air • Flights are available from Belém, Campo Grande, Cuiabá, Alta Floresta, Manaus, Rio Branco, Rio, Recife, Fortaleza, Salvador, São Paulo and a few other cities. The airport is located 13 kilometers from town. Taxis to downtown are readily available at the airport: the Tropical Hotel provides complimentary shuttle bus service for its guests. Airlines that fly into Santarém are: **Varig/ Cruzeiro** at *Rua Siqueira Campos, 227;* ☎ *522-2084 and 522-1084* (at the airport) and **VASP** at *Av. Rui Barbosa, 786;* ☎ *522-1680.*

Boat • See "River Cruises" below.

Bus • The *Rodoviária* ☎ *522-3392* is located on the Santarém-Cuiabá highway. Conditions permitting, bus service is available to Belém (through connections) and other points.

CAR RENTALS

Localiza/National
   Av. Mendonça Furtado, 1603; ☎ *522-1130.*

CITY TRANSPORTATION

Aquila
   (air and land taxis) ☎ *522-1848;* ☎ *522-2596 (at the airport).*

CLIMATE

Tropical temperatures vary between 68–92 degrees F in January and 69–90 degrees F in July. The dry season runs July–Dec.; the rainy season from July to Jan., when it precipitates copiously. March receives the most rain and, therefore, is the coolest month. The annual alternation of low and high tide that occurs every six months makes for exuberant ecological contrasts. From July–Dec., the meadows become excellent pastures for cattle and buffalo; between Jan.–July, wildlife must swim through swamps or be transported to *terra firm.*

MEDICAL EMERGENCIES

José Garcia, M.D.
   ☎ *522-1044.* This doctor specializes in tropical diseases and speaks English and Spanish.

João Otaviano de Matos, M.D.
   ☎ *522-5276.* This doctor specializes in internal medicine and cardiology.

MONEY EXCHANGE

No one officially changes money in Santarém (better to come with a sufficient pile of *cruzeiros*), but in emergencies, drugstores along Rua Siqueira Campos may comply; inquire of the owners.

POST OFFICE

Correio
   Av. Rui Barbosa, 1169.

PRIVATE GUIDE

A favored licensed guide these days is **Paulo Henrique Melchior**, who is fluent in both German and English, and particularly experienced in ecological tours. Contact him through **Lago Verde Turismo** ☎ *522-7577* or privately ☎ *522-6951*.

RIVER CRUISES

The oldest and still most common mode of travel in the region is boat, as witnessed by the 7000 vessels operating in the municipality, from small wooden diesel-powered crafts to large catamaran passenger ships owned by the ENASA Company. Luxury liners from the States and Europe are becoming a more frequent sight.

Larger boats and ships dock at the deep-water pier **(Docas do Pará)**, located at the far northern end of the Santarém-Cuiabá Highway. Most other boats leave from the area between the Market Place and the Praça do Pescador (Fisherman's Square). Though they are not always safe, two-decker *gaiolas* are the most popular way to journey downriver. Some have been known to sink from being overloaded with chickens, pigs and produce, but better precautions are taken these days to avoid the kind of tragedy that befell the **Cisne Branco** about eight years ago. (On a special New Year's cruise the ship sank, drowning everyone aboard when all the passengers moved to the right side at the same time to see the approaching port of Manaus. I must add, however, in 1991 I daringly took a cruise on the resurrected *Cisne Branco* and happily survived.) For any bookings for river cruises, contact **Lago Verde Turismo** or contact ENASA directly.

Most boats headed for Manaus or Belém offer a limited number of private cabins, and should be reserved as early as possible. The cabins in **gaiolas** are extremely small, but their virtue is privacy; if you rent one, you may also want to hang a hammock in the main galley to lounge during the hot days. Usually, there is an upper deck with a snack bar where you can sit and watch the banks pass by. More often than not, the price of the ticket includes meals, but do take a pile of bananas, oranges and cashews because the food may not be up to your personal standards of cleanliness.

Travel time by boat from Santarém: Belém 75 hrs., Manaus 75 hrs., Alenquer 6 hrs., and Monte Alegre 10 hrs.

Enasa Boats have been one of the most popular tourist excursions between Belém and Manaus (with stops in Santarém). Made for touring, the boats boast air-conditioned cabins with private bathroom, restaurant, telephone, video lounge, bar, sundeck, and swimming pool. The trip from Belém to Santarém runs three days; Santarém to Manaus two days. Schedules in the past have run once a month.

In Santarém contact **Representante ENASA**, *Tr. Francisco Correa, 34;* ☎ *(91) 522-1934;* in **Belém**, *Av. Presidente Vargas, 41;* ☎ *(91) 223-3011;* in **Manaus**, *Rua Mal. Deodoro, 61;* ☎ *(92) 232-4280.*

TELEPHONE COMPANY

Local and international phone calls may be made at **TELEPARA** *Av. São Sebastião, 913.*

TIME

Santarém is one hour earlier than Belém—a fact that sometimes confuses even airline officials.

TOURIST INFORMATION

Tourist brochures and information can be obtained at **Divisão Municipal de Turismo**, *Centro Cultural João Fona, Rua da Imperador, no number,* ☎ *523-2434.*

TRAVEL AGENCIES

Lago Verde Turismo Ltda.

Rua Galdino Veloso, 384; ☎ *(91) 522-7577; FAX 522-2118.* One of the premier agencies in Santarém, Lago Verde offers personalized packages to large and small groups. Good English-speaking management and guides are available for fishing, trekking, scientific expeditions, photographic projects and nature studies.

Agências Tropicais de Turismo/Hotel Tropical

Av. Mendonça Furtado, 4120, ☎ *522-1533.* This agency provides transfers from the airport to the hotel for its guests, as well as a variety of group tours, including half-day city tour, Alter de Chão, Meeting of the Waters, Belterra, piranha fishing and nighttime alligator hunts.

Amazon Turismo Ltda.

Trav. Turiano Meira, 1084; ☎ *522-2620, FAX 522-1098.* This company offers overnight trips to Monte Alegre in a jeep, and Alenquer in a wooden riverboat, as well as daytrips to Fordlândia and the National Park.

WHEN TO GO

From August–January, the flowers become increasingly more profuse and there's more sand on the beach. January is peak time, with **New Year's Day** celebrated with big bashes. **Festa do Sairé** occurs the first week in July. On June 29, a procession of *bumba-meu-boi* takes place during the **São Pedro** festival. In September there is the **International Tucunaré Fishing Championship**.

BELÉM

Belém effectively entered the 20th century in 1961, when Juscelino Kubitschek's highway from Brasília reached its final destination.
For centuries prior, however, the city, strategically placed on the Amazon estuary close to the mouth of the Rio Tocantins, had served
nobly as a natural port for the steady stream of products extracted
from the Amazon. Dating back to 1621, the city of Belém, which is
also the capital of the state of Pará, was christened on the feast day of
St. Mary of Bethlehem, and at times is still referred to by its long no-
menclature: **Nossa Senhora do Belém do Grão-Pará** or, at least,
Belém do Pará. The state, which is larger than most European countries, is the wealthiest in Brazil in regards to ore; even Indian tribes,
such as the Kayapó, are sitting on some of the richest mahogany and
gold reserves in the country.

It was the 19th-century rubber boom that transformed this natty
little port into a graceful, Victorian city of *fin de siècle* arches and Italianate palazzos. What makes Belém truly beautiful are its avenues
and plazas, shaded with magnificent *mangueiras* (mango trees) that
cool the cobblestones when temperatures soar above 80 degrees.
Even today, the historic quarter, which retains much of its art nou-
veau and neoclassical structures, is a pleasure to stroll through, butt-
ed on all sides by a thriving market. One need only step inside the
famed **Teatro da Paz**, the city's all-purpose theater, to appreciate the
ingenuity of the rubber barons who longed to recreate European
culture in the middle of the jungle. Yet it is the **Ver-o-Peso** market,
facing the waterfront, which outclasses any other outdoor marketplace in Brazil, and perhaps in South America. Crammed, chaotic,
and totally confusing to the uninitiated, the Ver-o-Peso is a veritable
lion's den of exotic sights and smells that could take days to exhaust.

Although most jungle-destined tourists have traditionally headed
for Manaus, Belém shouldn't be missed. Not only is the city more
navigable by foot, but the jungle expeditions I experienced here
should be considered some of the best in the region. Like Manaus,
Belém is hot and humid, but the locals here have developed a sense
of humor: They refer to themselves as fish because they feel they
breathe more water than air.

SIGHTS

ON FOOT

Hilton Hotel
    Belém is a perfect city to stroll through. Start your walking tour in front of

the Hilton. (If you're not staying there, you might take a peek at the lush breakfast buffet, open to the public but free for guests.)

Praça da República
The park is directly across the street from the Hilton. Once dense with tropical forest, the site was cleared in the 17th century to make way for Belém's first cemetery; later it became the city's principal park. There's even a *coreto*, an iron-grilled pagoda where brass bands used to entertain.

Teatro da Paz

Mon.–Fri. 8 a.m.–noon, 2–6 p.m. Dominating the square is the city's pride and joy, the theater, an unabashedly neoclassical opera house surrounded by Greek columns and adorned at its entrance with the four busts of the Muses. Inaugurated in 1878, the plush theater, with its bronze staircases and fabulous tiled floors was fueled by the ostentatious passions of the rubber barons who continually looked to Europe for style. Consequently, the foyer's crystal mirrors are Italian, the massive chandelier in the lobby German, the pastel, fluted light fixtures Art Deco. The theater's ceiling is an amazing marriage of Italianate painting and grillwork from which is suspended an eight-tiered, 1.5 ton crystal chandelier. The adjacent Salão Nobre is absolutely charming, once a salon for the elite balls and now the stage for chamber concerts and voice recitals. Note that the salon's ceiling painting is not from the original construction but was designed in 1960 by São Paulo artist Armando Balloni to reflect the wealth of Amazonian animals. Walk out to the balcony and look up to see the four Muses: from right to left, Comedy, Poetry, Music and Drama. In 1986 the building, after laboring under a blue facade for many years, was restored to its original pink color. Backstage, you'll see plaques honoring performances by the great ballerina Anna Pavlova in 1918 and the great Brazilian soprano Bidu Sayão. If you have the opportunity to catch a performance of theater or music, grab it; merely ask your concierge or check the daily newspapers for listings. Free tours are given continuously throughout the day, though only in Portuguese.

Bar do Parque
This outdoor café, on the side of the theater near the Hilton, is where the city's artists, singers and streetwalkers gather until the wee hours of morning. Nearby is a kiosk that sells bread and coffee in the morning and beer and *caipirinhas* in the afternoon.

Teatro Experimental Walder Henrique
Rua Pres. Vargas, 645; ☎ *222-4762.* Walking down **Rua Presidente Vargas**, you'll come upon this theater. Started in 1979, this experimental theater is a showcase for avant-garde music, plays and dance, with preference given to artists who are not yet professionals. Due to their struggling budget, shows are not given daily; they start around 9 p.m. when they do happen. Seats go for about $1.50.

Rua Santo Antônio
Walk down **Av. Presidente Vargas** to the right of the theater, passing a

travel agency, the **Varig** office at #363, and the **Monopólio Turismo Câmbio** (for exchanging money) at #325. Turn left on Rua Santo Antônio, a cobblestone street with no cars, down the middle of which are the remains of 19th-century trolley tracks. As the principal shopping avenue of the city (also called Comércio) the street overflows with shops and vendors hawking all kinds of third-world quality goods. As you wander, look up at the second-story houses, once 19th-century fashionable homes and still adorned with exquisite tile work and pastel-colored balconies and shutters.

Restaurante Vegetariano e Mercadinho Natural

At #264 on Rua Santo Antônio, you'll find the vegetarian market where you can stock up on natural shampoos, whole foods and Amazon teas. Upstairs, the restaurant serves only lunch Mon.–Fri. from 11:30 a.m.–3 p.m.

Paris N'América

Down the street from the market, do peek inside the Paris N'América, today a dry goods store but once a beautiful home constructed in 1906 for Francisco Castro by the Portuguese master Ricardo Salvador Fernandes Mesquita. From the sculptured ceilings to the dramatic grilled stairway, many of the details of the original architecture are still intact. The steel was imported from Scotland, the ceramic-tiled floor and mechanical clock from Germany, the bronze light fixtures from France, the crystal mirrors from Belgium, and the outside wall tiles from Portugal.

Praça Mercês

A few steps further on, you'll reach Praça Mercês, home to many finely restored buildings. Dominating the plaza is the church known as **Mercês**, founded in 1640. Despite the graffiti, you can see that the facade is still intact. This may be just the time that you need an ice-cold *água de coco*, which can be bought in front of the church.

Travessa Frutuoso Guimarães

Next, walk in front of the church on Rua Gaspar Viana and turn right on Travessa Frutuoso Guimarães. At #63, you can pick up decent mosquito nets and hammocks for about $6–14; white canvas hammocks with lace go for about $40.

Ver-O-Peso Market

Nearby, along **Av. Castilhos** facing the pier, you'll enter into one of the great third-world marketplaces of all time. To a first-world eye, the open-air market may look like a den of iniquity, but it's actually the epitome of Amazonian life: hundreds of tiny stalls selling anything and everything that floats up the river—from fruits and vegetables and Brazil nuts to snake skins, turtle soap and dolphin eyes (the last three all contraband materials). Begun as a checkpoint in 1688, the market received its name ("watch the weight") from the Portuguese habit of weighing all merchandise that passed through the port so that a tax could be charged. Today, the market is also a food bazaar, with scores of native women cooking aromatic dishes for the workers who cram into the tiny pathways. The air in the market is hot and dense and barely conducive to dining, but if you're brave enough, browse around until you find something that looks edible. The dark-maroon, soup-like juice sitting in the large tin pans is *açaí*, a true Amazon delicacy made with sugar and manioc juice (it tastes a bit like avocado and goes well with fried fish). Take a moment to watch the workers squeeze the water out of the ground manioc with a long straw tool called *tipiti* that works something like an accordion. As you walk through the market, each section will resound with its own sounds and smells. Daily life, not just business, is carried on here, with lots of flirting and cursing going on between stalls. A perusal of the tropical fruit stands will give you an idea of the enormous variety available here; note the Brazil nuts that come lodged in big brown shells, just as they're found in the forest. The large green spiny-looking fruit is a *graviola*. The herb section is particularly ripe with superstition and folklore. Good buys are small bottles of concentrated oils like *baunilha* (vanilla) and jasmine or more potent love potions like the *"Corre Atrás"* designed to make a man "Run After" you. *Tamaquaré* powder is a cooked lizard powder sprinkled on husbands to get them to calm down sexually— a hot-selling item in the Amazon. (Some women actually buy the live lizards you see in the market and cook them into potions themselves. Another trick is to place the live lizard in the same water where the man regularly washes his clothes.) On the opposite extreme, stall #54 sells perfume that comes complete with a boa constrictor inside, well known as a "fatal attraction" potion.

Insider Tip

Due to the tight space and general mayhem, this market can be dangerous. Go with little money on you, do not wear gold chains or jewelry, keep your bags close to you at all times, and be cautious about taking photos. Since a number of vendors trade in contraband items (particularly endangered species), they do not care to have their business recorded.

Meat Market

Don't miss the meat market nearby, a chrome-grilled structure brought from England in 1909; its cast-iron frame and Victorian turrets are souvenirs from the time when the British built most of the port a century ago. Inside, individual stands are manned by brawny workers who constantly yell at each other while slicing carcasses hanging from wires. The wet, smelly fish market in the same complex opens in the early morning and closes by 1 p.m.; here you can view full-sized samples of the region's most typical fish. Buyers receive their merchandise wrapped in large leaves from the *guarumã* bush, then supply their own plastic bag—a traditional Amazonian way of economizing on paper.

In general, the entire area near the pier is endlessly fascinating and ripe with photo ops. Outside the market you may see baby monkeys for sale (illegal) or even baby sloths (also illegal).

Boulevard Castilhos França

Make sure you walk down this boulevard next to the bay, where fishermen and merchants dock their schooners and canoes laden with goods. Unfortunately, a lot of trash litters the portside here, even though (or because) many people use their boats as floating lodges. You may even see rats scurrying about these barges to no one's apparent dismay. Do note the Texaco floating gas station in the bay, an omnipresent reminder of Western influence.

Praça do Relógio

Across from the pier near the market, this square, with its large, monumental clock tower, is often used by guides as a meeting place.

Insider Tip

ENASA boats to Marajó Island leave from the port on the other side of the market.

Praça Frei Caetano Brandão

Walk from the market past the mango and bamboo tree-filled Dom Pedro II Park to the Praça Frei Caetano Brandão, dominated by the 19th-century **Catedral de Nossa Senhora da Graça**. Sadly run-down on the outside, the cathedral boasts some of Brazil's finest paintings inside, though the lights are rarely turned on. *Hours for mass are Tues.–Thur. 5:30 p.m., Sat. 6:30 a.m. and 7 p.m., and Sun. 7 a.m., 9 a.m., 5 p.m. and 8 p.m.* It's from here that nearly one million strong begin their journey to the Basílica each year during the Círio festival. Nearby is the Igreja Santo Alexandrian, an 18th century church whose small collection of religious art may be open.

Forte do Castelo

Open daily 8 a.m.–noon, 2–6 p.m.: restaurant 11:30 a.m.–3 p.m., 6:30–11:30 p.m. This is a good place to end the walking tour. This fort marks the city's founding, as it was the first building constructed in Belém, strategically located at the confluence of the Guajará Bay and Guamá River on a hill commanding a view of the bay. Once headquarters for the military operations that expelled the English, French and Dutch, it also provided a refuge for the Caabanagem revolutionaries. Now the fort houses the **Círculo Militar Club and Restaurant**, open to the public. Actually, there's nothing to do here but sit and drink (better at night when the weather is cooler, though during the day the view of the port below is fantastic). From the perimeter of the fort you can also see the **Feira d'Açai** down below, where boats loaded with raw *açaí* start arriving as early as 4:30 a.m. You can also see large cargo boats transporting ceramics from the nearby islands and returning home laden with mineral water and sodas.

Cidade Velha (Old City)

The area around the market and cathedral is full of quaint squares and colonial homes with grilled balconies and colorful shutters. Browse at will, but do try to avoid **Rua da Ladeira**—not a safe street to walk through due to the prostitutes and homeless who frequent its alleyways. (During the day, it's more or less okay, but avoid completely at night.)

MORE SIGHTS

Basílica de Nossa Senhora de Nazaré

Praça Justo Chermont. Daily 6:30–11:30 a.m., 3–9 p.m. One of the most stunning churches in Brazil, this basilica is the end point for the annual procession of Círio de Nazaré on the second Sun. in Oct. The church, which was initiated in 1909, took 40 years to build—a majestic blending of Italian granite and mosaics, French stained glass and a ceiling of red cedar taken from the forest. The idolized statue of the Madonna, which is carried through the streets, rests above the altar in a circle of cherubs (a photo showing details can be found to the right of the altar). Devotion to the statue is so intense that you might see petitioners dragging themselves on their knees to the altar in payment of a promise. In front of the basilica is a modern, open-air complex consisting of high altar, ampitheater, pantheon and war monument, where mass during the Círio festival is held.

Museu Paraense Emílio Goeldi

Parque Zoobotânico, Av. Magalhães Barata, 376; ☎ *224-9233. Tues., Wed., Thurs., and Sat. 9 a.m.–noon, 2–5 p.m. (Tues. and holidays free in the a.m.), Fri. 9 a.m.–noon, Sun., 8 a.m.–5:45 p.m. Closed Mon.* Bélem's premier museum was initiated in 1866 to record the richness of Amazônia's flora, fauna, rocks, indigenous culture and folklore. The multimedia complex embraces a park, zoo and indoor museum. The park, planned after an Amazonian jungle, has fewer trees per square foot than the forest, but offers more species, including rubber trees, *guaraná* (from which the herbal stimulant is taken), *pau-brasil, cedro vermelho, castanha-do-pará* (Brazil nut), and the huge *sumaumeira* (the biggest tree in the South American jungle). At the desk of the permanent exhibition, ask for a guidebook in English, then tour the fine displays of stuffed birds, basketry, Indian artifacts and jewelry. Running freely outside in the zoo are *cutias* (a type of anteater with the frisky personality of a raccoon). Also to be seen is a dazzling array of tropical birds, alligators, cats, tapirs, manatees and electric eels. The souvenir shop is excellent.

Parque dos Igarapés

Conjunto Satélite WE 12, # 1000, Ananindeua, Pará. Office: Rua Manoel Barata, 704, Edifício Paes de Carvalho, #403, Belém, CEP 66020; ☎ *235-1910, 223-8324, 227-2588. Reserve only on Sun. or groups.* This tropical park owned by a private family is a welcome respite from the heat of the city and the ruggedness of the jungle. The $10 entrance fee can go toward food and beverages taken in the excellent open-air restaurant or beside the natural swimming pool (whose water was pronounced cleaner than the drinking water in Belém). Ecological walks can be taken through the forested grounds or you can hop in a canoe and navigate the narrow *igarapés* (streams) that seem to go everywhere and nowhere. Children will love the wood-log playground and there are so many animals here (including an *atú* (armadillo), *creatipurí* (squirrel) and *preguiçosa* (sloth) that a staff vet is required by law. Belemites flock to this complex on weekends when live bands turn the main arena into a outdoor nightclub.

WHERE TO STAY

Accommodations in Belém run from the ever-efficient, luxurious Hilton to the modest pousada. Air conditioning is de rigeur.

Expensive	**Over $75**
Moderate	**$50–$75**
Inexpensive	**Under $30**

Hilton International Belém

Av. Presidente Vargas, 882 (Praça da República) (Centro); ☎ *(91) 222-5611; FAX 225-2942.* The Hilton is Belém's first and only five-star—a luxurious relief from the heat and humidity of the cityscape. Service is geared towards those who wake up at dawn for river tours or stay up till dawn to dance; breakfast opens at 4 a.m. An impressive underground mall of stores includes a deli, famous for salamis, cheeses and exquisite pastries. The pool is small, but unusually shaped and is a magnet on the weekends for chic cruisers. The gym is the best in the city, with free weights, aerobic classes, sauna and massage. An elegant club serves exotic tropical drinks and offers live music on the weekends. Apartments are plush, with marble-topped bathrooms and comfortable beds. Normal rates for June 1995 are projected at $110 for singles, $140–$150 for doubles. Fielding's readers receive the following discount: $85 for singles or doubles. (361 apts.)

Expensive. All cards.

Equatorial Palace

Av. Braz de Aguiar, 612 (Nazaré); ☎ *(91) 241-2000, FAX (091) 223-5222.* This traditional four-star is located in a prime area of shady streets and chic stores, four blocks from downtown. Smaller and more intimate than the Hilton, the hotel boasts a fine, old-world restaurant, called 1900, famous for its Portuguese codfish. The circular, blue-tiled swimming pool is surrounded by a *churrascaria* and pool bar. The romantic piano bar is a favorite in the city. The older rooms, mostly used for long-term residences, have an old-world charm the newer apartments lack. Ignore the tacky lobby. Singles run $75, doubles $87. Fielding's readers receive 20 percent discount. (296 apts.) *Expensive. All cards.*

Novotel Belém

Av. Bernardo Sayão, 4804 (Guamá), 4 kilometer; ☎ *(91) 229-8011, FAX 229-8707.* Near the University of Belém, the Novotel is a good, medium-priced hotel, particularly suitable for families who make a one-day stop in Belém; most three-hour river tours leave from the harbor located in the hotel's backyard. The pool area, lined with *açaí* trees, is extensive, with a children's pool, playground and volleyball court. All rooms are air-conditioned and come with two double beds and an extra couch bed, color TV and a large desk. Make sure you ask for a room with a view to the river. Laundry service available. Standard doubles run $57, suites $73. Fielding's readers receive 20 percent discount if they pay in cash. (121 apts.)

Moderate. All Cards.

Zoghbi Park Hotel

Rua Pe. Prudêncio, 220 (Centro); FAX and ☎ *(91) 241-1800.* This small but adequate three-star offers a good low-priced option for discerning travelers. Rooms, all air-conditioned, are nearly monklike, but clean, with finely finished wood doors, closets and headboards. A good buy is the *especial*, with a fascinating view of the city's back streets. The bar doubles as a TV lounge. All room keys are electronic and safes are available at reception. Standard doubles run about $27, special doubles $32. (33 apts.)

Moderate. Cards: V.

Regente Hotel

Av. Gov. José Malcher, 485 (Centro); ☎ *(91) 241-1222; FAX 224-0343.* Centrally located within walking distance of the Praça da República, the Regente is a reliable low-priced hotel; nearby is the fine restaurant Lá Em Casa. Apartments, with color TV and minibar, are cheerful and overlook the city's rooftops. A good budget idea is the standard central for $23. Noise from the city traffic may filter up to the rooms. The restaurant offers standard fare without much style. Safes at reception. (149 apts.)

Inexpensive. All cards.

Vidonha's

Rua O' de Almeida, 476 (Centro); ☎ *(91) 225-1444.* A simple, small hotel that isn't at all seedy, Vidonha's has rock-bottom rates that can't be beat. Apartments come with minibar and color TV, and furniture in good condition. The only drawback are the small windows. Safes at the reception. Standard singles run $12, doubles $16, specials, which hold three beds and a partial front view, run $18. (48 apts.)

Inexpensive. Cards: DC, MC, V.

WHERE TO EAT

Expensive	Over $15
Moderate	$5–15
Inexpensive	Under $5

Lá Em Casa

Av. Gov. José Malcheer, 24 (Centro); ☎ *223-1212. Daily noon–3 p.m., 7 p.m–midnight.* Some folks say the only "native" food in Brazil can be found in Belém, where it was taught to the first colonists by the Indians. Owner Ana Maria Martin, who learned to cook from her grandmother (and even went upstream to the family farm to learn from Indian women) has received international raves for her *maniçoba*, a concoction of meat or fish mushed with manioc leaves that must be cooked for four to five days to extract the poison. Warm and voluble, Dona Ana Maria has installed two restaurants in this colonial-style house: the air-conditioned salon, called O Outro (The Other), which serves hot and cold buffets, and the back patio, called *Lá em Casa* (There at Home), with its gargantuan *flamboyante* tree in the middle.

The *Menu Paraense,* for about $10, gives you a chance to try all the different regional tastes. A special lunch plate is a steal at $4. *Pato no Tucupi* (duck made with a manioc sauce available only in Belém) and *patinhas de carangueijo à Milanesa* (fried crab legs) are excellent. The fish *tucunaré* is best eaten in Santarém.   *Moderate. All cards.*

Restaurante Círculo Militar
Praça Frei Caetano Brandão (Forte de Castelo); ☎ *223-4374. Daily noon–3:00 p.m. and 7 p.m.–11:00 p.m.* With its balconylike salon overlooking the bay, this is the perfect place to lunch away from the hubbub of the marketplace. Located in the Castelo Fort, it's especially romantic at night. A light lunch might be a crabmeat omelette, for under $6. *Polvo* (octopus), cooked in tomato sauce with potatoes and cooked eggs, is hearty. *Lagostim,* for about $7, is a small freshwater shrimp breaded with egg and stuffed with cheese. Try the native fruit juices like *cupuaçu* or *taperebá,* from the cashew family.   *Moderate. All Cards.*

Augustus
Av. Almirante Barroso, 493 (Marco); ☎ *226-8317. Daily noon–2:30 p.m., 7 p.m.–11:30 p.m., Sat. 7 p.m.–midnight.* Dark wood-beamed ceilings vie with tropical gardens in this chic restaurant. Beef, fish and shrimps run about $10 a plate. A specialty is *brochette misto à Piamonteza,* a mixed grill of steak, pork and sausage. Don't miss the *coco branco,* an intensely sweet concoction of shredded coconut glazed in sugar and spiked with cloves.
                    Moderate. All Cards.

Miralha Bar e Restaurante
Av. Doca de Souza Franco, 194; ☎ *241-4832. Daily 8 a.m.–4 a.m.* Hip Belemites come to this tropical beer garden after work for a drink (and a pickup). Families, however, will also feel at home. Music (usually MPB) is the best in the city with live bands starting at 9:30 p.m.; a $3 cover must be paid after 9:45 p.m. The special is Japanese food: *camarão na chapa miralha* comes with super-sized shrimp, vegetables and fries on a simmering grill. The bar is located near the docks in the Umarizal district.
                    Moderate. No Cards.

Hilton Delicatessen
Av. Presidente Vargas, 882 (Praça da República). Daily 11 a.m.–9 p.m., Sun. 10 a.m.–2 p.m. Takeout deli in the Hilton Hotel. Excellent pastries, salamis and cheese. Stock up if you're planning a river trip.
                    Moderate. All Cards.

VEGETARIAN

Alternativa Natural
Rua O. de Almeida, 306. Mon.–Fri. 11:30 a.m.–3 p.m., lunch. A nice, quick alternative for vegetarians—a natural foods buffet, including tropical fruit juices, noodles, soy meat, fried macaxeira, soup, salad and dessert for about $2. Unfortunately, the rice is white. The post office on Rua Santo Antônio is nearby.   *Inexpensive. No Cards.*

Nutribem Ltda.

> *Rua Santo Antônio, 264;* ☎ *224-3429.* Vegetarian restaurant and market for natural products.

ICE CREAM

One can't come to the Amazon without trying its most famous delicacy —ice cream made from tropical fruit flavors. Needless to say, it's the best way to beat the heat (and the parlors are usually air-cooled), but the flavors alone are unforgettable—ranging from delicate to sensuously ripe.

Tip Top

> *Travessa Pariquis at the corner of Padre Eutiquip (Batista Campos).* A tip-top ice cream parlor 4.5 blocks from the Hilton, with more than 150 exotic flavors. *Bacuri*, made from the hard-shelled fruit, is particularly delicious.

STREET FOOD

You're sure to see folks on the street slurping something from a shell. It's *tacacá*, made with dried shrimps and *tucupí* (a sauce made from manioc), served in a *cuia*, the dried shell of the fruit of the *calabaça* tree. *Tacacá* runs hot (both in temperature and in spices), and if you add pepper, you'll have even more sweat running down your brow—an effect strangely adored by locals.

NIGHTLIFE

Sabor da Terra

> *Av. Visconde de Souza Franco, 685;* ☎ *223-8620. Mon.–Sat. 9:00 p.m. Fee: $17 table, $5 tickets.* Come to dine on traditional Amazonian dishes or just enjoy the city's best folklore show, featuring backland dances like xote, forró, lundi, carimbó and lambada. The eight dancers are young and attractive and not at all bored. The show lasts about two hours; one fine number is a cowboy dance with lassos straight from Marajó Island.

Insider Tip

Check the newspaper for listings of local musicians like Nilson Choves, a singer/guitarist; Jane du Boc, an ex-volleyball player who sings like Zizi Possi; Rosanna, a wonderful singer of all types of music, Alibi de Orfeu, who sings Portuguese blues; Debson Tayonara, who sings MPB; and Oficina de Samba, an eight-man group that performs popular sambas.

Boite Lapinha

> *Trav. Padre Eutíquio, 3901;* ☎ *229-3290. Shows: Mon.–Sat. 8:30 p.m. Fees: $16 table for 4, tickets $5.50, bermudas not allowed for men.* The city's most famous nightclub hangs somewhere between funky and old-fashioned. A statue of Iemanjá surrounded by live ducks greets arrivals while inside, a 50s silver ball dominates the stage. The shows change every half hour, from comedy to live bands to striptease after 11:30 p.m., all introduced by a transvestite MC. The specialty is *língua de boi* (bull tongue), served with mashed potatoes. Dancing is fun, but beware of mosquitoes and be extra careful when you go to the bathroom: There are three

of them (men, women, and "others"), considered a major accomplishment by gays in Belém.

SHOPPING

MARKETS

The main city market is the **Ver-o-Peso** (see under "Walking Tour"). There's also an **artisan Fair**, *Praça da República. Fri.–Sat.*, not so big but worth a look. Good buys are drums, flutes, handmade jewelry and semi-precious stones. In the middle of the square is a monument to Brazil's independence. The **Palha Market** takes place every day near the Novotel Hotel—small but exceedingly third-world, with the intense smell of fish and dried spices.

CRAFTS

Cacique
Av. Presidente Vargas, 892; ☎ *222-1144.* The best artisan shop in Belém.

Insider Tip

Among local crafts are aromatic essences of oil, like Cheiro de Pará, made from Amazonian plants. Many of these oils are related to candomblé practices and often come packaged with promises of love, money, or good health. Roots and barks are also ground into pleasant-smelling powders and fashioned into dolls or simple sachets. Other good buys are leather-tooled jewelry, wood carvings and fiber crafts.

If you're in the market for an Amazonian icon, look for a *muiraquitã*—a piece of green jade (or ceramic) in the shape of a frog. Legend has it that once upon a time in the middle of the Amazon forest, a tribe of female warriors were desperately in search of men for reproduction. One full moon they waited for Yara, goddess of the water, who unearthed some green stones from the depths of the river. The women dived into the river to retrieve the stones, then shaped the jade (or malachite) into a frog, which they then wore as an amulet. (Since the jungle later became populated, we can assume the fetish worked.) Anyone who wears it today is said to enjoy protection and good luck. (Specimens in the museum were found on Marajó Island by the Aruã tribe who used them).

HERBS

Casa das Ervas Medicinais
Rua Gaspar Viana, 230. This "House of Medicinal Herbs" is veritably crammed with wooden bins of dried leaves, herbs, barks and seeds for every illness imaginable—even cancer. The owner has been in business for years, and even makes mixtures that come refrigerated in tall glass bottles (the tonic I bought did wonders for me). You can also buy a two-volume book (Portuguese only) called *A Flora Nacional na Medicina Doméstica*, which tells the story of each herb and what disease it cures.

Perfumaria Chamma
Rua Boaventura da Silva, 606; ☎ *224-7298* and **Artesanato Juruá**, across

the street from the Equatorial Palace Hotel on Avenida Brás de Aguiar, are both well known for natural soaps, shampoos, cosmetics and perfumes made from Amazonian plants. Celebrities and actresses, in particular, swear by the products at Juruá.

POTTERY

Stúdio Rosemiro Pinheiro

 # 100, Soledade (past Espírito Santo). On a back dirt road about 18 kilometers from downtown Belém (half-hour by car) is the village of **Icoracy**, an unusual community of craftsmen who maintain the age-old tradition of handmade pottery. One of twenty-odd master artisans in the area, 50-year-old Rosemiro Pinheiro works in a rundown shack that belies the extraordinary output of his "factory." (He personally makes 200 vases a day, while his 25-man team produces over 2300 pieces a month.) Young boys take their canoes down the igarapé in the backyard to find suitable clay, which is then brought back to be cleaned, fashioned on wheels and baked in brick ovens fueled by wood scraps. Children play around Senhor Pinheiro's feet while he fashions vases in the Marajó style, a technique he learned from his father, though he is constantly experimenting with new designs. In the front room is a showcase, from which you may purchase 45-piece feijoada sets, vases of all sizes, commemorative plates and even erotic beer mugs. Prices are extraordinarily low; shipping to the U.S. doubles the price.

EXCURSIONS

A JUNGLE ADVENTURE

Jungle adventures start early in Belém—4 a.m. at the Hilton, when my young guide Tony Rocha picks me up, threading his way through late-night revelers on their way to bed. We drive to the docks at the Novotel Hotel, then board a skiff in the moonlight, the humidity dense around us. Illuminating our way with flashlights, we set off down the Guamá River, passing caboclos *already on their way to* *market. Just 15 minutes later, Tony points out a brand-new island, recently sculpted by the six-hour tides that continually change the face of the Amazon.*

As the sky turns luminescent pink we settle in front of another island called Ilha dos Papagaios and watch as thousands of green parrots wake up, then fly off squawking in pairs. As the sun rises we catch glimpses of river life—women carrying baskets, children paddling to school. Soon we bank and I take my first plunge into the jungle. The feeling of being surrounded by literally millions of life forms—trees, shrubs, vines, birds, ants, bugs and whatever is flying in my face—is thrilling, if not a bit scary. Cutting the path with a machete, Tony points out the sumaumeira tree, an elephantine-like monster, whose trunks are used by natives to beat out messages. We inspect the leaves of the guaramá tree, which is used to wrap fish at market, and another tree whose bark exudes a drinkable milky substance. My boots sink deep into fungus. Despite the incessant cawing of birds, it's difficult not to appreciate the eery silence of the forest—what Peter Mathiesson once described as the "stillness of a cathedral."

A JUNGLE ADVENTURE

Cruising down the river again, we make a pit stop at a riverside grocery—a mere counter crammed with pinga, *the jungle's cure-all. The owners are an elderly couple, whose eyes are incredibly similar—wet and shining. "Maybe we're brother and sister," Senhor Tomé laughs. "When we were young, my father was very active." Their grandchildren, visiting from the city, scamper about in their marvelous backyard—the jungle. Don Palmira talks about the time she saw a white-suited stranger dive into the river late at night (obviously an enchanted* boto, *or dolphin). As a full eclipse of the sun is about to occur, we rush to the pier of an abandoned pepper plantation to catch the fantastic darkening over the river.*

At dusk, our boatman, named Branco, invites us to sleep at his riverside house. The moment the sun sets, mosquitoes attack us in droves, but we bat them off long enough to devour an excellent dinner of fried catfish cooked by his wife. Before retiring, we pump Branco for tales of the curupira, *the legendary master of the forest whose feet are turned backwards and who loves to befuddle humans. Branco tells of his troubles with a* matinta pereira, *a forest witch, who would never leave him alone until he finally married his present wife. At midnight I wake up terrified, since my hammock, which is strung over a boat anchored far up on the bank, is swinging wildly for no reason. Soon Tony's hammock goes out of control, too, driving us both to hysterics, when suddenly, both hammocks stop as fast as they started. At breakfast, Branco looks at us darkly and mumbles that the* matinta pereira *had paid us a visit. We don't laugh.*

After breakfast, we head out for the tiny streams called igarapés, *overhung with luscious green vines, just like in a Tarzan movie. Branco's nine-year-old nephew Fernando shows us how to climb a palm tree with a rope made from leaves. After a hot, sweaty trek over* terra firma, *we reach a* casa de farinha, *a manioc plantation, run by Dona Paula, a heavy-set woman with two grown daughters. Incredibly, the talk turns to the Gulf War, which she has just watched on her battery-powered TV. Before we head back, after a plate of hot manioc and beans, she warns us to watch for cobras—not a happy thought. By the time we return to the dock only 24 hours after we began, it feels like we've been gone a few lifetimes.*

Something similar to the above tour can be arranged through **Amazon Star Turismo** *(Rua Carlos Gomes, 14;* ☎ *and FAX 224-6244) which offers four kinds of tours: a half-day tour around Belém, in front of the Guamá River, including a forest walk, about $28 per person, including hotel transfer and two guides; an eight-hour (full-day) tour down the Guamá and Acará rivers, including a walk in the forest and lunch, about $48 per person; an overnight stay on the Guamá River and Parrot Island, about $70; and an early morning jaunt to Parrot Island, leaving at 4:15 a.m. and returning 8:30 a.m., about $38. Arrangements with Amazon Star Turismo can also be made in Rio through* **Expeditours** *at Rua Visconde de Pirajá 414;* ☎ *(21) 208-5559.*

MOSQUEIRO ISLAND

Eighty-six kilometers from Belém is **Mosqueiro Island**, the main bathing beach of the capital that is well-connected by road and bridges. Back in the 19th century, the first tourists to the island were Portuguese, French and English rubber barons enjoying the boom; today most of the village has still retained its mud-hut look. The hour's drive from the city takes you over a decent highway (BR 360) lined with verdant forests full of *açaí* and *dendê* palm trees (the red flag in front of houses signify they sell *açaí*); after you pass over the 1485-meter bridge, you'll be besieged by young boys hawking beer and bags of sun-dried shrimps. The bus from Belém stops at **Areão Beach**, where the city's main square and market is located, but most of the popular beach action takes place at Farol Beach, where the strand is the widest and rock concerts happen at night. The water here is a bay, where all rivers meet and flow to the ocean, causing an intense wave reaction big enough for surfing. **Murubira Beach** is considered the chic beach, where most of the jetskiers, ultraleve daredevils and windsurfers hang out. Swimming is considered relatively safe. During Carnaval, this beach is one of the hottest in the Amazon.

Since there are 16 *igarapés* in the middle of the island, the landscape is perfect for short jungle tours, which can be arranged through Carlos Alberto Ribeiro, owner of the **Maresia Restaurant**. For a mere $15 for 4.5 hours, you can tour the *igarapés* by canoe, visit a *caboclo*'s house and wheat plantation, and fish for fresh shrimp (you must provide your own transportation to the island). If you would like to spend the night, Senhor Carlos Alberto's colonial-style pousada offers an exotic hideaway on the beach for remarkably low prices (about $30). The restaurant itself, located on Farol Beach, serves a fine *caldeirada* (soup stew with fish, octopus, egg, potatoes, onions, shrimps and manioc flour) and a delicious *peixe tropical*, fish with Brazil nuts and the cream of Brazil nuts. Buffalo steak, another rare delicacy, must be ordered four to five hours in advance. For reservations for the tour and pousada contact the **Restaurante Maresia** at *Av. Beira Mar, 29;* ☎ *(91) 771-1463.* Crafts can be found on the Praça da Matriz from 8:00 a.m. to 9:00 p.m., daily.

When To Go • Mosqueiros Island seemed even hotter to me than Belém. After it rains at 1 or 2 p.m. (every day), the temperature cools a bit, making strolling more palatable. (In Belém the same shower is called the "three o'clock rain.") October is the hottest month, when crabs appear in the saltier water. High season lasts from July to November, with the best months of sunshine being August and September. The months notorious for rain are January and February.

How To Go • Buses leave hourly from the bus station in Belém (during vacations, every 15 min.). The trip takes about 1.5 hour by bus, or one hour by car. Return buses can be found on the Praça da Matriz, ☎ *(91) 771-1204.*

MARAJÓ ISLAND

Just across the bay from Belém is Marajó, an island the size of Switzerland, and fast becoming the major tourist destination of the North. The major attraction are the water buffalo ranches, where enormous herds graze the open plains—a species that first came to the island by way of shipwreck. Also in profusion are hundreds of rare bird specimens, as well as numerous alligators and monkeys, more easily seen here than in the jungle. Those who choose to stay along the coast are awarded with a roiling sea, whose crashing waves result from the confluence of the inland rivers and the ocean seas.

Those who want to truly feel the life of Marajó should go to **Bonjardim**, the most famous of the buffalo ranches. The owners, Eduardo and Eunice Ribeiro, are a charming couple who speak English, French and Spanish and love to sit down to lunch and dinner with their guests (invariably a groaning table of fine delicacies). During the day you can ride the range with the staff, birdwatch and fish for piranha; at night there are organized alligator hunts. Bookings can be made most easily through **Amazon Star Turismo** ☎ *(91) 224-6244.*

Beyond the ranch, the best pousada in the main town of Soure is **Pousada Marjoara** at *Rua de Soure, 33;* ☎ *(91) 741-1287.* In Belém, ☎ *(91) 223-8369.* It's walking distance from the waterfront and the center of town.

How To Go • The fastest way to get to Marajó Island is by plane. Air taxis, which can be reserved for any time, run about $200. Much cheaper are the regularly scheduled flights on TABA (about $30), which leave Monday and Wednedsday from Belém at 7 a.m. and return at 7:40 p.m. from Soure. On Friday the flight leaves Belém at 4 p.m. and returns on Sunday at 4 p.m.

You can also go by bus. Service leaves from Belém's bus terminal at 5 a.m. and includes a bus to Iguraci, a ferry boat to Câmara (across the Marajó Bay, about 3 hrs.), then a bus to Salvaterra and a small ferry to Soure. The return trip leaves from Soure at 2 p.m. Monday–Saturday.

ENASA boats leave Belém Wednesday and Friday at 8 p.m. and return on Thursday and Sunday at 4 p.m., as well as Saturday at 2 p.m., returning at 5 p.m. or 6 p.m. (from Soure). The trip is colorful, usually accompanied by screaming babies, squawking chickens and quacking ducks. Regional class is about $8, but tourist class (much preferred) runs about $18.

The easiest way to visit Marajó is to arrange a package deal through **Amazon Star Turismo**, 25 *FAX 224-6624,* who will provide transfer to the pier in Belém, trip by ferry boat to the island (three hrs., two buses) or boat (five hrs.), city tour, lodge with breakfast, half-day tour to a fazenda to see buffalos and horses, stops at one or two beaches, and a folklore show on Saturday night.

SALINAS

Two hundred kilometers from Belém, Salinas has one of the most beautiful Brazilian beaches and one of the longest, at 15 kilometers. The water changes its color and taste according to the season, due to the influence of the Amazon River. The best hotel is **Brasil Palace** at *Rua Ver. Corinto Pereira de Castro, 70 (Alvorado);* ☎ *891-1064.* An exuberant folklore festival with capoeira (the Brazilian martial art) takes place in August.

HANDS-ON BÉLEM

AIRLINES

Varig/Cruzeiro
  Av. Presidente Vargas, 768/3363 (across from the Praça da República);
  ☎ *225-4222; 233-3941 (airport).*

TABA
  Av. Gov. José Malcher, 883; ☎ *223-6300; 244-2866 (airport).*

Transbrasil
   Av. Presidente Vargas, 780; ☎ 224-6977; 233-3941 (airport).

VASP
   Av. Presidente Vargas, 620, loja B; ☎ 224-5588; 233-0941 (airport).

TAP
   Rua Senador Manoel Barata, 704, room 1401; ☎ 222-5304.

ARRIVALS

Cooperativos Taxis
   ☎ 233-4941. Located at the airport, taxis run about $11–$12 and can be hired at the last counter near the Paratur office. Buses run every 5 min. from the airport for about 25 cents. The name of the bus to downtown is "Perpétuo Socorro" (Perpetual Help).

CAR RENTAL

Avis
   Av. Brazil de Aguiar, 621; ☎ 233-2066; also **Hilton Hotel** ☎ 223-1276, ext. 7573.

CITY TRANSPORTATION

Taxis
   ☎ 224-5444, 229-4799.

CLIMATE

   Temperatures range from 82 degrees F. in the Amazonian winter (June–Aug.) to 90–93 degrees F. in summer (Dec.–Jan.). Rain occurs nearly every day around 3 p.m.; the months with heaviest rainfall are Jan. and Feb.

CONSULATES

U.S.A.
   Av. Oswaldo Cruz, 165; ☎ 223-0800.

Great Britain
   Rua Gaspar Viana, 490; ☎ 223-4353.

South Africa
   Av. Presidente Vargas, 351; ☎ 224-8282.

MONEY EXCHANGE

Casa Francesa
   Padre Prudêncio, 40; ☎ 241-2716.

Carajás
   Av. Presidente Vargas, 762; ☎ 225-1550.

Monopólio Turismo e Câmbio
   Av. Pres. Vargas, 325; ☎ 223-3177.

POINTS BEYOND

The **Rodoviária** (bus station) is located at the end of Av. Gov. José Malcher five kilometers from downtown (☎ *228-0500*). Buses are available to Brasília, Santarém, Salvador, Recife, Fortaleza, and Belo Horizonte, among others.

POLICE

POLITUR

☎ *224-9469*. This is a special division of the local police force that provides security for tourists.

PRIVATE GUIDE

Tony (Antônio) Rocha, *Filho Av. Antônio Everdosa, 1660 (Pedreira);* ☎ *233-1627*, gets my vote for best English-speaking guide in Brazil. A tall order to live up to, but his charm, knowledge and consideration made my first foray into the jungle a joy to remember. He can also be reached through **Amazon Star Turismo** ☎ *224-6244*.

RIVER TRANSPORTATION

The most utilized form of transportation in this region is boat. Wooden multi-deck cruisers called *gaiolas* regularly make trips down the Amazon River from Belém to Santarém and Manaus—a colorful way to make friends and enter into the heart of Amazonian life. Along with grandmothers, babies and traveling salesmen, you might share quarters with dogs, chickens and the family pig. Some boats rent only hammock space (you must provide your own hammock); others offer a few private cabins just big enough for a sink and two bunk beds, with a key to the private toilet. (Note well that the communal toilet is usually *beyond* description.) You might consider renting a cabin (for the privacy and the bathroom) and also hang your hammock in the main galley. During sunlight hours, the boats usually cruise near the banks so you can spot wildlife and peek inside the native homes; most people hang out on the top deck where you can buy beer and snacks. Most exciting are the brief stops at port, where you can watch lovers parting, children hawking fruits and homemade foods, and dockworkers loading the ship's goods.

ENASA touring boats with air-conditioned cabins and private bathrooms are popular ways to cruise from Belém to Manuas through Santarém. In Belém, contact **ENASA** at *Av. Presidente Vargas, 41;* ☎ *(91) 222-3995/224-0528*.

The **Amazon Clipper** is a riverboat built along traditional lines for cruising the Amazon and its tributaries. Eight double cabins with bunks accommodate 16 passengers, with night-time air-conditioning and private toilet facilities. Outboard-powered canoes are used for trips into lagoons, channels, and flooded forest. There's also an open salon, video, library and sundeck. Cruises run three, four and six days. Four-day trips include meeting native *caboclo* families to see jungle life up close. Contact **Expeditours** in Rio for more information ☎ *(21) 287-9697, FAX 521-4388*.

Safari Ecológico (*Rua Monsenhor Coutinho, 119;* ☎ *(92)233-3739; FAX 233-3739*) also offers two double-decked vessels—the Tuná and Fagra II—regional vessels with airconditioning, fully equipped kitchen, video lounge and library to penetrate the tributaries of the Amazon. Cruises from two, three, six and 15 days include close contact with local people; crews include a multilingual guide and a trained biologist. Day and half-day excursions can be taken on the Jacaré-Cu.

TIME

Belém is one hour later than Santarém.

TOURIST INFORMATION

A visit to **PARATUR** (*Praça Kennedy;* ☎ *223-6118; Monday–Friday 8:00 a.m.–6:00 p.m.*) won't be your typical boring trip to the tourist office. An ancillary park is full of native animals, particularly little monkeys called *saguis*, who will come eat from your hand. (They love peanut candy.) The primary handicrafts of the area are sold in an adjacent gallery. Of particular value are the ceramics, whose designs are native to the area. The style called *tapajônica* is characterized by fine line carvings and sculptured decorations, originally from Santarém but now made in Belém; they often resemble ceramics made by ancient civilizations. Of wider, heavier design, more colorful and slightly more modern is the *marajoara* style. It can be recognized by its low relief sculptures, often brightly patterned in red, black and white. You can also stock up on machetes and bows and arrows authentically crafted by native tribes in Amazonas. Brochures in English can be picked up at the information desk in the artisan store.

TRAVEL AGENCY

Most hotels do not have sufficient information regarding river and jungle tours. For the best service in Belém, contact **Amazon Star Turismo Ltda**. *Rua Carlos Gomes, 14;* ☎ *and FAX 224-6244*. Owned by French immigrant Patrick Barbier, the agency offers four kinds of river/jungle tours as well as package deals to Marajó and Mosqueiros islands. Special chartered tours can be arranged for specific needs. (For more information, see under "Excursions," below.)

WHEN TO GO

Best season to come to Belém is June–August, when there is sun in the morning and a little rain in the afternoon. December–March you'll experience the very wet side of the rain forest and will need rubber boots and ponchos.

Don't miss the Círio de Nazaré procession in the second Sunday in October, which attracts over a million religious devotees. The last two weeks of October are filled with celebrations. Make hotel reservations far in advance.

MANAUS

Cruising into Manaus along the Rio Negro is an awesome sight after spending even a few days in the jungle. I've often wondered what Indian or *caboclo* children feel when they first glimpse that skyline of twenty skyscrapers, the yellow construction cranes stretching to heaven, the improbable gold dome of the opera house, all towering over the pastel-colored shacks that cling precariously to the hillside. How could they possibly grasp the meaning of all that black smoke pouring from the refineries, the multicolored boats bobbing in the floating docks, the *desfile* of cars and trucks on the steel-girded bridge? One look, I think, and some of them must go reeling straight back to the forest.

For others, however, Manaus is the technological oasis of the Amazon. Located on the left bank of the Rio Negro, just above its junction with the Amazon River, Manaus is not only the political capital of Amazonas, it's practically the only city with any gusto of civilization. During the rubber boom, it enjoyed a few decades of nouveau-riche expansion; after a long decline, it's been gaining a grittier, if just as economically voracious, reputation ever since being declared a free trade zone in 1966. Just a few hundred meters from the docks, the center of the city is a beehive of activity—noisy stalls and shops selling everything from knock-off electronic equipment to Persian rugs and Taiwanese toys. A few years back, the international airport used to resemble the remains of a wholesale festival as passengers boarded planes loaded with enormous packages, but with the opening of customs to imported goods, the activity of the free zone has mellowed.

The eccentricities of the Rio Negro's ebb and flow sculpt the ever-changing face of Manaus' port. Subject to biannual tides, the river rises and falls as much as 40 feet within a six-month period; hence, the necessity of **floating docks**, a marvelous feat of British engineering (installed during the rubber boom) that responds to the tiniest variation of volume change. Many huts along the shore are actually built on rafts, some merely strung together by chains.

For many, the so-called **"meeting of the waters"** is an awe-inspiring sight—the junction of the Rio Negro and the Amazon, where two rivers of different colors flow together without mixing for miles. Blessed with a mosquito-free environ, the jungles around Manaus attract most of the Amazon's tourists, who usually head for the jungle lodges located three to six hours away by boat. Many visitors spend their first night in Manaus at the famed Tropical Hotel—a veritable palace replete with its own zoo. My suggestion is to stay there *after* your jungle expedition—to slowly acclimate yourself back to the luxuries of civilization.

Nineteenth-century biologists Wallace, Bates and Spruce all set out from Manaus; today the city is home to several hundred international scientists who actively study the forest in the hope of preserving both its fauna and flora. Though severely underfunded, INPA, the National Institute of Amazonian Research, staunchly perseveres in its multidimensional projects, including raising manatees, dolphins and rare sea otters that have been confiscated from illegal fishing expeditions. Many are on display to the public, and a swim-with-the-dolphins project is presently being planned, though its future may be bleak: Brazilians are uncommonly suspicious of the breed.

Unfortunately, the prospects for seeing substantial numbers of animals in their natural habitat near Manaus are somewhat discouraging. Frightened by loud motors and the sound of crunching boots, the smaller, more timid animals have for the most part retreated from the banks of the river while most of the birds are so high up in the canopy they are difficult to see. (If you are desperate for fauna, better go to the Pantanal.) Sadly, many animals in the Amazon have already become extinct; the endangered manatee, common in the time of Henry Bates, is now being illegally slaughtered by *caboclo* fishermen, who often torture the babies to attract the mother. More often seen on excursions (and definitely heard) are screeching howler monkeys and also capybaras, who can sometimes be glimpsed poking their snouts into vegetation. Jaguars are rarely encountered by tourists, but I was once lucky enough to be handed a live sloth to cuddle—an experience no one should ever pass up.

HISTORY

In the early 19th century, what is today known as Manaus was a garrison village called Barra that grew from a small fort the Portuguese had built in 1669 to monitor Spanish invaders. When botanist d'Orbigny stopped there in 1830, he noted that its three thousand ragtag inhabitants were impassioned traders in everything the region had to offer: dried fish, sarsaparilla, Brazil nuts and turtle oil. As rubber became an exportable commodity, Barra evolved into the provincial capital of Manaus, shipping nearly 20,000 tons of rubber abroad by the turn of the century. As rubber barons swelled the city to a population of 50,000, well-attired citizens in European fashions transacted business in gold coins. In 1897 electric trolleys clanged down 10 miles of tree-shaded avenues, and there were even 300 telephone subscribers, used by international stock houses competing for the price of rubber. In 1900 a chicken in Manaus cost about $27, and a bunch of carrots went for $9.

Between 1908 and 1910, when Manaus was at its peak, over 1.2 million square miles of forest, housing 80 million rubber trees, were being developed. With 80,000 tons of rubber exported annually, the country heavily depended on the city's export duties, which covered 40 percent of the national debt. But the rubber bust in 1923 sent Manaus reeling, with many declaring bankruptcy. Ironically, that very year, the 200-mile Madeira-Mamoré railway was inaugurated 1200 miles away to create an easier transport between Bolivia and the Brazilian city of Porto Velho. Called Mad Maria, it was an awesome accomplishment since everything—from charcoal from Wales, steel from Pittsburgh, and termite-resistant wood from Australia— had been shipped in by necessity. Sadly, the construction cost the lives of 6000 laborers and the collapsed market deadened any interest in pursuing the connection.

SIGHTS

Teatro Amazonas

Praça Sebastião; ☎ *234-2776. Daily 9 a.m.–6 p.m.* Imagine the chutzpah, the ingenuity, and the sheer persistence it took to build a grand opera house in the middle of the jungle. Inaugurated after 12 years of construction on Dec. 31, 1896, the Teatro Amazonas (660 seats, including boxes) is still a wonder of artful design, constructed completely with materials imported from Europe, except for the wood, which came from the Amazon forest. The original curtains, still intact, were painted by the Brazilian artist Crispim do Amaral in 1896 and represent the meeting of the waters of the Rio Negro and the Rio Solimões (the goddess in the middle is Yara, the water princess). The bronze chandeliers, which descend for cleaning, are from France; the pillars are made of English cast iron; and the ceiling was painted in Paris by two Italians, showing the arts of opera, tragedy, dance and music. Except for the theater chairs, everything in the house is original (the old wood and cane chairs were replaced when air conditioning was installed under the seats). The ballroom, now only used as a showpiece, consists of 12,000 pieces of Amazon mahogany. The wrought-iron staircases are covered with *guaraná* plants. The wall painting showing a group of Indians saving some desperate-looking Europeans is a scene from the Brazilian opera *I Guarani*, by Carlos Gomes. In olden times, musicians used to serenade guests from the balcony. In 1947 the Governor declared all public buildings should be colored gray; it wasn't until 40 years later that the front facade was restored to its original light mauve. The first opera given in the house was *La Gioconda*, performed by an Italian troupe imported for the occasion. Tours are given throughout the day at regular intervals (though rarely in English). The air conditioning is only turned on for performances, so bring a fan and prepare to swelter. The view from the balcony is wonderful, but be careful of flying pigeons, who may decide to use your shirt as a toilet.

The Port

The docks in Manaus often look like somebody threw all the people and goods up in the air and then let them fall back down willy-nilly, but actually there's a consumer's intelligence organizing the activity lining the waterfront. A stroll down the waterfront to the Municipal Market may well be one of your best moments in Manaus, as you elbow past brawny dockmen, tired fishermen, and even steely-eyed sailors eyeing the crowd for a little companionship. If you're daring, ask around to see which boats may be going out for the day; you could probably hitch a ride or, at the very least, charter one. During the day, walking around here is reasonably safe, but at night do avoid looking like you're loitering. Despite the enormous fluctuation in river volume, these floating docks, a miracle of British invention, can accommodate anything from canoes to ocean liners all year round. Nearby is the Customs House, prefabricated in Britain, then shipped to Manaus piece by piece.

Feira da Manaus Moderna

Around 10 p.m. nightly a fantastic commotion takes place behind the Municipal Market as the port fills up with fishermen unloading their day's catch from canoes. Often the fishermen throw some of their fish away, and dolphins lurking nearby leap out of the water to catch them. You can even rent canoes here and row around to inspect the activity. Make sure, however, that your boat doesn't have a hole in it, and take precautions with your valuables. A block away is the new market where the fish are sold.

Mercado Municipal

Located at the corner of Rua Rochas dos Santos and Rua dos Barés, the Mercado Municipal is a concrete-and-steel structure built in 1906 and painted the pastel gray of all government buildings. Small cubbyholes manned by swarthy-looking merchants sell fruits, beans, wheat, sweets and popcorn in big burlap sacks; it's a good place to stock up on supplies if you're headed for the jungle. You can also buy camping gear here, including paddles and hammocks. Good prices for Indian and *caboclo* crafts also can be found here (bargaining is de riguer). Check out Store #67, teeming with fresh and dried herbs for medicinal purposes; #30 is an *Umbanda* store selling candles, incense and other paraphernalia for calling up the spirits. Be careful with your own worldly goods here, however. A merchant cautioned me to carry my backpack in *front* of me because several persons were eyeing it longingly.

Fish Market

The fish market next door to the Mercado Municipal is wet and slimy, full of merchants, women and children all juggling for a good price. Here you'll see *pirarucu* just off the boat, as well as many fresh counterparts to the stuffed fish on view at the Science Museum.

BEACHES

Manaus is hot and humid because it labors three degrees south of the equator, 100 feet above sea level and 1000 miles from the ocean. But you can find a beach, nearby **Ponta Negra**, to which locals flock during the dry season, June-November. About ten miles from the airport is the city's elite bathing grounds, **Dourado Beach**. Do ask locals about swimming conditions so you don't run into unexpected piranhas or electric eels.

MUSEUMS

FLORA AND FAUNA

Museu de Ciências Naturais (Museum of National Science)

Colônia Cachoeira Grande (Aleixo); ☎ *244-2799. Tues.–Sun. 9 a.m.–5 p.m., closed Mon. Fee: adults $2, children $1.30.* Founded in 1988, this exceedingly creative and well-maintained museum was the brainchild of a Japanese businessman who came to Brazil 15 years ago and immediately fell in love with Amazônia's flora and fauna. Located 15 min. from downtown, the museum is situated in a Japanese community where children still speak Japanese and traditional customs are maintained. The museum's air conditioning makes it a most attractive location to plant an overheated nervous system, and if you're heading off for some serious fishing, this is a great place to get oriented. All notations are in English, Japanese and Portuguese. Among the 20 stuffed and 15 live species of fish housed in a gorgeous outdoor aquarium you'll see the *pirarucu*, the largest scaled fish in the world (up to 440 lbs.); the vicious *canjirú*, a small leathery fish that is extremely carnivorous (the species of the *gnus Vanellia* are feared by people living along the river because they can enter the genitals of unsuspecting swimmers); the *tucunaré*, a very delicious fish whose coloring confuses other fish as to which end is its head. The insect room is straight out of a horror movie, featuring locusts, scarabs and elephantine beetles. The butterfly mounts are extraordinary, including some species whose coloring resembles leaves and owls. The souvenir shop is one of the finest artisan stores in Manaus; though the goods are pricey, the quality is superlative. No cards are accepted, but traveler's cheques, dollars and yen are welcome. Groups may make arrangements to come at night.

INPA

Al. Cosme Ferreira, 1756; ☎ *236-9400. Mon.–Fri. 8 a.m.–noon, 2 p.m.–6 p.m. Tours 9 a.m.–11 a.m. only. Free lectures (some in English) are given every Tues. at 3 p.m.* The Instituto Nacional Pesquisada Amazônia (the National Institute of Amazonian Research) is a forested park utilized by research scientists who are studying the survival and maintenance of the Amazon region. Many foreign scientists are working here, and guests are welcome during the morning hours (9 a.m.–11 p.m.), when free tours are given. You may see manatee pups in captivity that have been saved from fishermen who tried to use them as bait to capture their mothers, and there are usually several tanks of dolphins. A good show is always given by the *arainha*, a diva-like otter who seems to have a special ability to amuse itself in front of adoring onlookers. In the past, tours of the sawmill belonging to Center for the Study of Forest Products have been given upon request, and guests have sometimes been presented with free boxes containing many different types of Amazonian wood. Fine T-shirts with slogans like "Preserve the Manatee" can be purchased on the grounds. Permission to enter the INPA grounds must be obtained from the security police at the front gate. In 1995, more opportunities will be open to the public, so call about programs.

Eco Park

Praça Auxiliadora, 4, AP 203; ☎ *234-0939; FAX 633-3170.* You will probably see more animals at this privately owned 4500-acre preserve operated by the nonprofit Living Rainforest Foundation than in the "real" jungle. Opened in 1991 for purposes of conversation and education, the aquarium and botanical garden is still under construction; the orchid garden is complete. There's also a visitor center, bird sanctuary, a restaurant designed as a gigantic Indian hut, and even bungalows to house overnight guests in the forest. The 150 monkeys in the Monkey Jungle, who might use your back as a rest stop, were rescued from areas that have been flooded or burned down as a result of development. They receive medical attention and are given time to acclimate in the region before being released into the wild. You can hike six miles of trails leading through 4500 acres of forest, accompanied by trained guides; a full-day tour called the "survival course" emphasizes the techniques of indigenous people in obtaining food, water, shelter and medicine from the forest. To reach the park, you must take a half-hour boat ride from the Hotel Tropical. Half-day excursions run about $25, full day $50, boat transportation included. Two-day, one-night stays costs $155 per person, based on double occupancy, and includes two-day tours and all meals, a five-day, four-night visit (which requires a minimum of eight persons) is $425 per person and includes two days in the park and a two-day river cruise. The Tropical Hotel also offers packages starting at $180 a person, double occupancy. Each night includes a one-day tour of the park with lunch. Another package includes a night tour with dinner and an Indian dance show.

For more information regarding Eco Park or these packages, contact Max Blankenfeld at Eco Park's office in the U.S.: *9434 Old Katy Road,, Suite 230, Houston, TX 77055-6300;* ☎ *800-255-4326, FAX (713) 468-1213.*

NATIVE CRAFTS

Museu do Homem do Norte

Av. 7 de Setembro, 1385 (Centro); ☎ *232-5373. Mon. 8 a.m.–noon, 1–6 p.m., Fri. 1 p.m.–5 p.m. Minimal fee.* This hot and sweaty, two-room museum was founded in 1985 to show the culture and way of life in the north. If you can brave the heat, you'll find the Indian artifacts fascinating, especially those from the Xingú tribe, which Noel Nutel collected over a 30-year period. Most impressive are the ritual clothes and masks, among them an exquisitely beaded mask used to celebrate a girl's passage to puberty, and an ant-filled glove called *Luva de Tocandira*, into which young boys put their hands in order to prove their manhood. There is also a room full of *bumba-meu-boi* costumes and a typical manioc house. A guaraná display shows the development of the plant as well as its many uses. There is no guide, but we did locate a worker who spoke a little English.

Museu do Índio

Rua Dq. de Caxias/Av. 7 de Setembro; ☎ *234-1422. Mon.–Fri. 8:30 a.m.–11:30 a.m., 2–4:30 p.m., Sat. 8:30 p.m.–11:30 p.m. Minimal fee. To film or take pictures, you must pay an extra 30 cents.* Another non-air-conditioned museum in Manaus—this one owned by the Salesian nuns who run an Indian mission along the Rio Negro. Each of the six rooms is dedicated to various facets of Indian life; there are fantastic ceramics, baskets and weapons, and even a model of a Yanomami house, a circular, straw-roofed dwelling where between 30–250 people live. The museum's store sells crafts from tribes up the Rio Negro and from *cablocos*. Rumor has it you can buy here the best *guaraná* (an herbal stimulant) in Amazonas (called Marou de Maués). One interesting novelty is a *Pega Moça* ("catch the girl"), an Indian wedding ring that looks like a Chinese knot and is placed on the woman's finger to pull her along. Also fascinating is the display of a *paje's* instruments—the magical tools of the tribal shaman, including various powders, rattles and medicine pouches. Among the musical instruments are panpipes, maracas, turtle-shell rattles, rain sticks and instruments made out of the brain of a buck. The last room is full of neon-colored butterflies and humongous-sized creepy crawlers.

Insider Tip

Ponta Negra, the river beach next door to the Hotel Tropical, is the city's hot spot on weekends. Between Oct.–Mar., when the river is low, you'll even find sand for fresh-water swimming.

JUNGLE EXCURSIONS

What's the best way to "do" the jungle near Manaus? You have basically two choices: lodges or package cruises. Jungle lodges are pousada-type accommodations located deep in the jungle (usually near the shore of a tributary), where trekkers stay for two to three days. Quality ranges from the semiluxurious to the primitive; meals are generally served in an open-air communal dining room. If you like to cruise, you may be happier (and cooler) if you take a package boat tour where you sleep in tight (usually "cramped") quarters and take meals on board prepared by a crew member. (The schedule may include a night of sleeping in the forest.) Excursions from both the lodge and the boat tours are usually similar: canoe treks through tiny streams, piranha fishing in the afternoon, alligator hunts at night, and the proverbial walk through the forest. During rainy season, consider that the lounging space on a boat becomes even *more* cramped. Private boat cruises usually sleep up to eight, not including crew.

There is a third category of tourists who fantasize about renting their own canoes, meeting up with crazy explorers and riding the rapids to the mouth of the Amazon. Before you do, make sure you read Joe Kane's compelling account of his own hazardous trip in *Running the Amazon*. The Polish daredevils he traveled with now have their own agency called **CanoAndes**, *310 Madison Avenue, NY, NY 10017;* ☎ *212-286-9415*. They arrange trekking, rafting and wildlife and cultural expeditions for all levels of fitness and expertise. Just be forewarned that their guides run on the wild side.

CRUISE PACKAGES

There are over 150 travel agencies in Manaus that offer river excursions. Some of the best are listed below.

For those in a hurry, there are excellent one-day cruises out of Manaus, which go to the January Ecological Park, leaving from the docks at 9 a.m. and return 3 or 4 p.m. (lunch included, about $20). You see the meeting of the waters, tour around water lilies and take a canoe ride to the *igapós*. For more information call **Selvatur** *Av. Gétulio Vargas, 725 A;* ☎ *(92) 233-8044, FAX 622-2177*. Also **Amazon Explorers** *Rua Nhamunda, 21 (Centro);* ☎ *(92) 233-4418, FAX (92) 233-4418*.

Several different kinds of cruising options are offered by Fontur, located at the *Hotel Tropical/Estrada da Ponta Negra;* ☎ *(92) 656-2167, FAX (92) 656-2167*.

Some of the best tours outside Manaus these days are being offered by **Amazon Nut Safari** *Av. Beira Mar, 43 (São Raimundo);* ☎ *(92) 671-3525, FAX 671-1415*. It's best to write or FAX for their itineraries, but schedules can accommodate any number of days, from 3 day/2 nights to 5 day/4 nights, as well as private rentals. (The 5-day jaunt tours the Anavilhanas Arquipelago, the biggest archipelago in fresh water, formed by 400 islands.) Among their boats is the *Cassiquiari*, a double-decker river schooner which sleeps 24, with private, airconditioned bedrooms. Trips leave from the Tropical hotel, and include a visit to Novo Ayrão, a tiny town where the company's owner maintains a farm inhabited by an Indian family. The *Iguana* is a ten-person boat, with remote engine controls, hydraulic steering, and a satellite navigation center. You can also hire *Catuque*, a small regional motorized boat, for abot $100 a day.

For information about Amazon Nut Safari's jungle lodge, see "Apurissara Floating Lodge" under "Lodges" in the Manuas section.

EXCURSIONS FROM MANAUS: ORNAMENTAL FISH

Ever wonder where the neon fish in your aquarium come from? Thousands of collectors and vendors swarm the area near **Barcelos, Amazonas** (pop. 7000), 300 miles northwest of Manaus, along the Rio Negro for its enormous stock of ornamental fish. In 1993 about 16 million cardinals were exported. The first ornamental fish festival was held in January 1994, and the second one will be held in 1995 (see below). Studying these fish at the Dr. Herbert R. Axelrod Foundation in Barcelos is **Dr. Ning Labbish Chao**, who can be reached through his **Bio-Amazonia Conservation International**, *Caiza Postal 2310,69,061, Manaus, Amazonas;* ☎ *and FAX (92) 644-1138*, or *3204 Beamont Drive, Tallahassee, Florida 32308-2806, USA;* ☎ *and FAX 904-668-8225*. Arrangements can be made for groups (such as aquarium societies or classes) to visit Barcelos and work at Dr. Chao's lab. Charter boats to Barcelos are also available.

From January 27–29, the city of Barcelos will host the Second *Festa de Peixes Ornamentais (Festival of Ornamental Fish)*. Participants can buy aquarium fish collected by *piabeiros*, or collect their own (a license is required). Visit the fish and plant show, trade crafts, workshops, contests for children, sportfishing and boat excursions, music, dancing, and a tour of the aquarium business in Manaus. Beautiful water and bog plants, and especially wild orchids and bromeliads, are to be found everywhere. Turtles may be available for sale, but do note that their trade or transportation is illegal. For more information contact: **II Festa de Peixes Oranamentais, Prefeitura do Municipio de** Barcelos, *Av. Tenreiro Aranha, 204; Barcelos, Amazonas Brasil (CEP 69,700); tel (only Portuguese) 011-55-92-7221-1200, FAX 721-1191.*

Travel arrangements and boating accommodations can be made through Miguel Rocha da Silva, **Amazon Nut Safari** *Av. Beira Mar, 43 (São Raimundo) Manaus, Brazil; tel (92) 671-3525/233-7282; FAX 671-1415.*

EXCURSION FROM MANAUS:
SAO GABRIEL DA CACHOEIRA

Situated on the upper Negro, 1.6 thousand kilometers (by river) to the northeast of Manaus, the region of São Gabriel possesses tremendous natural attraction. For those who have already visited the Amazon, or are looking for a riskier adventure, this may be it. In this region, the Negro River contains many rapids, with rocks on the riverbed and islands that emerge during the low-water period. The relief here is very different with the formation of the mountain range similar to **Morro dos Seis Lagos** (Hill of the Six Lakes) and the **Bela Adormecida** (Sleeping Beauty)—so called because it resembles a reclining woman. It is located only thirty minutes from the city. In the region of **Natauracá** to the northeast of this municipality is found the beautiful **Serra do Padre** (Priest's Ridge). The region is rich in flora and many species are still unknown by researchers. The subsoil is known for its high mineral concentration such as gold, and the largest reserve of the world's supply of niobium. Along the course of the Negro, the German naturalist Alexander von Humboldt, discovered the Orinoco Canal, which links the river to its headwaters.

In São Gabriel there is the **Pico do Neblina** (Fog Peak) National Park, the second largest in the country. There are also the National Parks of **Pico 31 de Março** (March 31st Peak) and **Pico Guimarães Rosa** (Guimarães Rosa Park), as well as the forest reserve of the Rio Negro region. The region is distinguished by the presence of indigenous people. There are at least thirteen large indigenous groups in the Upper Negro Region. Among them are the Tukano, Baniwa, Yanomami and the Tariano, all who produce excellent handicrafts.

Nature Safaris, an agency based in Brazil, offers several kinds of excursions and expeditions for all levels of expertise. A ten-day hiking journey up the Pico da Neblina Mountain includes motorized canoeing on remote rainforest rivers where you'll truly feel off-the-beaten path. The trip is not for the faint of heart, and travelers should be in excellent condition for trekking through dense humidity. There is also the lighter Humboldt Trek, which includes a visit to the famous Casiquiare Channel discovered by the German naturalist/explorer Alexander von Humboldt. A 3 night/4 day Jungle Survival Course is also popular. An Amazon first is the unique mountain bike trip for experienced bikers, which includes a jaunt through the Park of the Pico da Neblina Mountain, and ends with a hike up the 600-meter "Cucui" Rock for an eagle-eye view of the entire region of São Gabriel da Cachoeira. For more information contact **Nature Safari** *Av. N.S. de Copacabana, 330/1001, Rio de Janeiro, Brazil;* ☎ *(21)235-2840, FAX (21)236-5285.*

Brazil Nuts, a fine American-based agency, offers tours of the Amazon, and has included São Gabriel da Cachoeira in some itineraries. Contact them for their present schedule. (For the address, see under "Specialty Tours" in the back of the book.) Also offering popular excursions is **Expeditours,** the Brazil-based eco-travel agency.

JUNGLE LODGES

Ariaú Jungle Tower

2 kilometers from the archipelago of Anavilhanas, 60 kilometer from Manaus (3 hrs. by boat). The Amazon jungle's premier accommodation, Ariaú is the brainchild of a Brazilian businessman who longed to be not only in the jungle but above it. The entire complex of 45 wood apartments are interlinked by wooden catwalks between the trees, affording a unique communication with the flora and fauna. Towering 35 meters (130 ft.) above ground is an observation deck (the only one in Amazonas), which allows you to see the magnificent canopy of the forest from above—a thrilling experience. A special Tarzan House on top of a 120-ft. chestnut tree was especially erected for guests who want to live out tree house fantasies. All rooms, with air-ventilators only, have private bathrooms and verandas. The duplex Presidential Suite, where the owner stays when he visits, boasts a downstairs dining room, TV, VCR and lush leather furniture. Upon arrival from the river, you'll no doubt be greeted by the resident monkeys, macaws, and *coatis* (charming anteaters with raccoon tails); just watch out for the monkeys, who love to rip off eyeglasses and throw them in the water. Two day/one night packages for about $280 include all meals (except drinks), a visit to a *caboclo* village, an alligator hunt at night, forest walks and fishing. (Longer packages are available.) One warning: the manager was dumbfounded as to why Americans never seemed to eat their food. For reservations contact the main office in Manaus: **Rio Amazonas Turismo** *Rua Silva Ramos, 41 (Centro)* ☎ *(92) 234-7308; FAX (92) 233-5615.*

Amazon Lodge

Lago do Juma, about 100 kilometers from Manaus (4.5 hrs. by boat). This is a two-story rustic pousada that actually floats on the water. The 17 apartments share two bathrooms (cold water only) and use candles for illumination. Various treks into the jungle are part of a package. In Manaus, contact: **Transamazonas Turismo** *Rua Leonardo Malcher, 734 (Centro);* ☎ *(92) 622-4144; FAX 622-1420.* In U.S. contact **Brazil Nuts** ☎ *(800) 533-9959* or **Expeditours** in Rio ☎ *(21) 287-9697, FAX 521-4388* or direct ☎ *(92) 622-4144; FAX 622-1420.*

Amazon Village

Lago do Puraquequara, 60 kilometers from Manaus (2 hrs. by boat). These 64 wood apartments in neat cabanas are favorites of Germans and Swiss who appreciate the excellent service and reputedly good food. Perched on a small hill at the bend of an *igarapé*, it's located 2–4 hrs. from Manaus, depending on the river's condition. There are no electric lights, no air conditioning, no doors and no windows. The "main building" is a large, open-thatched shed with a dining area, living room, bar and mini-museum, all open to the wind. Guests sleep in cottages scattered around the main building, easy to find with flashlights. The house jaguar even eats in the dining area and loves to be stroked like a kitten. A five-star banquet can be held in the middle of the jungle if you ask. In Manaus, contact: **Transamazonas Turismo** *Rua Leonardo Malcher, 734 (Centro);* ☎ *(92) 622-4144; FAX 622-1420.* In the States contact **Brazil Nuts** ☎ *(800) 533-9959* or **Expeditours** in Rio ☎ *(21) 287-9697, FAX 521-4388* or direct ☎ *(92)622-4144; FAX 622-1420.*

Acajatuba Jungle Lodge

Lago Acajatuba, Rio Negro, 70 kilometers from Manaus (4 hrs. by boat). More primitive than the Ariaú, these recently built 16 apartments are contained in three grass-roofed huts with private bathrooms, all illuminated by gas lanterns. Two day/one night packages for $140 include all food and mineral water, as well as piranha fishing, alligator hunt, river tour and jungle walk. *No cards* accepted, but traveler's cheques, dollars and *cruzeiros* are welcome. In Manaus, contact: **ECOTEIS** *Rua Dr. Alminio, 30 (Centro);* ☎ *(92) 233-7642, FAX 233-7642.* Contact **Expeditours** in Rio ☎ *(21) 287-9697, FAX 521-4388* or **Amazon Explorers** in Manaus ☎ *(92) 232-3052.*

Pousada dos Guanavenas

Ilha de Silves, 320 kilometers from Manaus (4.5 hrs. by car). The Hilton Hotel of jungle lodges, these 20 apartments overlooking the Urubu River sometimes embarrass tourists who come to the forest to escape air conditioning, minibars and excellent food. On the other hand, the two-story roundhouse with screened porches and hewn-log verandas has received architectural raves for its structure made entirely from regional materials. From Manaus, it's a 3.5-hour trip by jitney to Itaquatiara, where you must board a flat-bottomed boat for another 1.5-hr. ride. You may also arrive by sea plane or take a bus to Itacoatiara and continue by boat. Packages include all meals and guided jungle excursions, such as alligator hunts and piranha fishing. In Manaus contact the main office: *Rua Ferreira Pena, 755;* ☎ *233-5558* or **Expeditours** in Rio ☎ *(21) 287-9697, FAX 521-4388.*

Terra Verde Lodge

This is an attractive lodge with two towers and five exotic grass-topped cabins on stilts located in The Forest of Life, a large ecological reserve of virgin jungle situated among the richly contrasting ecosystems of the Negro and Solimões rivers. Electric lights, complete bathroom facilities, floating pool for swimming, and facilities for fishing and horseback riding are available.

The owner is the famous film director and ecologist Zygmunt Subitrowsky. Contact **Agencia de Viagens e Turismo Terra Verde** at *Rua Dr. Moreira 270/207;* ☎ *(92) 234-0148; FAX (92) 238-1742.*

Apurissara Floating Lodge

Rio Cueiras. Owner Miguel Rocha was a world traveler who used to invite his friends to cruise the Amazon with him. Today he still leads tours, along with his sons and daughters, using a squad of four kinds of boats. Their flagship property is a floating lodge (about 5 hours by slow boat, one hour by fast boat) on the Rio Cueiras, a tributary of the Rio Negro. The style is primitive chic, with 14 beds, some private bathrooms, and a thatched-roof dining area with a 360-degree view of the river. A 4-day program includes transfer from Manaus, a canoe trip through the woodlands, night-time alligator hunts, visit to a native house, an orchid search, and an overnight stay in the jungle. The lunch I ate here, cooked by a local, was nearly haute-cuisine. Swimming in the river is encouraged, and kayaks are available. On rainy afternoons you can curl up with one of the many ecological books on board. For more information on their cruising boats, see above, under Cruising. For reservations, contact in Manaus: Miguel Rocha da Silva c/o **Amazon Nut Safari** *Av. Beira Mar, 43 (São Raimundo);* ☎ *(92) 671-3525/233-7282; FAX 671-1415.*

Lago Salvador

On the right bank of the Rio Negro. This floating restaurant on the banks of the river, with 12 cabanas, is more luxurious than the average. An excellent resting place with a superb view; locals go just to feel at home in the jungle. For reservations, contact: **Fontur (Hotel Tropical)**; ☎ *(92) 658-5000, FAX 658-5026.*

WHERE TO STAY

Manaus is one of the hottest places in the world (and I grew up in Houston!). So, there are several points to remember in selecting a hotel.
• The air conditioning must work
• A good pool will be appreciated
• Cleanliness is sacred (this close to the jungle, you should think twice about what bugs end up in your bed)
• Laundry (no one has ever returned from the jungle without the devastating need to wash clothes).

Considering all that, good deals can be found in Manaus, but at least one night at the Tropical is *de rigeur*. If you can't afford that, at least drop by for a drink beside the fantastic wave-pool.

Very Expensive	**Over $100**
Expensive	**$75–$100**
Moderate	**$40–$75**
Inexpensive	**Under $15**

Tropical Manaus

Estrada da Ponta Negra (Ponta Negra), 18 kilometer, ☎ *(92) 658-5000; FAX 658-5026.* The palatial oasis of the Amazon jungle—if you have the money, spend it here. The hacienda-like hotel is a sprawling maze of 608 rooms; a newer building built six years ago doubled the capacity. Dominating the lobby is a three-story atrium housing a great white heron and tropical ducks who do tricks between 6–7 a.m. A magnificent pool complex famous throughout Brazil sports waterfalls gushing over rock cliffs. A mini-zoo features jaguars and pumas. Minimal differences exist between standard and deluxe rooms, both lavishly appointed, with a chic-rustic allure. (Rooms in the older section are slightly more expensive, but sometimes retain a musty smell that cannot be removed.) The three restaurants are spectacular: a barbecue buffet poolside for about $16, a candlelit gourmet restaurant and a charming coffee shop. Tennis courts are open from 9 a.m.–9 p.m. daily. A travel agency arranges river and jungle tours, and a Varig office is open during business hours. Standard doubles run $118, superiors $142, deluxes $165, suites $236– $284. (605 apts.)

Very expensive. All cards.

Taj Mahal Continental

Av. Getúlio Vargas, 741 (Centro); ☎ *(92) 633-1010; FAX 233-0068.* Opened in 1991, the Taj Mahal is the premier property of a famous Indian family who also owns the Plaza and the Imperial. All apartments have a view of the city; standards and deluxes barely differ. Furniture is streamlined and functional. Special rooms are equipped for the handicapped. The roof pool is about three strokes long. A nightclub is being built. The restaurant delivers a fantastic view of the Opera House, and an upper level slowly rotates for a panoramic view. Standard doubles run $92, deluxe doubles $106. (190 apts.) *Expensive. All cards.*

Imperial Hotel

Av. Getúlio Vargas, 227 (Centro), ☎ *(92) 622-3112; FAX 622-1762.* Brass sculptures of the Buddah adorn the lobby of this Indian-owned hotel in downtown Manaus. Standard rooms sport brightly flowered spreads, but the rugs are not uniformly clean. The medium-sized pool looks up to the hanging laundry of the neighboring apartment. The best *tacacá* in Manaus—a native dish of tapióca, manioc juice, garlic shrimps and pepper—is located right outside the front door, between the Plaza and the Imperial. Doubles run $90–$102. (100 apts.) *Expensive. All cards.*

Plaza Hotel

Av. Getúlio Vargas, 215 (Centro), ☎ *(92) 622-3314; FAX 622-1761.* Owned by the same family as the Taj Mahal, the Plaza carries over the Indian decor in its colorful tapestries and bedspreads. Service is friendly. Superior rooms are substantially larger than deluxes, with an extended area for an extra couch bed. Although the rooms are well cooled, the corridors are as hot as a sauna. A rectangular pool is covered by a glass ceiling, which keeps the pollution out. Laundry service, a travel agency and an imported-foods store are also on premises. Deluxe doubles run about $71, superiors

about $86. Fielding's readers receive a 20 percent discount. (80 apts.)
Moderate. All cards.

Hotel Amazonas

Praça Adalberto Vale (Centro), ☎ *(92) 622-2233; FAX 622-2064.* This four-star seems to be particularly accommodating to children, who were running their electric cars all over the lobby when I visited. Best bets are deluxes, with verandas offering a fantastic view of the port; standards are a bit depressing. Special discounts are available for those who eat lunch and dinner. A hair salon, barbershop, pool, luncheonette and drugstore accommodate guests. Children up to five are free. Children 5–12 years old are half price. Standard doubles run about $76, deluxe $92. (182 apts.)
Moderate–Expensive. All cards.

Slaass Flat Hotel

Av. Boulevard Alvaro Maia, 1442; ☎ *(92) 233-3525/3519, FAX 234-8971.* This gorgeous three-star is such a steal for its price that one is left wondering, what's wrong with this picture? Built initially as an apart hotel (with kitchenettes), the Slaass, about six minutes by car from downtown, suggests an elegance almost unknown in Manaus. Doubles are incredibly spacious, with attractive wood floors and a breezy veranda overlooking the city's rooftops. Apartments for four include three bedrooms, two bathrooms, kitchen and living room. Special long-term rates are available. The rooftop bar makes a great perch. A pool and shopping center are being planned. Restaurants within walking distance include Florentina (Italian), Canto do Peixada (fish) and Miako (Japanese). Singles run $40, doubles $47. *Inexpensive. All cards.*

Hotel Monaco

Rua Silva Ramos, 20 (Centro); ☎ *(92) 622-3446; FAX 622-1415.* The classic Hotel Monaco is something out of a Jim Jarmusch movie, where the receptionist resembles a hooker and the quirkiest people emerge from the rooms. Still, the rooftop restaurant is one of the great spots to witness the city's fabulous sunsets, and you're sure to meet characters. Standard doubles run $52, deluxe doubles $56. 112 apts. *Moderate. No cards.*

Pousada Monetmurro

Rua Emilio Moreira, 1442 (Praça 14 de Janeiro); ☎ *(92) 233-4564.* This pousada, in a middle-to-low-class residential neighborhood, is a viable budget option. A white stucco building holds six kitchenettes and three suites, all air-conditioned, with sculptured stained-glass windows. Suites are the best bet, with an outer room that includes a couch, dining table and crazy photos of the Swiss Alps. All apartments have color TV and tiled bathrooms; only the suite has a phone. Breakfast (included in the rate) is the only meal served, but a tiny luncheonette is located across the street. A sunning patio with potted plants relieves any sense of claustrophobia. Singles run $10.50, doubles $13, suite $20. *Inexpensive. No cards.*

Hotel Dona Joana

Rua dos Andrades, 553; ☎ *(92) 233-7553.* If you're looking for a cheap night, this simple three-story pension might do, but check your room before you sign on; grunginess is in the mind of the beholder. There's no elevator, and the stairs are steep, but the deluxe on the third floor has a good breeze and great view of the river. You pay extra for hot water but the spacious rooms should all have air conditioning. Across the street is a famous fish restaurant. The lobby is more funky than tasteless, but do note: This is no place to leave valuables. Deluxe doubles run $13, (extra bed $4); suites with hot water, minibar and color TV $18. (60 apts.)

Inexpensive. No cards.

Hotel Rio Branco

Rua dos Andradas, 484; ☎ *(92) 233-4019.* Located across the street from the Dona Joana Hotel, this pension is the hangout for hard-core adventurers, with 90 percent of the clientele European. All rooms have private bathrooms, and if you're seriously backpacking, who cares if the rooms are a little musty, the showers cold, and the breakfast room small? PR man Christopher Charles Gomes organizes jungle tours with expert guides; among his best is Jerry Hardy (part Brit, Indian and Brazilian) who owns his own boat. Three day/two night tours run about $150. Reports from the bush have been raves. Doubles with air conditioning run $10, with fan $8, singles $5–$6. Bedrooms with three or four beds, a *coletiva*, run $5 per person; all rates include breakfast (coffee, bread and milk only). A pay telephone, which you can use for three minutes a shot, is in the lobby, as are safes.

Inexpensive. No cards.

Hospedaria de Turismo Dez de Julho

Rua 10 de Julho, 679; ☎ *(92) 232-6280.* Located walking distance from downtown, this youth hostel for all ages is perfect for trekkers. All rooms are air-conditioned, and come with tile floor, two beds, and clean baths. Breakfast is included, and laundry service is available. Pay phone in the lobby. Janete Tôrres the director, is a lovely, gray-haired lady who speaks some English. Singles go for $16, doubles $18. (13 apts.)

Inexpensive. No cards.

WHERE TO EAT

No one really goes to Manaus for a memorable meal. However, if you're just coming out of the jungle, any food that's more sophisticated than a ham sandwich will probably taste great. The finest cuisine can be found at the Tropical Hotel, which features an impressive (but pricey) outdoor barbecue, indoor Italian restaurant, coffee shop and several bars, all open to the public. Throughout the Amazon region be careful to avoid raw vegetables, salads, sushi and unpeeled fruits.

Expensive--- **Over $15**

Moderate -- **$5–$15**

Inexpensive -- **Under $5**

La Barca

Rua Recife, 684 (Parque 10); ☎ *236-8544. Daily 11:30 a.m.–3:30 p.m., 7 p.m.–midnight, Sun. 11:30 a.m.–4 p.m.* This popular fishery is set in an open-air, white stucco building, with a glimpse of the encroaching forest seen through open arches. *Costela de tambaqui grelhado* (grilled fish) is native to the Amazon—big enough for three, and one of the best fish I had in Brazil. People with colds (everyone seems to get one in Manaus because of the heat and the air conditioning) will love the steaming bowl of *canja da galinha* (chicken soup). Beef, chicken, strogonoff, and omelettes are also available. Those who can't take the heat or the traffic noise can escape into an air-conditioned salon.   ***Inexpensive–Moderate. All cards.***

Churrasco/Tropical Hotel

Estrada da Ponta Negra (Ponta Negra); ☎ *238-5757. Daily 7 p.m.–midnight.* This barbecue buffet held under a tent-like roof is a little steep at $16, but the quality of the meats, fish, chicken and salad bar is superb. One meal could last you two days.   ***Expensive. All cards.***

Búfalo

Rua Joaquim Nabuco, 628A (Centro); ☎ *232-3773. Daily 11 a.m.–3 a.m., 6 p.m.–midnight, Sun. 11 a.m.–3 p.m.* An air-conditioned *rodízio*—all-you-can-eat meat for about $14 per person.   ***Moderate. All cards.***

Tarumã

Tropical Hotel, Estrada da Ponta Negra; ☎ *238-5757. Daily 7 p.m.–midnight.* Old-world romance with Spanish-style lanterns and high-beamed ceilings makes a welcome, i.e., air-conditioned, oasis. The cuisine rates as one of the best in the city: roasted duck with a cashew-spiked sauce was memorable. Desserts are first-class. Music from a grand piano and strings wafts down from the upper staircase.   ***Moderate. All cards.***

Fiorentina

Praça da Polícia, 44 (centro); ☎ *232-1295. Daily 11:30 a.m.–11 p.m., closed Monday and first Sunday of the month.* In the heart of the duty-free zone, this is the closest you'll get to an Italian cantina in the Amazon—cheerful tablecloths, bustling waiters, wood-slat chairs and the inevitable fan. Air-conditioned room upstairs. Menu in English and Portuguese, with pizzas ranging from $6–$12.   ***Moderate. All cards.***

Hakata

Rua Jonathas Pedrosa, 1800; ☎ *233-3608. Tues.–Fri. 11:30 a.m.–2 p.m., 6:30 p.m.–10:30 p.m., Sun. 11:30 a.m.–3 p.m.* "Na chapa" (or table-grilled) is the specialty at this air-conditioned Japanese restaurant. *Camarão na chapa* comes with six shrimps, fried cabbage, and fried rice—a bit greasy but filling.   ***Moderate. No cards.***

Restaurant Palhoça

Estrada da Ponta Negra; ☎ *238-3831.* An open-air restaurant with excellent views overlooking the river and obsequious waiters who present your fish to you before cooking it. Specialties include the *caldeiradas* (fish stews) and *pato no tucupi* (spicy duck). Entrees run $4–8. ***Moderate. All cards.***

Panorama

Rio Negro Boulevard, 199; ☎ *624-4626.* Half the price of La Barca (see above) and Amazonian fare almost as impressive. Plus a wonderful view of the city.

Canto da Peixada

Rua Emilio Moreira, 1677 E; ☎ *234-3021.* Situated in an old house with a veranda, this very good fish house specializes in such Amazonian delicacies as caldeirada, a kind of fish stew.

Restaurante Suzuran

Rua Senador Alvaro Maia, 1683 (Adrianópolis); ☎ *234-1693. Hours: 11:30 a.m.–2:00 p.m., 6:30 p.m.–11:00 p.m., Sunday 11:30 a.m.–3:00 p.m., 6:00 p.m.–10:00 p.m., closed Tuesday.* Best Japanese restaurant in the city. Personally, I wouldn't eat raw fish here, but I'm in the minority.

Churrascaria Búfalo

Av. Joaquim Nabuco, 628; ☎ *232-3954. Hours: 11 a.m.–3:45 p.m., 6:00 p.m.–midnight, Sunday 11 a.m.–3:45 p.m.* A fine steakhouse rodízio-style. ***Moderate. All cards.***

Bar "Galo Carijó"

Rua dos Andradas, 536. Daily 10:30 a.m.–3 p.m., 5:30 p.m.–9 p.m., closed Sun. Also known as O Rei Jaraqui Frito, this open-air dive across from the Hotel Dona Joana is just a roof and tables, but it's famous citywide for fish. The ones I saw were bigger than the plates, with the head and tail hanging over. Tastiest is the *pirarucú*, one of the largest fresh-water species, for about $5; the small *jaraqui* runs about $2.50. Fish is normally served lightly fried, with tomatoes, onions and a mixture of rice and beans. ***Inexpensive. No cards.***

ICE CREAM

Beijo Frio Ice Cream Parlor

Av. Getúlio Vargas, 1289 (Centro). Daily 8 a.m.–midnight. People go to Manaus just to indulge in the numerous tropical fruit-flavored ice creams. This air-cooled parlor features 36 exotic tastes like *cupuaçu, goiaba, tucumã, tapioca, graviola, castanha de cajú, açai,* and *maracujá* as well as five diet flavors. Scoops run about $1; sundaes and banana splits are delicious. Take your time tasting flavors.

Alema

Rua José Paranaguá at the corner of Doutor Moreira. Located near the Free Zone, this is a good pit stop for cold tropical juices, desserts and ice cream.

Insider Tip

Do try tacacá–a street dish famous in the region, made with tapioca, cupí (manioc juice and pepper), garlic and shrimps. The most famous vendor is located on the corner between the Plaza and Imperial Hotels.

NIGHTLIFE

Nightlife is limited in Manaus, but not nonexistent. Clubs appear and disappear in less than a year, so check out the latest hotspots with your concierge or locals.

Maloca

Estrada da Torre, km. 6 (Marina Tauá). Hours: Monday–Saturday 9 p.m The major folkloric show of Manaus, set in a grass-topped open-air theater, telling the legend of guaraná (the Amazon herb used as a stimulant) through song, dance, and fantastically feathered costumes. Fixed prices include dinner, transportation, arround $42; tickets available for show only. Buses to the show leave from the Hotel Amazonas. With one exception all songs are sung in Sateré-Maué, a native dialect. Free brochures with translations in various languages are distributed.

Hotel Tropical

Estrada da Ponta Negra (Ponta Negra); ☎ *658-5000.* You won't find many locals at the hotel's fine disco (due to the high price), but it's considered the best in the city. Just hanging out beside the wave pool and having a drink can be fun, even if you aren't a guest.

Hagae 39

Rua Djalma Batista. This was the top bar in 1994.

Kalamazon

Highway to Itacoatiara. Thur., Fri. and Sat., action starts after midnight. Fee: about $4. This is the best club to dance *lambada* and *forró*, situated on the road to Itacoatiara—a substantial taxi drive from downtown. All ages are welcome and sometimes folklore bands from Paratins perform *toadas*, songs from the *boi* festivities.

Jet Set

Rua 10 de Julho, 439; ☎ *234-9309.* Manaus' version of tropical striptease; women welcome. Locals consider the show "cold," but tourists seem to get a kick out of it.

Sabor Brasil

Rua Leonardo Malcher, 1840. Friday and Saturday from 10:00 p.m. on; Sundays at 7:00 p.m. Club to dance Samba and Pagoda.

Insider Tip

Live bands can often be found at Praia da Saudade on the weekends.

GAY MANAUS

Turbo 7, a well-known gay bar, has served at least three generations of gay clientele, near the docks.

SHOPPING

DOWNTOWN

The main street downtown is **Rua Eduardo Ribeiro**, full of large department stores like **Mesbla** (the Macy's of Brazil) and the even cheaper **Lojas Americanas**. The majority of banks are located along **Rua Djalma Batista**. Duty-free shopping (not of particular value to the foreign tourist) is concentrated in the Calçadão area around the streets of Doutor Moreira, Marcilio Dias and Guilherme Moreira, crossed by Quintino Bocaiuva.

NATIVE CRAFTS

Centro de Artesanato Banco e Silva

Rua Recife (no number); ☎ *236-1241. Mon.–Fri. 8 a.m.–7 p.m. and Saturday 8 a.m.–1 p.m.* Located in Parque 10 de Novembro, these 20 stores carry various indigenous Indian and *caboclo* artisanry.

Museu do Índio

Av. 7 de Setembro at the corner of Duque de Caxias. Fine Indian artisanry, such as headdresses, bows and arrows, and jewelry, have been collected by the Salesians nuns who run the museum. Reasonable prices and considerably cheaper than the Science Museum store.

Eco Shop

Amazonas Shopping Mall. Unbelievably expensive, but you'll find lots of good quality handicrafts from Amazonia and Alta Floresta, including fine specimens of Indian art.

Artíndia

Praça Aldaberto Vale, 2; ☎ *232-4890. Monday 8 a.m.–noon and 2:00 p.m.–6:00 p.m.* In front of the Amazon Hotel, this old white building houses the Funai store, with excellent prices and good variety. Amazon Indians from all over provide earrings, necklaces, pottery, straw baskets, bows and arrows, and tangas made from seed. The ambiance effects the boisterous spirit of an outdoor market.

HERBS, COSMETICS AND WHOLE FOODS

Chapaty

Rua Saldanha Marinho, 702-A (Centro), ☎ *233-7610.* This natural health food store specializes in herbal medicines, teas, whole breads, whole wheat pastas and natural sweets. Also, extraordinary shampoos made from Amazon products.

Prönatus do Amazonas

Rua Costa Azevedo, 11 (Centro), factory at Rua Visconde de Porto Alegre, 440 (Centro); ☎ *234-8754.* Inspired by the richness of Amazônia, this company has developed an exclusive line of herbal pills and cosmetics culled from the plants and fruits of the jungle. All products are hypo-allergenic, and their processing is all done with respect to the cycles of the forest. Soaps and shampoos made from tropical herbs make great gifts, as do herbal formulas for anything from impotence and diabetes to weight control.

SHOPPING MALL

Amazonas Shopping Mall

Rua Djalma Batista, on the corner of Rua Darcy Vargas (Chapada). Hours: Monday–Friday 10 a.m.–10 p.m., Saturday 10 a.m.–10 p.m. On Sunday leisure and movies open at noon, shops 3 p.m.–9 p.m. Ten minutes from downtown by car (20 minutes from the Tropical Hotel), this new shopping mall is shockingly chic for Manaus. Six movie theaters, food fairs, fine clothes stores, even a one-hour photo shop, pharmacies, and a store that sells American cosmetics. Go just to get out of the heat.

Insider Tip

Best place to buy hammocks is along Rua dos Bares. For international magazines and newspapers, try the Livraria Nacional on Rua 24 de Maio and the kiosk near the Teatro Amazonas.

HANDS-ON MANAUS

ARRIVALS

Aeroporto Internacional Eduardo Gomes

Av. Santos Dumont, ☎ *212-1431.* Receives flights from Rio, Belém, Brasília, Campo Grande, Cuiabá, Fortaleza, Natal, Recife, Porto Velho, Recife, Rio Branco, Salvador, Santarém, São Luis, São Paulo and a few others. From the United States, Varig flies direct from Miami, and a new flight was recently installed from San Francisco and Los Angeles.

The Hotel Tropical provides shuttle service (bus) to and from the airport for guests.

Varig

Rua Guilherme Moreira, 278/86; ☎ *621-1136.*

VASP

Rua Guilherme Moreira, 179; ☎ *621-1355.*

Transbrasil

Rua Guilherme Moreira, 150; ☎ *621-1356.*

TABA

Av. Eduardo Ribeiro, 664 (Ed. Zulmira Bittencourt); ☎ *621-1480; 232-0806.*

Air France

Rua dos Andradas, 371, first floor, ☎ *234-2798.*

BUSINESS HOURS

Mon.–Fri. 8 a.m.–noon, 2 p.m.–6 p.m. Banks are open Mon.–Friday 9 a.m.–3 p.m. Stores are also open Sat. from 8 a.m.–1 p.m.

CITY TRANSPORTATION
Car Rentals

Hertz ☎ *621-1376.*

Nobre ☎ *233-6056.*

Taxis

Amazonas ☎ *232-3005.*

Coopertaxi ☎ *621-1544.*

Buses

City buses run from 5 a.m.–midnight.

CLIMATE

Manaus is a sauna—hot and humid all year long with temperatures that start at 80 degrees F and rise without mercy, sometimes up to 115 degrees F. November–March is the rainy season, with precipitation a daily occurrence. Temperatures are a bit cooler in May and June, with the water level reaching its peak in June, Dry season occurs July–November. During dry season, you may have to change routes. Canoe trips may be cancelled in downpours. In an open river with a real storm, don't go out in a canoe because of high winds.

EXCHANGE HOUSE

Casa Cortez
   Av. 7 de Setembro, 199; ☎ *232-2695.*

Banco do Brasil
   Rua Marechal Deodoro and at the *airport* (24 hrs.) exchanges dollars at the tourist rate.

GUIDES

Emamtur, the official tourist board, requires officially sanctioned guides to take three months of training, including courses in history, jungle survival, ecology and Red Cross. If you hire a nonofficial guide, make sure he is reliable and knowledgeable or you will regret it dearly. Some recommended private guides are: **John Harwood** (☎ *236-5133),* a British scientist formerly at INPA, who now works with cruise lines as well as individuals; Brazilian-born **Claudia Roedel** (☎ *244-2455)* formerly an ecology student who now guides treks into the jungle with her husband. **Christopher Charles Gomes** conducts tours and individual expeditions that may be reserved through the **Hotel Rio Branco** at *Rua dos Andradas, 484;* ☎ *233-4019.* (See more information under "Hotels").

Special interest groups may contact **Sherre P. Nelson** at **Solução**, *Rua Monsenhor Coutinho, 1141;* ☎ *234-5955, 5400.*

LUXURY CRUISE LINERS

A number of luxury cruise liners dock in Manaus or travel up the Amazon River, among them: Odessa America Service Co., Sun Line Cruises, Regency, Royal Viking, Ocean Princess, Society Explorers, Saga Fjiord, Stella Solaris, Berlim and

Fairwind. (For more information, see "Cruises" under *Specialty Tours* in the back of the book.)

MOSQUITOES

The Amazon River has an acidity content that prevents the breeding of mosquitoes, but the white waters of the Solimões are seriously infested. There, mosquitoes attack mostly at dusk and after dark, when repellant is absolutely necessary. Most legitimate tours avoid this area at those times. (Also see the "Amazon Survival Kit," in *Amazônia.*)

Yellow fever, transmitted by mosquitoes, is considered endemic in Brazil, except around the coastal shores. Health authorities advise that the most infected areas are Acre, Amazonas, Goiás, Maranhão, Mato Grosso, Mato Grosso do Sul, Pará, Rondônia and the territories of Amapá and Roraima. Vaccinations are good for 10 years and are essential if you are traveling either to the Amazon or the Pantanal. You may be required to show proof of vaccination when entering the country from Venezuela, Colombia, Ecuador and Bolivia; it's best to always travel with the document. (For more information on malaria, see the "Amazon Survival Kit".)

For a list of other gruesome diseases carried by bugs, see Alex Bradbury's book *Backcountry Brazil* (Hunter Publishing, 1990). As far I could tell, I never encountered any of these bugs on the normal tourist excursions, except perhaps for a few tics.

PHOTO DEVELOPMENT

Foto Nascimento

Av. 7 de Setembro, 1194; ☎ *234-4660, 234-4995.* Film development in one hour. Major makes of cameras are for sale.

TELEPHONES

To make international calls, head for the telephone company **Telamazonas** *Rua Guilherme Moreira, 326 (downtown). Daily: 6 a.m.–11:30 p.m.* Another branch is located on the corner of Av. Getúlio Vargas and Leonardo Malche. Both are downtown.

TIME

Manaus is one hour behind Brazilian standard time (two hours behind between Oct.–Mar., when the rest of Brazil is on summer time).

TOURIST INFORMATION

Emamtur (state tourist board) is located at *Av. Tarumã, 379 (Praça 24 de Outubro);* ☎ *234-2252, FAX 233-9973.* An information post is also located at the airport Eduardo Gomes. An information booth is also located across from the Opera House at the intersection of Eduardo Ribeiro Ave. and José Clemente. For information regarding native tribes and permission to visit reservations, contact **FUNAI** *Rua dos Andradas, 473;* ☎ *234-7632.*

TRAVEL AGENCIES

Amazon Explorers (*Rua Quintino Bocaiúva, 189;* ☎ *232-3511*) arranges boat excursions, overnight jungle treks, fishing trips, city tours and excursions specially tailored to the needs of clients. English-speaking staff available.

The **Hotel Tropical** (☎ *238-5757*) maintains a fine agency for guests and non-guests alike.

Another full-service agency is **Selvatur** at *Praça Adalberto Vale (Hotel Amazonas);* ☎ *234-8984.*

WHEN TO GO

June 12–30

Folklore Festival of Paratins. Often as spectacular as Carnaval in Rio, these festivities divide the cities into rivaling groups with parades, typical foods and music. Best time to go is the last three days.

July 15–30

Folklore Festival of Amazonas.

August–December

Best month to visit to avoid rain. In July the river starts to recede and beaches sprout up.

September 21–28

Agricultural Fair.

September 27–29

Itacoatiara Festival of Song.

January (last weekend)

Ornamental (Aquarium) Fish Festival, in Barcelos.

ALTA FLORESTA

In the southernmost part of the state of Mato Grosso, the grit-and-grizzle town of **Alta Floresta** is something right out of the Old West. The business at hand is gold. For the last twenty years, thousands have converged on the area to try their luck; some make it after two years; others are still following pipe dreams. Luck, not persistence, seems to be the deciding factor in these parts, and as one local explained, a kind of inbred culture prevails where rules are not made to be broken. "There are no thieves here," he told me matter-of-factly, "because if someone takes something, he dies." A pale orange dust storm seems to have perpetually enveloped the city; even the children playing outside are covered with it. The major activity during the day takes place at the **Aurim Gold Exchange**, where *garimpeiros*, from the slick to the mud-slung, come to exchange their gold nuggets for cash. Around 10:30 in the morning, you'll see *garimpeiro* wives, dressed in cut-offs, high heels and lots of gold jewelry, forking over the husbands' hard-earned nuggets to be weighed and processed.

Alta Floresta is also fascinating because you can actually see rain forest burning. Perhaps that's not everyone's dream vacation, but there's nothing like ramming home the reality of the earth's plight than by seeing it close at hand. Just traveling the roads out of town will bring you past scorched earth and burnt trunks, and you'll no doubt see not only smoldering grass but groves of trees and shrubs in actual flames. I actually saw one farmer setting fire to a plot of land so he could plant cotton, but the most shocking scene I witnessed was that of a three-year-old playfully setting a tiny pile of twigs on fire with a match—just like his dad.

There is, however, access to a wonderful jungle near Alta Floresta and the best way to see it is to book a stay at the **Floresta Amazônica Hotel**. This resort, unusually stylish for the area, is located on the junction of the **TeleSpires** and **Cristalina Rivers** and is owned by a large landholder who is passionate about preserving the forest (she even hires as guides young professional botanists who do extensive research over their six-month internships). The complex is most unique for the multidimensional perspectives of Amazonian life it offers its guests, who can look forward to widely different adventures, depending on the season (routes navigated during the dry season by jeep are cruised by canoe during the rainy season.) A day trip may be taken to a nearby *fazenda* that features an unusual zoo as well as an exciting display of *garças* roosting in the leafy trees at dusk. Other excursions include a coffee plantation and the muddy dregs of a gold mine, where you'll probably get a chance to speak with miners. Overnight excursions into the jungle are the most exciting: Guests are escorted down the Cristalina in a canoe to a location in the jungle, where they bed down dormitory-style (beds or hammocks). Just waking up to the symphony of cawing birds will be thrilling, not to mention the nightly orchestra of bullfrogs. Fishing expeditions and fresh-water swimming are also available. This resort is particularly fine for families.

CULTURE

The Forest People

The following interview was made with Luiz Pereira Andrade, a 57-year-old guide who lives with his wife, daughter, son-in-law and grandchild in the forest connected to the Floresta Amazônica Hotel. He is a big, burly man with gray, bushy eyebrows and a paunch that pushes out of his shirt. He has lived in the forest for twenty years.

"Here, in Alta Floresta, we call the matinta pereira *the* pai do mato *(father of the forest). The first clue to being in contact with him is when you are in the forest and suddenly feel lost. You go home and get something to give him—food or anything—and put it where you felt strange. If you don't do this, you'll be lost forever and won't find your way back home. He's invisible but you can feel him. When I fish at night, sometimes I hear strange sounds, like tools falling, or somebody coughing, but there's nothing there. I never feel afraid—I just don't know what it means. Many times I've seen strange lights. When I'm fishing at night, a spot of light, yellowish with a blue tail, comes up behind me, goes to the river, then disappears in the water. This light is very strong and illuminates the whole river. Some people say it's the Gold Mother. Me, I don't know.*

"Do trees and animals have spirits? Com certeza. *If they are alive, they have spirits. Trees have a natural capacity to take energy, others to receive. When I embrace a tree, I feel it. I learned this by myself because one time I went to the shade of a tree when I was very nervous and suddenly calmed down. You saw that when you went to hug the* embauba *tree, it released your negative energy and when you hugged the* castanha *it gave you positive energy. How could trees do this if they don't have souls?*

"When you go to the forest and watch birds, they are happy so you start to be happy. You start to join with their happiness. When you are unhappy and you go to the forest and look around, you feel human is not that big. You are just a small piece in this world. I will live in this forest till I

am 90 because here the old people become young. We don't miss anything from the city. I just feel unhappy I didn't come sooner."

A Gold Mine

The following interview was made with the owner of a gold mine in Alta Floresta, a well-dressed man in his late 50s who was waiting to exchange gold. His slicked-back gray hair, good linen clothes, diamond ring and gold watch made a sharp contrast to the rough, desperate-looking young men with muddy feet who were also waiting in line.

"I came here nine years ago from Paraná just for gold—eight in the mine, one year making money. In the beginning you don't know much. You usually lose money. You get friends to work for you, but usually they steal from you. But I was lucky. I have a good life now—a good house, car. I was rich also in Paraná—I had a shop of tools for cars. But I think life was better there. The city here doesn't have much society, but my wife likes it better here because it's hotter. I had malaria five times. Only last year did I have it badly—at Christmas, I was very ill. Is it worth the pain? For me it's been good. Garimpo is like a vice. When you start you can't stop. And sometimes you lose all your money just because you have to reinvest it to try again."

WHERE TO STAY

Floresta Amazônica Hotel

Av. Perimetral Oeste, 2001; ☎ *(65)521-3601; FAX 521-3801.* A clean, cheerful resort that is about as comfortable as you'll find for thousands of miles. An outdoor dining area looks out onto a pleasant pool complex; meals can also be eaten inside a stylishly rustic restaurant. Excursions include jungle hikes, coffee farm and gold mine. The landscape is an ebullient profusion of pink and blue flowers and the lobby sports a few caged spiders and snakes. Trained biologists serve as guides. Fishing and freshwater swimming included. Reservations can be made through Expeditours in Rio ☎ *(21) 287-9697, FAX 521-4388.* The following rates contain a 50 percent discount: single deluxes run $24, doubles $30, VIP apartment $43.
Moderate. Cards: V.

HANDS-ON ALTA FLORESTA

ARRIVAL

Air

Alta Floresta is serviced by the airline **TABA** *Av. Ariosto de Riva;* ☎ *(65) 521-3360/521-3222 (airport)* with flights from Altamira, Belém, Cuiabá, Itaituba, Jacareacanga, Juará and Santarém.

Bus

The Bus Station is located at *Av. Ariosto da Riva;* ☎ *521-3177/2710.*

Connections can be made from Campo Grande, Cuiabá, Paranaiba and others. If you take the bus from Cuiabá, some parts of the road are not paved and you may feel like you will never see civilization again. "Luxury" buses called *leitos* are available from São Paulo to Cuiabá, where you must change buses. At Colida, you change to an even more primitive bus for another three hours (total trip from São Paulo runs 12–14 hrs., about $76).

Air Taxis

Jato ☎ *521-3903* or **Penna** ☎ *521-2584.*

WHEN TO GO

The rainy season runs October–March; mosquitoes are rampant after heavy rains. Best time to visit is May–October. The coolest months are August–October.

Insider Tip

Mato Grosso is one of the most malaria-infected states in Brazil, and Alta Floresta has its fair share (mostly around the gold mines). Do come protected with prophylactics and wear plenty of mosquito repellant, reapplying it before dusk. Keep windows shut at night. (Personally, I never had a problem, but I did take prophylactics.) (See Health Kit in the back of the book.)

THE PANTANAL

Caiman crocodile makes its home in Pantanal swampland.

Although nearly obscured by the eco-media's blitz on the Amazon rain forest, the Pantanal—an immense kidney-shaped swampland in Western Brazil—is perhaps the country's greatest natural resource. Officially known as *O Grande Pantanal*, the region, which cuts across the states of Mato Grosso and Mato Grosso do Sul (as well as western Bolivia and northeastern Paraguay) is a multifaceted ecosystem that changes its alluvial face every six months—not unlike the Everglades in Florida. During the rainy season (October to March), torrential rains inundate up to 85 percent of the region, causing rivers, lakes and ponds to merge into an inland sea. Five months later, the effect of the burning tropical sun and the north-south flow gives way to verdant grassy plains dotted by water holes teeming with fish, tall wading birds and alligators. As such, the Pantanal during the dry season becomes an acutely visible arena for the playing out of Mother Nature's food chain. Simply, what the Amazon is to flora, the Pantanal is to fauna. If you want to see Brazilian wildlife at its most exotic, come to the Pantanal.

A BIRD'S EYE VIEW

There are many ways to visit the Pantanal—all of them rugged, muddy affairs, but well worth the effort for a die-hard eco-tourist. At least once in your stay, you must traverse the grand **Transpantaneira Highway**, a feat of civil engineering completed during the dictatorship (1964–85) that unwittingly created a stunning ex post facto reserve. The 150-kilometer road, elevated two to three meters above the flooded plains, starts right after the quaint village of Poconé, where the asphalt road suddenly turns into what Pantanal vets sardonically call an "all-weather" highway. In the rainy season, the road becomes a linear refuge for wildlife; when the waters recede, millions of fish are trapped in the roadside trenches, offering a smorgasbord for predator and scavenger alike. During the dry season, riding over the bumpy highway with its bomb-sized craters is like journeying through a zoo on the moon—every few meters, another "oh-oh-oh" experience. Large mounds become islands of refuge for snakes, capybaras, antbears, and jaguars, while caimans and great wading birds retreat to the artificial pools below to wait out the dry season. Seeds borne on the wind and in the guts of birds create the landscape of squat trees and scrub—a dried-out *cerrado* that nearly resembles parts of East Africa. The highway ends abruptly 150 kilometers south of Poconé at Porto Jofre on the banks of the Cuiabá River.

There are few people and no other towns in the Pantanal, so a look around Poconé is well warranted. Dating back to the 18th century, Poconé is a picturesque, well-kept colonial town, where most of the houses have traditional roofs and horse-drawn carts still meander down the cobblestone streets. A blue church dominates the main square, around which are situated general stores and the mayor's office. Just as it was 150 years ago, gold was "rediscovered" in Poconé about five years ago, turning the town upside down. Convinced there was gold hidden in the walls of the church, miners actually tore it down, finding only enough to rebuild a new church. Today, signs of *garimpeiros* are everywhere, from the picks and axes in the country stores to the smell of mercury in the air.

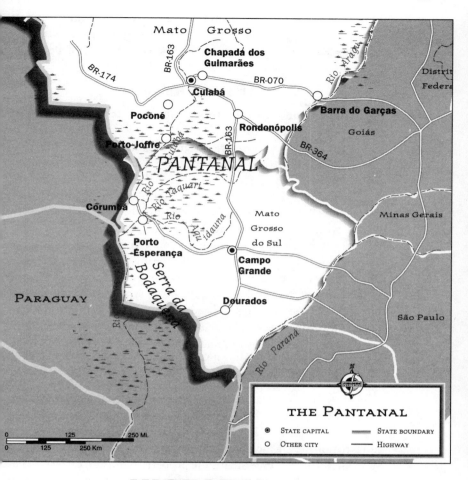

HISTORY

Although the word "pantanal" is usually translated as swampland, in actuality the Pantanal is a sedimentary basin into which drain numerous rivers, including the Rio Paraguay and its tributaries, as they make their way south to the Rio de la Plata and the Atlantic Ocean. More than 65 million years ago, the region was completely ocean; 7500-year-old animal bones have been found here, as well as the remains of a 10,000-year-old human fetus. As recent as 500 years ago, Kayapó, Iguato and other tribes were known to migrate along the border with Amazonas. In the early 18th century, rumors of fist-sized emeralds and diamonds magnetized the first *bandeirantes* from São Paulo, though it was gold that was finally discovered along the banks of the Cuiabá River. After a 30-year rush, most miners moved on, but the few who stayed started sugarcane plantations and huge cattle ranches, piquing the interest of the King of Portugal, who established a captaincy in 1719 to collect taxes.

A WILD WEST FANTASY

It would take another century until anyone intentionally returned to the Pantanal. As 17th- and 18th-century expeditions found the way nearly impassable, the region gained a certain wildcat reputation. In 1925, Lt. Colonel Percy Fawcett, one of the most indefatigable explorers, mysteriously disappeared while searching for the legendary city of El Dorado, but that didn't deter big-city slickers during the 1930s and 1940s from zooming down in their German-made seaplanes to fish and bag game. With the construction of the highways between Cuiabá–Santarem and Cuiabá–Porto Velho, the Pantanal's fortunes, and especially those of Cuiabá (Mato Grosso's capital) improved dramatically. The booming frontier town, situated on the banks of the Cuiabá River, became a symbol of Manifest Destiny, a Wild West fantasy for those trapped in the drought-ravaged Northeast. Roads were planned for 150,000 new residents, but many more thousands were spellbound by the lure of gold, lumber, cattle and diamonds. Nearly all had to pass through Cuiabá on their way to the yellow-brick plains.

Today, as the Pantanal loses its reputation as an intractable swamp, it is fast becoming the focus of enormous political and economic intrigue. Although two Brazilian areas are officially protected—a remote national park near Bolivia and a small ecological reserve in Mato Grosso—the rest remains the property of private cattle ranches where frontier law prevails. Illegal hunters, miners and commercial fishermen continue to blatantly exploit the region in the face of lax federal enforcement. The health of residents is threatened by mercury poisoning from goldmining, agrochemical pollution from crops, and malaria epidemics. Violent outbreaks take place daily between goldminers and native tribes, the latter which are being forced further and further into the interior. Sadly, with the exception of Pantanal Alert, an activist group made up of artists and musicians in São Paulo, there are very few private organizations dedicated to conserving the Pantanal with the same fervor as that of the Amazon rain forest.

Whether the land in the Pantanal is even economically viable is being hotly debated today behind closed doors. Although most of the land had been traditionally owned by a few families, it is now being divvied up into smaller plots, at great loss to the new owners. Rumor has it that, since such a large percentage of the land is flooded for most of the year, substantial agriculture is nearly impossible, and the exorbitant cost of constantly relocating grazing cattle makes for unprofitable business. Some factory owners are now using their newly claimed property merely as tax dodges. Beyond the great ranches, the only other residents of the region are poor fishermen, who eke out a subsistence level of existence. Eco-tourism is the Pantanal's brightest hope for the future.

WHOS' WHO IN THE PANTANAL: FAUNA AND FLORA

FAUNA

The outstanding changeability of the Pantanal's weather patterns and ecology makes for a dramatic appearance of wildlife ever in contact with the life-and-death struggle of Mother Nature. While the following guide to the region's abundant animal life emphasizes individual characteristics, do stay attuned, as you travel through the countryside, just how each animal plays out its role in the overall plan of ecological balance—what in the words of one poet has been called the "terrifying beauty of God's irrevocable Plan." In that way, you may come to see and feel and hear the Pantanal as intimately as its own inhabitants do.

Capybara

The world's largest rodent is not shy and may well be the animal you most sight on your Pantanal voyage. The name means "master of the grasses" in the native dialect of the Guarani Indians and perfectly describes how the mammal mows down tall grasses with its four large incisors and grinds them with a set of specialized molars. Looking lovable, but dumb and extremely slow-moving, this bear-like creature always lives near water (therefore, good for sighting from canoes), but it flees when threatened, letting loose a series of grunts, snorts and snuffles. Capybaras are expert swimmers and divers and tend to rove into small bands of up to 20 individuals.

Jacaré

The Tupi Indians gave the name *jacaré* to the reptiles of the alligatoridae family which includes the African crocodile and the North American alligator. You will see hundreds of *jacarés* on a boat trip; the first one will scare the living daylights out of you, particularly if he is following your canoe; by the time you sight the fifth one you'll feel chummy; the twentieth, nonchalant; and the thirtieth will bore you stiff. Awkward and easily threatened on land, the jacaré gains its true strength in the water. Its best protection is its sharp teeth and its thick, leathery skin that is nearly impenetrable. It feeds on whatever it can catch, from fish and birds to mammals and reptiles, as well as decaying meat. Its extreme taste for piranha helps keep the population of the voracious fish relatively balanced. Females can lay up to as many as 30-50 eggs at one time. Since alligators have been known to crawl across roads, where they are sometimes run over by vehicles, be careful if you camp outdoors. At night, if a light is shined on them, their eyes shimmer like a sea of red specks of light. One of the pastimes of some boat tours is to go "alligator-hunting" at night in canoes. Don't try this yourself, but your guide will probably stick his hand in the water, pull out a baby, and show you the genitals. It's supposed to be very bad luck for men if they pull up a male jacaré.

Pantanal Deer

One of the region's most beautiful (and largest) animals, this deer roams the extensive plains where the buriti palm tree is found. Long on the endangered species list, the deer population is fast disappearing, since they succumb to cattle diseases, such as foot-and-mouth disease.

Felines

Among the felines in the Pantanal are the ocelot, the cougar, and the jaguar, the latter now on the endangered species list as a result of hunting. Even today, some farmers will not hesitate to kill a jaguar, claiming it is destroying their herds of cattle. A characteristic figure of the region is the *zagaieiro*, a "jaguar hunter," who kills the feline with a kind of primitive iron spear attached to a long hardwood handle. Locals usually hold the *zagaieiro* in awe for his almost inhuman courage. When wounded or cornered, the jaguar hurls itself against the hunter, who is waiting for it with his *zagaia* firmly planted in the ground.

Monkeys

White-headed capuchin monkeys fill the trees of the riparian forests; its name comes from the fact that it has a thin, nail-like penis. Black howlers, or *guaribas*, also abound in the crowns of the tallest trees, a big-bodied ape weighing over 8 kilos. They live particularly near Manaus. Every morning, the howlers stake out their own territory by emitting roars that unnerve the most macho traveler (the sound even did entomologist Alfred Wallace Bates in), a thunderous cry that leaves no question who owns the forest. You'll hear the roar throughout the night, and especially at dawn. An excellent place to see and even

touch monkeys is at the Eco Park in Manaus, a research reserve where the monkeys will actually jump all over you.

Tapirs

The largest of land mammals, the tapir has a snout that extends into a flexible trunk and its ears are as movable as a horse's. It eats all kinds of vegetable matter as well as wild fruits; it's been known to invade planted fields.

Anaconda

Smaller than the Amazonian species, this still enormous snake in the Pantanal reaches 3-4 meters long. It is not poisonous, but it uses its tremendous strength to squeeze the life out of its hapless victims.

Vibora

Looking a little like an iguana, this aggressive lizard is erroneously thought to be poisonous. Moving as easily on dry land as it does in the water, it feeds primarily on mollusks and crabs.

Sinimbu

A member of the iguana family, this prehistoric-looking lizard grows to about one meter, more than half of which is its tail. An expert swimmer and diver, it can leap gracefully over tree branches as well. Its diet consists mainly of fruit, leaves, insects and small animals.

Pantanal Cattle

Bred freely on native pastures and allowed to roam freely, this is a type of cattle which adapted well to the region's adverse conditions. The first head of cattle, imported in the early part of the 18th century, were from Europe. In the early part of the twentieth century, the Pantanal cattle started to be crossbred with zebu, mainly that of the Nelore species. One of the most exciting things to happen to a traveler in the Pantanal is to be caught on the highway or backroad in the face of an oncoming herd of cattle being escorted by cowboys on horseback.

Pantanal Horse

This special breed of horse was introduced over four centuries ago. Rustic and rugged, it has an acquired ability to graze below the surface of the water in partially flooded fields.

FISH

There are over 400 different species of fish in the Pantanal, making it one of the world's richest resources. There are strict restrictions on fishing, so you must inquire at local authorities or follow the advice of your hopefully trustworthy tour guide, who certainly does not want to be fined for illegal actions. Among the species are:

Piranha

This vicious-looking and acting fighter fish is a committed carnivore, aided by razor-sharp teeth. Amazonian rivers, marshlands and bays are full of piranhas. They are delicious to eat, but do avoid swimming near them, especially if you have open wounds—they attack ferociously at the smell of blood. The most common species include: black piranha or red piranha, which measure up to 35 centimeters in length, the yellow piranha, which changes color, and the white piranha.

Dourado

Considered by anglers as the "king of the rivers," the dourado in the Pantanal can weigh up to 30 kilos, giving a huge and valiant struggle when it is caught.

Pacu (Pacupeva)

This is a round-shaped fish that enjoys digesting the wild fruits of soft fig-trees and inga-trees growing on the riverbanks. Pantanal residents adore its savory meat.

Scale Fish

Among the varieties of scale fish are piraputanga, curimbatá, piau, piava, piavaçu and lambari.

Skin Fish

Also known as siluridians, these skin fish have no scales (hence their name), but rather barbels or "feelers" near the mouth. Nocturnally active, their instincts are driven more by taste and smell. The best representatives of this species are the jaú and the pintado, the latter whose meat is quite tasty. Other skin fish include the abrado, jurupensen, chara, palmito and the beautiful yellow mandi or golden mandi.

BIRDS

Bird-sighting is one of the great joys of Pantanal travel. Aquatic birds, who can move easily from place to place, are especially adaptable to the demands of the region, with its alternating cycles of flooding and drought. The climate and hydrological changes in the Pantanal strongly affect the feeding and mating habits of birds. As such, the best time for bird-watching is during the mating and egg-laying season. During the dry season, from July-September, thousands of tall-legged birds, from egrets to herons to spoonbills and American wood-storks come to breed in colonies known as nesting grounds, or bird sanctuaries. At this low-water period, when the waters return to the riverbeds, the juvenile fish attempt also to return to the rivers, but many fail, crowding into the remaining shallow bodies of water—easy prey for scavenging birds.

This dry season is also a marvelous time to glimpse nests, themselves wonders of construction and resourcefulness. Mud, wood chips, grass and twigs are made into a variety of shapes and sizes, from the spacious two-room "house" made of earth and cow dung by the **rufoud hornero** to the hollow made in the grass by the **southern lapwing**. Saliva is often used by **hummingbirds** and **swallows** for gluing materials together. Some exciting nests to look for are the sack-like structures of all the **icteridae** species (**orange-backed orioles**, **crested oropendola** and **yellow-rumped cacique**) that dangle from the tips of long palm branches by bunching together the individual strands of leaf. During the dry season, nests of different species sometimes occupy the same branch. A highly dramatic scene, the nesting grounds, full of thousands of birds, are also stalked by a vicious round of natural selection, as **crested caracas** and **black vultures** snatch eggs and chicks directly from the nests, while down below on the ground, alligators wait patiently for any helpless chick that has fallen out. *Excellent places to sight birds are along the shores of the Miranda River, downstream from Passo do Lontra, along the Vermelho and Cuiabá rivers, and down the Transpantaneira Highway.*

Egrets and Herons

Dynamic symbols of the Pantanal, these graceful, svelte, lanky-legged birds with multicolored plumage are omnipresent, but often difficult to photograph. They usually live near water, especially shallow swamp waters or marshes where they search for prey, in particular small fish and other aquatic animals, including insects. To keep their luscious plumage looking good, nature has provided them with a kind of comb alongside their toes. To watch a heron walk, slowly and pointedly, is a lesson in meditation. At dusk, a memorable sight is a flock's en masse return to its collective roost high up in a tree.

Great Egret

One of the symbols of the Pantanal, this entirely white bird has a yellow/orange bill, legs and feet. They are the most commonly found species in the Pantanal, and can be seen especially well during the dry season—July to October—when hundreds travel side by side next to alligators, around a *coriso* or "bay," swarming with fish. During the breeding season, they develop decorative dorsal feathers, called "egrets," whose plumes flow down their backs like a wedding veil.

Snowy Egret

Sometimes associated with the great egret, the snowy egret is a bit smaller and has a black bill and legs and yellow claws. It lives either in fresh or brackish water and sometimes on the beach. When it is mating, a tuft of fine feathers appear on the back of its neck and longer "egrets" with upturned tips down its back.

Cattle Egret

This idiosyncratic egret also has white plumage but is less slender than the snowy egret, has a thicker neck, and yellow bill and legs. It was first sighted in Brazil in September, 1964, on the island of Marajó in association with buffaloes. The species tends to walk in the fields following cattle and eat insects (for example, grasshoppers), which they rout.

Whistling Heron

Also known as the "singing hero" because it sings as it flies, this species has a distinctly melodious whistling voice and a spectacular multicolored plumage Often seen in couples, it hunts for insects in dry fields where it sometimes associates with buff-necked ibises.

White-necked Heron

The largest of the herons, it boasts a 180-centimeter wingspread. It has no song, and only makes noise, a shrill cry, when frightened and sometimes while flying

Black-crowned Night Heron

This heron of the night boasts large red eyes, gray wings, black crown and back, and a white underbelly. A voracious eater, it has been known to gobble up an enormous number of frogs as well as fish longer than its own body.

Ruffescent Tiger-heron

Young specimens can often look like leopard-skin due to their brown and beige-patterned plumage. The name "socó-boi" (ox heron) was derived from its cry, a deep monosyllabic mooing resembling that of an ox. When attacked, it tends to stand motionless, as if in the hope that its cryptic plumage will succeed in camouflaging it from an observant predator. Its neck can often resemble a perfect "S."

Storks

Storks, from the ciconidae family, are master gliders, all the more impressive since they have robust, big bodies, long bills and elongated necks.

Tuiuiú

Pronounced "too-yoo-yoo," this stork is the largest of the species and is considered the symbol of the Pantanal. Also called jabiru, it is forced to build its nest on very tall, leafless trees because of its huge size. A jabiru builds one nest in a lifetime and refurbishes it every year at mating season, which usually starts in June. Their nests can often be found near a jatobá or a piúva tree destroyed by the floods. Though they mostly feed on fish, they sometimes catch baby alligators and steal small specimens of anacondas to their nests. When they are frightened, they clasp their bill, emitting a sound like that of a castanet. Rumors abound in the Pantanal about a jabiru that actually attacked a horse and rider.

Ibises

Ibises belong to the same family as the sacred ibis (*Threskiornis aethiopicus*), the ibis found in Egyptian hieroglyphics, a startling-looking bird with a snow-white plumage that was revered as a god of wisdom. Today ibises are characterized by long-legged creatures of various sizes who have long, curved bills, slender, graceful bodies and varicolored plumage. They build their nests in redbuds, bushes or trees, in large colonies, in small groups, or alone.

Roseate Spoonbill

This ibis sports a remarkable bill that resembles a long cooking spoon and a magnificent pink plumage which darkens during the breeding season. Searching for food in shallow waters, they revolve the mud with their spatula-like bills, looking for small fish, crustaceans and mollusks, plankton, insects, and larvae. The number of roseate spoonbills in the Pantanal has been sadly reduced since their nests are constantly plundered by the crested cascara and black vultures.

Buff-necked Ibis

The "alarm clock" of the Pantanal, is often seen carousing with the plumbous ibis. When the flock come together to spend the night, they screech in unison and throw their heads back at the peak of passion. This buff-necked bird will scour dry fields looking for spiders, beetles, snakes, mice, sand-lizards, toads, etc. Upon sensing human presence, it also emits a shrill cry.

Green Ibis

A dark shiny green, this ibis also sports a jade-colored bill and legs. A forest species, this ibis prefers to remain close to river shores and lakes deep inside the forest. Its diet consists of worms, plants and insects.

Bare-faced Ibis

Black-greenish plumage with a light red forehead and a curved whitish bill are the identifying features of this ibis. This species lives in the marshland where it eats seeds and leaves, searching in shallows by walking slowly along with its bill in the water. At certain times of the year it is one of the most frequently seen birds.

Passerines

The living jewels of the Pantanal, the passerines are arguably the most attractive and ornamental of all birds. They also are essential to ecological balance since they form a protective shield against the invasion of the planet by insects. There are nearly 400 species in the Pantanal (5100 worldwide). Among them are:

Black-capped mockingthrush

Part of the Mimidae family, this is a singular bird that lives in marshes and along riverbanks where the piri plant grows. Both sexes rise early and sing magnificently in unison while flitting through tall grasses. Sometimes they even dance together, fanning and swinging their tails.

River Warbler

A species of the Parulidae family, this one-centimeter-long bird can be found along the forest creeks, groves of buriti palm trees, and flooded riparian forests. It skips and hops onto roots and alights down on branches overhanging the water, rabidly flicking its tail while flapping its spread wings.

Yellow-throated Spinetail

About 14 centimeters long, this passarine of the furnariidae family, sports a rusty red color. Its nest, built above or very near the water, consists of a mound of twigs accessed through a vertical tube or chimney. The male and female sing in unison.

White-headed Marsh-Tyrant

This species inhabits swamps and marshes, usually perching on branches as opposed to scavenging the ground. The male is easily recognized by its white head and black coat; the female is ash-gray in color.

Chestnut-capped Blackbird

This passerine is glossy black with crown, throat and breast tawny-rufous to chestnut. It often sings while gliding with wings and tail tautly stretched. They are often seen in flocks numbering hundreds.

Gulls and Terns

Terns consist of several species of long-winged birds of the Laridae family (the same as gulls).

Of ten species living today in Brazil, two can be found in internal waters, on the shores of major rivers and their tributaries, and in the Amazon and the Pantanal. In general, their color is white mixed with pale gray; the bill and legs are yellow. Feeding on fish and crustaceans, they fly low and quite slowly over the water searching for prey. Without warning, you might see them suddenly flapping their wings while hovering over water and swaying their bodies vertically, with the head at a right angle to the body, as if their gaze is penetrating the river floor. Then, like a missile, they will dive straight down, almost up to one meter below the surface, to snag their dinner. The nests they build, on the ground, are little more than holes dug into the sand, not far from water's edge. Varieties include:

Black Skimmer

This species spends most of the day lying in the sand, waiting till twilight to search for food. Its extremely narrow bill sports a mandible (lower part) much longer than the maxilla (upper part). As it flies just above the surface of the water, it keeps the mandible partially in the water, as if it were plowing.

Large-billed Tern

This tern is unmistakable due to the considerable size of its lemon-yellow tail. It may be glimpsed in the company of common stilts or the caraúna.

Jacana and Lapwings

Closely related to collared plovers, brown snipes, gulls and terns, these Charadriiformes comprise a large number of cosmopolitan birds of heterogenous characteristics, usually aquatic, both in salt and fresh water. Many have the capacity to fly great distances.

Southern Lapwing

A graceful and perky resident of marshes and pastures, this species is characterized by long feathers on the back of its head and red spur on the bend of its wings. The bill and legs are remarkably red. Its song is nearly metallic, and closely resembles its name in Portuguese: *téu-téu*. The bird is often seen squatting ever watchful for enemies; when it does sense a threat, it silently runs off along the fields and takes flight a good distance away. Then it screams loudly as if its nest were there. If a predator does try to snatch its eggs, it swoops down with large shrills and strikes him with its wing spurs. Humans have been known to be attacked in such a manner.

Wattled Jacana

One of the most common birds in the Pantanal, this small waterfowl has a strikingly elegant shape with a very light body, tall thin legs, and a yellow beak topped by a red shield. This long-legged bird spends its whole life within a one-kilometer distance. Protective of its own environs, it emits a great shrill and simultaneously raises its wings as soon as a threat is sensed. Most wattled Jacanas live in pairs along marshes or small bogs like those formed by excavations alongside roads.

Common Stilt

Marked by extremely long legs, this is the sole representative of the Recurcirostridae family. The size of the white patch on its head and back vary with the bird's age, season and geographic location. They are found in the muddy shores of lakes and marshlands.

Hawks

Hawks are omnipresent in the Pantanal; it is impossible to travel any distance without seeing one. Species range from the pearl kite, the smallest falcon, to the stately and impressive harpy eagle. Astute hunters, they boast strong hooked bills and powerfully sharp claws that are most suitable for ravaging flesh. Extremely sharp vision and a majestic flight help in their quest for nourishment. Among varieties are:

Crested Caracara

Plentiful in the Pantanal, this bird takes its name from the sound of its call. A voracious eater, it often preys off the catch of the black vultures; it has been known to wander into houses to snatch food off the table. Large numbers often gather on riverbanks when fishermen clean their catch, patiently waiting to feast on the discards.

Snail Kite

This is one of two species of hawks in the Pantanal that can also be considered an aquatic bird, since it feeds on mollusks. The plumage of the adult male is slate-gray. The female and fledglings have whitish eyebrows and throat, underparts streaked buff, resembling an immature savannah hawk. A mound of crab and mollusk shells around a fence post is often the sign that a snail kite had been present.

During the breeding season, they often perform elegant exhibition flights full of loops and dashes.

Harpy Eagle

The world's most powerful hawk, the harpy eagle has a majestic bearing and unrivalled strength. Its wing spread can reach as much as two meters. Like most hawks, its retinas are 4 to 8 times more sensitive than a human's, making it the creature endowed with the greatest visual acuity.

Black-collared hawk

Often seen in the Pantanal, this species haunts the bays and swamps where they use long claws to catch mollusks. The adult has ferruginous plumage, a buffy white head and a black patch on its throat. Fine, thorn-like warts cover the underside of their toes, enabling them to easily hold onto fish they catch.

Turkey Vulture

Known in the Pantanal as "sole-leather head," this vulture can often be sighted standing over the carcass of alligators.

Cormorants and Anhingas

Relatives of the pelican, cormorants are expert fishermen; indeed they eat only fish. Unlike the majority of other waterfowl, they will descend underwater and swim while chasing a fish. Since their feathers are not waterproof, you can often see them perched on a rock or tree, drying out their spread wings. Among the species are:

Anhinga

Also called a snack-neck bird, this species has a very thin, long neck with twenty vertebrae which makes it extremely mobile, enabling forceful and rapid strikes similar to a snake's. Its bill is so straight, sharp and long, that the anhinga can directly spear fish on its side. When sensing retreat, the anhinga dives under water, then emerges only part of its head some distance away. Because of the shape of its neck, it often resembles a water snake in this position.

Neotropic Cormorant

Basically fish-eaters, groups of Neotropic cormorants band together for collective fishing expeditions, swimming side by side in the same direction in order to block a channel or river inlet, thus preventing the fish from escaping. You can often see them flying in V-shaped formations, or lined up one after the other. While underwater, they propel themselves only with their feet and use their long, stiff tail as a rudder.

Owls

Great horned Owl

This is the largest owl on the continent and lies on the edge of wooded areas., in groves and fields, usually near water.

Burrowing Owl

This owl has daytime habits and builds its nest in holes in the ground.

Ducks

Ducks in the Pantanal are by necessity migratory for several reasons: the availability of food changes widely with the water level, as do safe havens for sleeping and the moulting period (when they are unable to fly).

Muscovy Duck

The South American domestic duck is descended from this species, which is found in small groups or sometimes in pairs, in rivers and lakes, surrounded by forests, or close to them. They often spend the night perched on the branches of defoliated branches, like those of the embaúba tree; sometimes they use the location as a daytime lookout. Nests are built in trees, which can accommodate up to 14 eggs. Since they are avidly hunted by humans, they have developed skittish and distrustful personalities.

White-faced Whistling Duck

One of several ducks known for nocturnal habits, this species is quite gregarious, forming groups of 10-20. They search for food at night, which includes grass seeds, as well as mollusks and small crustaceans. When disturbed, they stand more erect than most ducks, stretch their necks out, and let loose a repeated three-note whistle. Other varieties include the fulvous whistling duck and the black-bellied whistling duck.

Brazilian Duck

A small duck about 40 centimeters, this species roams the swamps and weirs of the Pantanal, which are chock full of low dense vegetation. Depending on how the sunlight hits them, their wing covert can appear black, green, or shiny blue. The female sports a blue-tinted bill and two white spots on her face while the male's bill is red.

FLORA

Bromeliad

The vegetation of the Pantanal is not a typical homogeneous formation; rather, the unusual combination of plants and flowering trees is known as the "Pantanal Complex." Patches of forest, thick brush, and open prairie vie for space through a vast plain. Elements characteristic of the shrub lands in the Amazon forest as well as in Central Brazil freely mix with plant species that have adapted to the swampy lowland environment. In addition, a xerophytous flora has developed on shallow calcareous overgrowth and higher terrain, with results similar to that of the "caatinga," a characteristic dried-out terrain of Northeastern Brazil. In regards to flora, the Pantanal is best seen, not as a mere swamp, but as a homogenous combination of vegetal growth, which inspired by peculiar soil conditions, floods, and topography, create a stunning, yet delicate ecological balance.

The alluvial plain of the Pantanal lies between 100-200 meters above sea level. On the Brazilian side (east, north, and west), it is surrounded by a plateau, approximately 600-700 meters in altitude, covered with *cerrado* (bush savannah vegetation). To the south, lies the Paraguayan depression, a rolling plain with an extensive hydrographic network, formed by countless tributaries of the Paraguay River. These alluvial plains are so wide that drilling in this area has reached 83 meters without hitting the bedrock.

The Pantanal's vast prairies, or *campinas*, as they are called, are filled with slender meadow grasses, forming a natural pastureland boasting only an occasional ligneous plant. In general, these prairies are mostly found in the more humid areas subjected to flooding. In contrast, the shrub lands, restricted by nature to higher and drier areas, remain out of the water, giving rise to tiny islands of vegetation.

Clusters of thorny bushes, dense forests and palm tree groves complete the terrain of these prairies. The most common palm tree is the **carandezaias**, formed by specimens of the **carandá**, a stately palm tree with fan-shaped leaves, that grows to about 10 meters. The **buriti** is another popular palm tree, which also sports fan-shaped leaves. In densely forested areas called capões, we also find the **aroeira fig** trees marked by twisted, almost sculpture-like trunks, the **piúva**, which blooms flamboyantly in shades of pink, lilac and purple in the month of July and August, and the **cambará**, which is remarkable for its golden yellow flowers.

Another type of grove, called **paratuda-is**, sports trees with more slender trunks, thick and wrinkled bark and twisted branches. The most common variety is the **yellow ipê**, known in the Pantanal as the **paratudo**.

Wild Cashu Fruit

Flanking both sides of the region's many waterways are the **riparian forests**. Among the trees here are the **genipapo fig trees**, **inga trees**, **the silver-leafed embaúbas** which flourishes beside anthills, and the **tucum**, a small palm tree of the Bactris genus. The **acuri palm** tree provides a delicious delicacy in the form of fruit to the blue macaws, and the **pau-de-novato** significantly contributes color to the riverbanks with its cluster of pink or red flowers. The name "novato" (or newcomer) refers to the danger awaiting the indoctrinated who do not know that if you cut the tree down with an axe or hang your hammock there, that the plant's movements will cause hundreds of tiny ants to fall upon you without mercy. Their sting is intensely fiery.

On the higher plains, calcareous rock formations pierce the surface, creating a mosaic of xerophytic and deciduous, succulent cacti and spiny, rigid-leafed bromeliads. Here you can find smaller groves of Bromeliacae and Cactacae.

Among stunning examples of flowers, the **pond-lilies** are floating aquatic plants typical to the region, forming clusters that collect in ponds and watercourses. Their various blues and purples are a welcome color addition to the green vegetation. As in the Amazon, there are numerous **Vitória-régias**, enormous lily pads that look like Alice-in-Wonderland-type pie plates.

CULTURE

The rugged, die-hard faces of the Pantanal's cowboys, farmers and fishermen tell it all. Due to the great distances between ranches, the typical inhabitants of the region have had to accustom themselves to lives of solitude and isolation. Facing the unforgiving climate and obstinate terrain daily has created a breed of resourceful, independent people. By intermarrying with the Guarani, Paiaguá and Guiaiató Indians, the Pantanal local has inherited physical agility and a deep respect for nature, though a certain streak of hunter's-style machismo still reigns supreme. Among the skills of the typical resident are the ability to deftly maneuver a flat-bottomed boat or canoe, horsebackriding, and oxen-herding over both dry and swampy terrain. Most locals drive jeeps with unwavering courage and seem to preternaturally know when and where fauna will appear.

The typical Pantanal farmhand primarily chows down on meat. A local breakfast might include jerked beef with rice, coffee and milk, and at times a typical biscuit of the region called *maria-chica*. Before he sets off for a day of work in the fields, a farmer will pack an *empamonado* (made of minced jerked beef and manioc flour). Barbecues are thrown at even the hint of a potential celebration. To offset the overconsumption of beef and aid in digestion, residents in the northern section of the Pantanal drink a mixture of guaraná powder, water and sugar. In the south, more preferred is the *tereré-mate*—a Paraguayan tea brewed in cold water and served in a bull's horn.

Because roads are often impassable, the majority of farms communicate by radio and even have their own airstrip to avoid complete isolation. Due to the lonely life-style, single women traveling through the region alone should probably be careful how they conduct themselves. From experience, I suggest to women that they travel in the company of a known and trustworthy male companion or take a package trip as outlined in the "Options for Travel;" and the "Where to Go" sections (even then, be careful around guides).

OPTIONS FOR TRAVEL

RIVER EXCURSIONS AND LODGES

Besides trekking the Transpantaneira Highway, there are several other travel options in the Pantanal. Cuiabá is only one of three gateways to the Pantanal; the other jumping-off points are Campo Grande and Corumbá. From any one of these cities you can journey into the interior and choose among several types of accommodations. Favorite among fishermen and birdwatchers are the two to four day river cruises in **botels** (floating lodges, really just boats), like the one I took with Expeditours. Or you can choose to stay in a **rustic lodge** from where you can initiate treks by foot, horseback, or canoe—usually preferred by those who sleep more comfortably on dry land. A variety of lodges in all price ranges are available, from the most primitive ranches, where meals are cooked over an open fire, to the luxurious **Pousada Caiman**, the most famous lodge in the Pantanal. Package deals are usually the cheapest and the most sensible way to go; just make sure the lodge provides transfer from the airport.

THE FAZENDA EXPERIENCE

I step off a 10-seater plane in Corumbá and find a rugged, silent-type cowboy waiting for me in the lobby. He piles my gear in the back of his truck, and soon we're off on a wildly bumpy ride to reach the **Fazenda Xaraes**. During rainy season, more than half this trek would be made by canoe, when the annual rains flood the plains leading to the farm.

After a dead-to-the-world sleep in my air-conditioned cabana, I fortify myself with a mule-teamer's breakfast, then hop in a truck to see the countryside. Julio, our driver, seems to have a preternatural sense where the wild animals are, even before he sees them; along the highway we discover cobra skins, contemplate the jaws of alligators from bridges overhead, nearly get crushed by herds of cattle running Pamplona style.

Capybaras sometimes plant themselves in our way; birds fly right in front of the windshield, barely surviving. If we were traveling at night, our guide informs us, we'd run smack into gators looking for food. Twice we see toucans streaking past. In mid-sentence Julio jumps out of the running jeep to race after an armadillo, catching him by the tail so we can inspect the armored body. If you go to Bolivia by train, he says, they'll serve you *armadillo na casca* (in the shell). Soon we discover it's not just humans who scavenge the Pantanal. We drive past about 20 black urubus (vultures) feasting on the remains of a jacaré (crocodile).

THE FAZENDA EXPERIENCE

In the afternoon, a canoe trip takes us through the leafy waterway of an igarapé—a miraculous vista at dusk when a crop of trees lining the banks becomes home to roosting garças who fly in for the night. The next day we comb the enormous grounds of the Xaraes Fazenda on both horseback and foot, exploring forests that seem nearly primeval—home to hundreds of monkeys, capybaras, and rodents who scurry under the brush as we approach. From our guide, we learn that the only way to hear the voice of the Pantanal is to descend into silence—a kind of Zen in the wild. Crouching down behind bushes, we suddenly hear the terrifying screech of howler monkeys, a sound that even unraveled the botanist Henry Bates.

Fazenda Xaraes

Rio Abobral, 130 kilometers from Corumbá. Reserve in Campo Grande ☎ *(67) 242-1102 or São Paulo* ☎ *(11) 246-9934, or through Expeditours in Rio* ☎ *(21) 287-9697, FAX 521-4388.* This well-maintained, three-star lodge is rustic enough to be authentic and clean enough to be comfortable. Owned by the same group as the Nacional Hotel in Corumbá, it features wood-and-tiled rooms with shutters open to the river. The air conditioning is solid, and whatever dirt you trail in seems to mysteriously disappear in a matter of hours. The dining room is surrounded by screens so you can see and hear the chirping birds. Most impressive is the salt-of-the-earth staff, some of the nicest people I met in Brazil. Packages include all meals and a variety of daily excursions. Rates per person per night range from $57.85 (doubles $51.05); transfers from Corumbá $61 per person or $40 for doubles; three-hour horse treks for 2.5 hours run $8, boat trip, $40. two-day/one-night package, including one boat tour, runs $89; three-days/two-nights per person is $200 (doubles $162).

If you arrive in Corumbá, the staff will pick you up and transfer you by truck (or canoe during rainy season) to Fazenda Xaraes. You can also take the bus to Morro do Azeite, which leaves you out in the middle of the road, 31 kilometers (45 minutes) from Xaraes, where the staff will pick you up. Flights to Corumbá are offered by VASP from Belo Horizonte, Brasília, Campo Grande, Cuiabá, Goiânia, and São Paulo.

Insider Tip

Avoid January when there are the most mosquitoes. August and September are the coolest months.

Pousada Caiman

236 kilometers from Campo Grande, Mato Grosso do Sul. The five-star accommodation of the southern Pantanal, situated on a serious working ranch, is the eco-dream of Roberto Klabin, the energetic scion of a rich Brazilian family who wanted to create for his friends and tourists the height of luxury-in-the-wild. Of the ranch's 53,000 hectares, 7000 (15,400 acres) has been set aside as an ecological reserve, but much of the land remains range for the 65 staff cowboys who live in a village adjacent to the lodge. The U-shaped hacienda (formerly the Klabin's family residence) houses 22 guests and offers every deluxe amenity, from swimming pool and Italian-tiled floors, to comfy leather furniture, satellite-dish TV, and stylish apartments with excellent air conditioning; the cuisine is superb. The grounds have been called "an oasis for birds," since a large variety of species can easily be seen. Guests are led on morning and afternoon excursions on horseback, in canoe, and on foot. The lodge is located about four hours by car from Campo Grande; transfers by air-conditioned micro-buses are offered every Saturday and Wednesday from Campo Grande between 1:30 p.m.–2:00 p.m., and after breakfast from the lodge. (Campo Grande may be reached by commercial flights from Belém, Brasília, Corumbá, Cuiabá, Rio Branco, Santarém, São Paulo and others.) Three-day packages run from Wednesday–Saturday; four nights from Saturday to Wednesday. In New York, contact **Brazil Nuts** (see the chapter, *Specialty Tours,* for address). In São Paulo, contact **Roberto Klabin Hotéis e Turismo** *Rua Pedrosa Alvarenga, 1208, first floor, CEP 045531;* ☎ *(11) 883-6566.* In Rio contact **Expeditours** ☎ *(21) 287-9697, FAX 521-4388.*

Fazenda Boa Sorte Região de Abobral

☎ *231-1120* (in Corumbá)*;* reservations can be made through **Expeditours** ☎ *(21) 287-9697 (Rio) or (65) 381-4959 (Cuiabá).* A rustic (read "primitive") farm without frills near the Fazenda Xaraes gives you a home-on-the-range ambiance. Sleep outdoors in hammocks, inside tents, or under grass-roofed huts with wood-slat floors. If you don't want to bathe in the river, there's a communal bath. Three daily meals are cooked over a wood fire; don't pass up a glass of freshly milked cow juice. The farm's parrots will sit happily on your shoulder and even the wild ducks and toucans are friendly. During the day you can make excursions on horseback, sleep in other fazendas, and take canoe trips. A three-day package for $70 includes all meals and treks.

Fazenda Beira Rio

Rod. Transpantaneira, 150 kilometers from Poconé, 205 kilometers from Cuiabá. Reserve ☎ *(65) 322-0948, or* ☎ *(11) 35-4157 (in São Paulo), or* ☎ *(67) 725-5267 (in Campo Grande),* or through **Expeditours** ☎ *(21) 287-9697, FAX 521-4388.* Located on 3700 hectares of land right off the Transpantaneira Highway, this is considered the best pousada in the region for cleanliness and trek options. The hotel is two years old, owned by the grizzly but *simpático* Senhor Valdo de Luis. Running next to his property is the Pixaim River, which you can traverse by motor boat ($25 an hour), or canoe (monkeys upstream, herons downstream). You can also rent horses ($7 per hour) or explore the grounds by foot. Guides accompany guests without charge. Housed in a one-story white stucco building with traditional tile roofs, the simple rooms are all air-conditioned and come with minibar, TV, and attractive tile floors. Suites sleep five. If you come through a travel agent, the package deal includes horse treks and boat excursions; otherwise, you pay extra. There are no phones, but there is radio communication with Cuiabá. Rates are about $50 per day, including all three meals; packages available. (13 apartments.)   *Moderate.*

Hotel Santa Rosa do Pantanal

Transpantaneira Highway, 150 kilometers from Poconé. Reserve in Cuiabá ☎ *(65) 322-0513/0077; in São Paulo (11) 231-4511.* Once a luxurious (for the region) hotel, this is still the best in Porto Jofre, located at the end of the Transpantaneira Highway on the banks of the Cuiabá River. One travel option is to trek or hitch your way here, then rent boats, horses, or guides at the hotel. The owner of the nearby campgrounds also rents boats. (54 apartments.)   *Moderate. No cards.*

NEW FOR 1995

After nearly 20 years of working in the Pantanal, André Von Thuranyi of **Expeditours travel agency**, has now started his own lodge program in collaboration with native farmers in the Pantanal wetlands. A four-day/three-night package at the Araras Farm lodge, a private reserve off the Transpantaneira Highway, offers treks by foot, canoe, horseback and jeep. An extra night in Cuiabá and/or a tour of Chapada dos Guimarães (highly recommended) may be added. Transports to the lodge leave the Expeditours office in Cuiabá every day at 3:30 p.m. For more information about this lodge and others, contact Expeditours *Rua Visconde de Pirajá, 414 (Ipanema), Rio de Janeiro;* ☎ *(21) 287-9697, FAX 521-4388, or in Cuiabá: Avenida Governador Ponce de Arruda, 670;* ☎ *(65) 381-4959/381-5674 in Cuiabá.*

Insider Tip

If you are traversing the Transpantaneira in a group tour, make sure the driver and your guide know you want to savor every scene. This will slow down the trip considerably, so if you have flights to catch later in the day, leave a few hours earlier. You may never see anything like it again.

BOTELS AND BOAT CRUISES

An alternative to bunking down at lodges is to take a package cruise. Expeditours offers the Pantanal Ecological triangle tour, a fine five-night/ four-day package on the Pantanal Explorer, a modest, low draft boat that sleeps 12 including crew (four air-conditioned bunks for passengers, with two shared bathrooms, sun deck, and kitchen/bar, contact **Expeditours** in previous paragraph). During the day, you can sight birds and other wildlife from the top deck of the boat; at night special alligator expeditions are conducted in canoes. Tight quarters make sociable personalities a must, but humor is provided by outgoing guides who are able to identify most of the animals and birds sighted. Food is surprisingly good: a mixture of beef, fish, chicken and pasta. The most exciting part of the trip is the roller-coaster ride over the Transpantaneira Highway—a must for Pantanal-goers. Among animals to be sighted are savanna hawks, Amazon kingfishers, snowy egrets, toco toucans, black-headed vultures, wood storks, herons, parrots, woodpeckers, cormorants, marsh deer, capybaras, caimans, iguanas and lizards. The highway's 114 bridges are sometimes portraits of imminent disaster—weatherbeaten washboard planks crossed by moldy timbers, but the anything-can-happen ambiance is part of the fun. An hour and a half beyond Poconé you'll pass the São João ranch owned by Sebastião Camargo Correia, one of the five richest men in the world. Ask if you can visit. A stop at the gold mines near Cangas, 10 minutes from Cuiabá, is also an eye-opener. For more information, see *Hands-On Cuiabá*.

INDEPENDENT TRAVEL

The independent's way to see the Pantanal is to combine different options. First, hire a good guide who is ready to go anywhere, then improvise. You can go by car from Poconé to Barão de Melgaço, then rent kayaks and paddle to Porto Cercado, or if you're crazy enough, all the way down to Porto Jofre (about four to five days). This way you can stop and take time to talk to the locals, who are usually friendly. Have a car waiting at Porto Jofre and go over the Transpantaneira Highway to Pixaim, camping or staying at a lodge. To do it right, you'll need about eight to ten days. The price for such a trip with guide and transportation will probably cost as much as an Expeditours boat tour for four days, but you must come prepared with your own food. To find a guide, call a travel agency and just ask for the names of reliable guides without explaining exactly what you want, then make private arrangements with the guide.

Insider Tip

Hitchhiking the Transpantaneira Highway (as opposed to traversing it in a prearranged tour) seems to be the beloved pastime of male travel writers and photojournalists who are mad for adventure and great photo-ops. Maybe I'm a sissy, but frankly, I wouldn't suggest hitchhiking, at least not on your first trip to the region. Sure, you'll find a friendly ride eventually, and you'll meet lots of colorful cowboys, native fishermen, and even a few federal agents, but in the meantime you could be overcome by sunstroke, exhaustion, bee attacks, hungry capybaras, dazed jacarés, and swarms of malaria-ridden mosquitoes, not to mention sudden floodings. You might even stumble on illegal poachers who would like to scramble you for breakfast. Better on your first attempt to go with a reputable guide, in well-maintained vehicles (trucks, boats, planes) with responsible drivers who know the terrain. The driving is rough; even Brazilian tourists have been known to topple over their jeeps. Since there are no towns, no restaurants, and no phones on the highway, getting stuck will mean a very long wait.

PANTANAL SURVIVAL KIT

CLIMATE

Between April–October, which is the dry season, temperatures average between 68°F and 75°F, but temperatures can rise over 50 degrees in just a matter of hours. The hottest months in the Pantanal are *December–February*, when temperatures average between 110°F and 112°F. During dry season it's important to drink lots of liquids to avoid dehydration. Starting in *November*, weather alternates between torrential rains and scalding sun. The most animals can be seen in *December and January*.

MEDICAL EMERGENCIES

It's best not to have them while you're in the Pantanal. Decent hospitals will probably be boats, planes, and torturous jeep rides away. Take your own medicine kit (including gauze, antiseptic, allergy pills and antihistamines, calamine lotion, aloe vera lotion for cuts and bruises, a snake bite kit, TANG™ for dehydration, and Pepto-Bismol™ for diarrhea, etc. Make sure you've had all the necessary inoculations (tetanus, yellow fever, typhoid, polio). And pray. (Hospitals are listed under *Hands-On Cuiabá.*

BEES

Anyone going to the Pantanal should read Vic Banks's riveting description of the "bees from hell" in his book *The Pantanal* (Sierra Club, 1991). According to Banks, 300–400 people a year die from bee stings in Brazil, more than from any other animal attack. In the Pantanal, Europa honeybees have interbred with African killer bees, making them capable of attacking aggressively en masse, even if just one drone is disturbed. Truly, Banks' encounter was most unfortunate, but I frankly never met one bee in the Pantanal.

WHAT TO PACK

Follow guidelines for Amazon treks (see *Amazônia* chapter), but also dress in layers (for cool nights, a jean jacket and sweater is sufficient). Binoculars, telephoto lenses and high-speed film are essential in the Pantanal. (Those magnificent close-up shots of birds seen in books and brochures are surely taken by professionals who spend days waiting silently under a bush for just the right moment.)

WHEN TO GO

Fishing season runs February-October.

Bird Watching season runs year-long, with best times beginning in the middle of May and peaking from the middle of June through the middle of October.

Reptile-watching season runs yearly, with peak times from September-December.

Mammal-spotting season runs year-long, with peak times from January through May.

WHERE TO GO IN THE PANTANAL

CUIABÁ

The capital of Mato Grosso, **Cuiabá** (pronounced Kwee-ah-bah) is the major gateway to the Pantanal, located about 102 kilometers from the northern entrance of the Transpantaneira Highway. Even so, it's not exactly a destination in itself, though a day or two stuck here won't feel like the end of the world. Most visitors use Cuiabá as a trampoline to visit other parts of the region, like the magnificent rock sculptures in the **National Park** and the caves and waterfalls of **Chapada dos Guimarães**, one of the most beautiful sites in all Brazil. Once a frontier town, Cuiabá has boomed to over 330,000 people (some reports claim up to one million in the surrounding area); you will discover fine regional restaurants here, as well as some of the best crafts stores for Indian artifacts in the region.

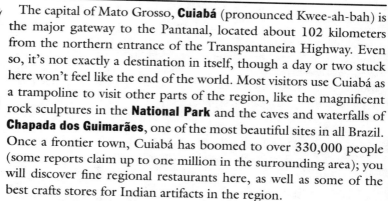

The first *bandeirantes* in the early 18th century came in search of Indian slaves but soon forgot their objective when they discovered gold. A Paulista, Pascoal Moreira Cabral, established the first settlement in 1719, having braved disease, mosquitoes, floods, and intense heat through his arduous five-month journey from São Paulo. Soon, thousands more were traveling the 3000-kilometer route, boosting the population of Cuiabá far beyond that of São Paulo between 1719–1730. Because of the navigation systems, however, ties with Bolivians, Paraguayans and Argentinians soon became tighter than with fellow Brazilians, resulting in a kind of trans-Latino culture. The flotillas of canoes and medium-sized ships that arrived laden with supplies and slaves invariably departed from Cuiabá groaning with gold.

In 1979, **Mato Grosso** was divided into two states, Mato Grosso in the north and Mato Grosso do Sul in the south. Since then, Cuiabá has enjoyed enormous development in education, tourism and construction. In 1989–1990, three shows on TV claiming that gold had been found on the streets (!) of Cuiabá magnetized a stream of Northeasterners and Mineiros, who arrived with little more than dreams in their pockets. As a result, a rash of frontier towns rose up, most of them approximating slums. One such town is **Cangas**, ten minutes from Cuiabá on the Cuiabá-Santarém highway, the site of six or seven **gold mines**. Founded about seven years ago, Cangas today is a scene straight out of a wild west movie, with two big bars, three small snack bars, one school, three churches, three gas stations, and a single public phone (for all 5000 people). As one local told me, "There's only one phone because most people here have no one to call."

During the dry season, airplane descents into Cuiabá can be turbulent due to the smoky warm air from fires set by cattle ranchers every dry season to burn off undesirable vegetation and promote fresh grass for fodder. August is the peak month for these fires, and sometimes flights are canceled for several weeks, forcing travelers to take five-hour bus trips from the nearest open airport. During the rainy season, flights may be delayed due to inclement weather.

A BIRD'S EYE VIEW

Cuiabá is nicknamed the Garden City because of its many trees, including 200-year-old palms. The main plaza, Praça da República, is dominated by an old church, the city, the Hotel Excelsior, and a 12-story television tower on a nearby hill. Next to the tower is the alabaster minaret of a Muslim temple. From the Igreja de Bom Jesus dos Passos, an 18th-century church with an exquisite Gothic facade, you can see a vista of the city. The tourist office, TURIMAT, is located off the main plaza near the Igreja Matriz.

SIGHTS

Praça Moreira Cabral (Geodesic Center)
Although the *mirante* in Chapada is considered a more scenic representation of the geodesic center of South America, the exact point is located here, in Cuiabá. The site is marked by a monument and pyramid in a small concrete park facing the Legislative Assembly and is considered to include a 50-kilometer radius (of which Chapada forms one end). The Praça can be entered from Rua Barão de Melgaço.

Fish Market
Buying and selling the day's fresh catch takes place along the Rio Cuiabá daily from 4:00 a.m.–6:00 p.m.

Horto Florestal Bairro Coxipó (City Park)
At the confluence of the Rio Coxipó with Rio Cuiabá; access through Avenida Fernando Correa da Costa. Daily 7:00 a.m.–5:30 p.m. Guides available 2:00 p.m.–5:00 p.m. The future park of the city is being planned on this tropical landscape where children can scamper around playgrounds made from logs. On the docket for the future is an orchid greenhouse, an exposition of seeds and plants natural to the forest, and a special display of medicinal plants.

Comunidade São Gonçalo (Crafts Commune)

Located near the Fazenda de Mato Grosso, this primitive community sits on the banks of the Rio Cuiabá and supports itself totally through artisanry (especially pottery) and folkloric presentations. Visitors are always welcome; just seeing the rural lifestyle should prove fascinating. The community's major festival is held on January 10, the Feast of São Gonçalo, when colorful boats proceed upriver to herald the arrival of the saint.

Insider Tip

If you want to eat regional food, see a folkloric museum, and buy regional crafts all in one stop, try the complex that houses the Casa do Artesão, the Museu de Artesanato, and the Regionalíssimo restaurant, located on Praça Maj. João Bueno.

MUSEUMS AND ZOO

Museu de Artesanato

Rua 13 de Junho, Praça Maj. João Bueno. Tuesday–Sunday 10:00 a.m.–3:00 p.m., 6:00 p.m.–11:00 p.m. Next door to the Casa do Artesão (a fine crafts store) is a museum of folkoric art situated in a frontier-styled, brick-and-wood house, complete with an antique kitchen. Featured are ornaments and weapons from the Xavantes and other Mato Grosso tribes, as well as leather goods from the home-on-the-range culture. Especially intriguing is the leather *bornal*, a contraption that was strapped around a horse's mouth so it could walk and eat millet at the same time.

Museu do Indio Marechal Candîdo Rondôn

Located at the University Federal of Mato Grosso this museum displays artisanry, weapons, and ornaments crafted by the state's indigenous peoples.

Universidade Federal do Mato Grosso (Mini Zoo)

Avenida Fernando Correa da Costa, best times to visit: 6:00 a.m.–8:00 a.m. and 3:30 p.m.–7:00 p.m. To avoid sunstroke (1:00 p.m. is deadly). An indoor environ is open daily 7:00 a.m.–11:00 a.m. and 1:30 p.m.–7:00 p.m., closed Monday. UFMT displays the fauna and flora of the region in an outdoor natural environment that features snakes, jaguars, monkeys, birds, and ostriches. On the far side of well-secured fences, animals such as capybaras, egrets, garças, alligators and land turtles all seem to live in harmony, although some tend to look collapsed from the heat. A university restaurant near the parking lot goes on strike a lot but is a nice place to meet young people. To reach the zoo, take the city bus labeled "*Copamel Universidade*" or "*Santa Cruz.*"

WHERE TO STAY

If you don't want to find a veritable zoo in your hotel room (i.e., frogs in your toilet and cockroaches the size of capybaras in the closet), you'll have to pay for a bug-free environment in Cuiabá. In the hot clime, air conditioning is essential, and if you are returning from an excursion, you'll appreciate a good laundry service.

Expensive	**$30–$50**
Moderate	**$10–$30**
Inexpensive	**Under $10**

Veneza Palace Hotel

Avenida Coronel Escolástico, 738 (Bandeirantes); ☎ *(65) 321-4847; FAX 322-5212.* This perfectly respectable, impeccably clean three-star has an oriental lobby and a genial staff. The carpeted apartments are small, but the air conditioning is ice-cold, and the wood furniture attractive. All rooms come with color TV, minibar and carpet. Safes are at the reception. Laundry is available. The restaurant, which favors international cuisine, serves an excellent *canja de galinha* (chicken soup). There's also a pool, TV/playroom, and an American bar. Superior singles run $46, doubles $61. (78 Apts.)   ***Moderate. All Cards.***

Hotel Fazenda de Mato Grosso

Rua Antônio Dorileo, 1200 (Coxipó); ☎ *361-2980.* Located only 6 kilometers from the city, this farm-like complex is surrounded by 19 hectares of forested land—a kind of "civilized wilderness." The rustic apartments are housed in one- and two-story buildings with traditional tiled roofs; all have air conditioning, color TV, minibar, and phone. Clean and attractive, the bathrooms are appointed in tile and marble. On the grounds is a mini-zoo with snakes, garças and capybaras; there's also a large pool and playground surrounded by tropical vegetation. Horses, paddle boats and other sports are included in the daily rate, as is breakfast. Transportation to the city is provided for groups who hold conventions here. (50 apartments.)
Moderate. All cards.

JJ Palace Hotel

Rua Alziro Zarur, 312; (Boa Esperança); ☎ *(65) 361-1858.* For budget travelers only. A single in this three-story hotel is absolutely basic—little closet space, a slight mustiness, somewhat dirty walls, but a well-equipped minibar. Location is near a pharmacy and several restaurants. Singles with fan run about $10, doubles with air conditioning $20.
Inexpensive. No Cards.

WHERE TO EAT

Moderate	**$5–$15**
Inexpensive	**Under $5**

Recanto do Bosque

Rua Cândido Mariano, 1040; ☎ *323-1468. 11:30 a.m.–3:00 p.m., 7:00 p.m.–midnight.* Trees grow right through the middle of this open-air restaurant, the best rodízio in town, situated under a grass roof. Eighteen cold salads and all-you-can-eat meat; Saturday features *feijoada.* After 5:00 p.m., beer is half price and barbecued fish is included. Buffet runs about $4–$5 per person, discounts for groups of 15 or more.   ***Moderate. All cards.***

Taberna Portuguesa

Avenida XV de Novembro, 40; ☎ *321-3661. Daily 11:00 a.m.–2:30 p.m., 6:00 p.m.–11:30 p.m., Monday lunch.* Located about one kilometer from the center of town, this cozy, air-conditioned Portuguese tavern is piquant with the smells of home cooking. Codfish runs about $9, *caldeirada* (a thick fish soup made with white wine, potatoes, onions, pimentos, and tomato sauce) runs about $13, an award-winning paella about $20. Dishes usually serve two.   ***Moderate. No cards.***

O Regionalíssimo

Rua 13 de Junho (Praça João Bueno); ☎ *322-3908. Daily: 11:30 a.m.–2:30 p.m., 7:30 p.m.–11:00 p.m., live music Thursday–Sunday, closed Monday.* Situated next to the Casa do Artesão, this charming adega features some of the best regional cuisine in Cuiabá. Local folkloric musicians serenade the buffet, which changes daily; you might find fried fish, *peixe ensopado, farofa de banana, carne de sol,* and other delicacies. Alas, no air conditioning, but a steady breeze whips through the open brick arches.   ***Moderate. No cards.***

Mamma Aurora

Rua Miranda Reis, 386; ☎ *322-4339. Daily: 6:00 p.m.–midnight.* Best pizzeria in town. Live music.   ***Inexpensive. No cards.***

NIGHTLIFE

Nightlife in Cuiabá is as hot as you will find in the Pantanal, or even in Mato Grosso—north or south.

Discoteca Logan

Best disco for the 18–40 set.

Get Up Dance

Avenida Fernando Corrêa da Costa, 1953; ☎ *323-3335.* Another dance spot.

Mirante Bar

Avenida Miguel Smith, in front of the Plaza Motel. For local bands and solo singers performing MPB.

SHOPPING

Casa do Guaraná

Avenida Mário Corrêa, 310; ☎ *321-7729.* Situated in the *bairro* of Porto, the oldest district in Cuiabá, this "House of Guaraná" makes a facinating showcase for Brazilian ingenuity, featuring products made from the plant most known for its stimulating kick to the nervous system. Here you can buy "sticks" of guaraná that you can grate into a powder in the traditional way, or you may buy the powder already formed. *Xarope de guaraná* is a syrup that is drunk as juice (just add water). The store also features *licor de Pequi* (a liqueur made from a typical fruit of the *cerrado*), as well as *serrin-*

has de unha (nail files made from fish scales). You can also stock up on natural herb shampoos and cosmetics, as well as stunning Pantanal T-shirts.

Casa do Artesão
Rua 13 de Junho, 315; ☎ 322-3908, 321-0603. Founded in May 15, 1975, this store, situated in an 18th-century blue-and-white colonial house, features some of the best crafts for sale in the region. Good buys include *ganzas* (scraper-like percussion instruments made of wood) and handmade pottery. Absolutely exquisite are the embroidered hammocks that go for about $200—steep, but so lovely you could hang them on the wall as decoration. Also for sale are indigenous Indian crafts such as bows, arrows and basketry. A special room features homemade sweets and liqueurs; don't miss the antique sugarcane machine in the garden. Next door is the Regionalíssimo restaurant.

Artíndia
Rua Comandante Costa, 942; ☎ 321-1348, near the Praça Rachid Jaudy. The artisan store of FUNAI features crafts from the indigenous tribes of the Pantanal.

Mercearia Banzal
Avenida Generoso Ponce (no number), Mercado Municipal Box 1/2/3 (downtown); ☎ 321-7518. Macrobiotic and natural products including brown rice, miso and tofu are sold here.

HEALERS
Cuiabá and Chapada dos Guimarães have attracted a steady stream of holistic health practitioners during the last 10 years. Among the best are those listed below.

Centro de Vivências Para Integração do Ser
Rua Balneário São João, 323 (Coxipó da Ponte); ☎ 361-2215. The city's most active alternative health center, offering a fine acupuncturist, Décio Cesar da Silva, as well as other practitioners in the fields of rebirthing, oki-yoga, massage, etc.

Ma Prem Dwari
Rua Doze, 297 (Boa Esperança); ☎ 361-5274. Excellent masseuse and practitioner of Bach Flower Remedies.

HANDS-ON CUIABÁ
AIRLINES
Flights to Cuiabá can be arranged from Alta Floresta (TABA), Belém, Belo Horizonte, Brasília, Campo Grande (Varig), Natal, Porto Alegre, Rio Branco, Rio de Janeiro, Salvador, Santarém, and São Paulo, among others.

Varig/Cruzeiro
Rua Antônio João, 258; ☎ 321-7333.

VASP
Rua Pedro Celestino, 32 (Downtown); ☎ 624-1313, ramal 112.

Transbrasil
  Rua Barão de Melgaço 3508; ☎ *381-3347.*
TABA
  Airport; ☎ *381-2233.*

ARRIVALS

Aeroporto Marechal Rondôn is situated at *Avenida Governador Ponce de Arruda (Várzea Grande);* ☎ *381-2211.* The Rodoviária (bus station) is located at *Avenida Mal. Rondôn (on the road to Chapada dos Guimarães),* ☎ *624-2085.* For more information see *Points Beyond* below.

CAR RENTALS AND AIR TAXIS

Nobre can be found at the airport; ☎ *381-1651.* There is also an office at *Avenida Governador Ponce de Arruda, 980;* ☎ *3811-2821.*

Localiza Nacional
  Avenida Dom Bosco, 965; ☎ *381-3773; at the airport, open 24 hours.*

Air Taxis

Abelha
  ☎ *381-122.*
Guará
  ☎ *381-2863.*

CLIMATE

Weather can change very quickly within hours in Cuiabá. Basically, summers (December–February) are hot and humid (temperatures over 100°F) while winters (June–August) are cool and dry (temperatures dropping to 60°F).

MONEY EXCHANGE

If you're flying into the state of Mato Grosso from a major Brazilian city, it's best to exchange money before you arrive; rates will undoubtedly be better. Traveler's cheques can be exchanged at **Banco do Brasil** at *Rua Barão de Melgaço, 915.* In addition, good exchange rates for dollars are offered at the **Abudi Palace Hotel.**

MEDICAL EMERGENCIES

Hospitals are generally to be avoided in this region. For emergencies:

Hospital Geral e Maternidade
  Rua 13 de Junho, 2101; ☎ *323-3322.*
Pronto-Socorro Municipal
  Rua Gen. Valle; ☎ *321-7404.*

PHARMACIES

Drogaria Avenida
  Avenida Getúlio Vargas, 280; ☎ *624-1305.*
Farmácia Bezerra de Menezes
  Avenida Ten. Cel. Duarte, 326; ☎ *322-7779.*

POINTS BEYOND

Buses

Buses run regularly between Cuiabá and Chapada dos Guimarães. (For times, see under *Hands-On Chapada*). Buses are also available to São Felix do Araguaia, São José dos Quatro Marcos, Guiratinga, Rio do Casca, Paranatingam, Paxaréo, and D. Aquino, among others. You can also reach the Véu de Noiva (a waterfall and mountain) by local bus, which will leave you off after Buriti if you tell the driver in advance.

Air

Flights are available to Alta Floresta, Belém, Brasília, Belo Horizonte, Corumbá, Fortaleza, Manaus, Porto Alegre, Recife, Porto Velho, Rio Branco, Rio de Janeiro, Salvador, Santarém, São Paulo, and others.

PRIVATE GUIDES

Amilton Martins da Silva

☎ *322-3702.* For the names of city guides who speak English, call the president of the Guide Association, who is a very good guide himself.

Carlos Wolff

☎ *661-1469.* Another English-speaking guide.

TELEPHONE

Local and international phone calls can be made from the telephone company **Telemat** *Rua Barão de Melgaço, 3195* during commercial hours. There is also an office located at the bus station and the airport.

TRAVEL AGENCY

Cidade Turismo

Rua Duque de Caxias, 59 (Alvorada); ☎ *(65) 322-3702.* Director Amilton Martins da Silva specializes in cinematography, film crews, ecological tours, and VIP service. Arrangements for treks by boat, jeep, or plane can also be made. Four-hour city tours run about $37, including lunch at a regional restaurant.

Expeditours (Pantanal Explorers)

Avenida Ponce de Arruda, 670 (near the airport); ☎ *(65) 381-4959, 381-5674.* Perhaps the leading eco-tour agency in Brazil, Expeditours mans an office in Cuiabá near the airport, where clients headed for Pantanal river cruises and Chapada dos Guimarães are received. (Their base office is in Rio.) One of the most serious eco-tour operators in Brazil, owner André von Thuranyi is not only deeply commited to preservation, but is also well tuned to the mystical aspects of the countryside. His efficient English-speaking staff can arrange accommodations at any of the pousadas listed below, as well as transportation and accommodations throughout the country, including the Amazon.

TOURIST INFORMATION

The state tourist board **Turimat** is located at *Praça da República, 131 (downtown);* ☎ *(65) 322-5363.* Information booths can also be found at the airport and the bus station. You'll find maps and some general assistance on car rentals and hotels. For major excursions, it's best to contact the travel agencies above.

WHEN TO GO

July presents a Winter Festival in Chapada.

CHAPADA DOS GUIMARÃES

Chapada dos Guimarães is simply an extraordinary place. More than 800 meters above sea level, it boasts a variety of microclimates that allow for the coexistence of an enormous variety of plants and animals. Geological studies have shown that life existed here over 45,000 years ago, and mystics predict that future civilizations will be born here. Exactly what that means for the average visitor remains obscure, but it can't be denied that most tourists immediately feel a strong sense of clarity and well-being here, and many are inclined to stay longer than they had initially planned. Frankly, it's my favorite place in Brazil, if not the world.

Chapada is located at the 15th degree parallel, on line with such cities as Porto Seguro, Bahia (the birthplace of Brazil), Brasília (the futuristic capital), and Ilhéus, Bahia (near the site of the Transamérica Hotel, the most luxurious resort in Brazil). Such a location is rendered symbolic among Brazilians; many prophecies have suggested that Chapada dos Guimarães will be the birthplace of the Third Millenium. If you're a fan of Sedona, Arizona, you might recognize some of the same kinds of "vibrations"—a mixture of gorgeous landscape and mystical energy generated by numerous psychics, healers and "Green People" who have moved to Chapada over the last 15 years. Not surprisingly, spiritual beliefs run rampant here. Some locals even believe there's a magnetic "hole" over Chapada that allows for communications with extraterrestrials. Indeed, something magnetically fishy is going down here since car batteries and cameras are notorious for malfunctioning on cloudy days (mine did). Without much effort, you're sure to find residents who claim to have personally tape-recorded conversations with ETs; the topics generally seem to concern saving the environment.

HISTORY

Chapada's recorded history began when the Jesuits built a little chapel in 1751. By 1779, Chapada had become a primitive baroque city, its newly built cathedral marked by two imposing towers that were later felled by heavy rains. *Bandeirantes* from São Paulo swarmed over the area, looking for gold to mine and Indians to subjugate; the first sugarcane plantation was established, later becoming famous for its *cachaça*. Supplies were so limited in this isolated region that locals were often forced to trade large hunks of gold for the simplest foods imported from São Paulo.

In the 1930s, a group of Americans left Bahia to found an evangelical mission at Buriti, Chapada's first farm. Today, the pastoral estate is an agricultural school, but the American-made church and colonial houses still look like something out of New England. In more recent times, *Chapada has become famous for its waterfalls, rock formations, and UFO sightings.* Every year a Winter Festival brings artists and craftspersons to the region during the month of July.

A BIRD'S EYE VIEW

The town of Chapada is located 73 kilometers north of Cuiabá, (with access on MT 251). No one quite knows how many people live there; some say about 6000, but it's rumored another 15,000 live in the surrounding area. The main square is full of flowers and trees and makes a peaceful core to the town; the main restaurants are located here, as well as the oldest church in Mato Grosso, the Igreja de Senhora Sant'Ana, built in 1779 with the help of the local Indians. Today chickens scratch around in its courtyard, but inside is a magnificent dusty old chapel. Of particular note is the statue of Joseph wearing boots, a symbol of the goldminers who lived in the area. During my visit, an old couple was valiantly trying to clean the church from the soot that continually blows in from the burning fields—a sad reminder of the forest's destruction.

SIGHTS

The drive from Cuiabá to the National Park of Chapada dos Guimarães offers some of the most thrilling vistas in Brazil. Taking MT-2551 (Cuiabá–Chapada Road), you'll first pass verdant rolling hills and glimmering lakes, behind which looms a massive mountain range washed in purples and blues. Suddenly, the rocky skyline is accentuated by vertical cliffs standing like sentinels—a dramatic contrast to the shrunken brown-and-green shrubbery lining the highway. This is the beginning of the **Planalto Central** (Central Plains) of Brazil, 10,000 years ago a magnificent inland sea that gradually dried to its present state.

Salgadeira

The first stop you must make is at this weekend spot, originally built by the government for tourists, but now a private enterprise. Nicknamed the "Beach of Mato Grosso," the area boasts a stupendous man-made waterfall where bathers can take a dip, as well as a restaurant complex with four bars, ice cream stands, bathrooms, and playground. Walking along a path into the forest, you'll come upon a turbulent double waterfall, and at every angle another mystical nature scene, including steamy falls, natural grottoes, and macumba offerings tucked inside coves. Campgrounds are available, but please don't litter; policemen keep close watch. A few years back, the "Green" community made a fuss here when trees were cut down to build the complex, but the environs are still so beautiful that it's hard to complain.

Portão do Inferno (Hells' Gate)

Nearby is this truly awesome canyon sculpted into dramatic shape more than a thousand years ago by natural erosion. The lookout point, a few meters beyond, is replete with gossip. Legend has it that the federal police threw "undesirables" off this cliff during the dictatorship, and at the beginning of Sarney's administration, a lot of Brazilians were rumored to have thrown *themselves* off when they lost all their money. Even today, a yellow car can be seen at the foot of the pit, reputed to have accidentally veered off the cliff, killing four or five people. These days, police maintain strong surveillance against further incidents, but locals claim they can still hear the spirits of the departed crying at night. Three to four centuries ago, Indians roamed these areas, and the rock formations, which rise like phallic symbols along the highway, have given rise to various legends. Local mystics like to think they are street signs for landing extraterrestrials. The big holes in the ground, however, are definitely made by local rodents. If you're intent on climbing these hills, be careful because the rock is soft.

Cachoeira Véu de Noiva

Six kilometers after Salgadeira, take a right turn onto a red dirt road and go a few hundred meters from the rock formations. The road takes you down to an open canyon graced with a slender 60-meter waterfall that looks like the veil of a bride (hence its name). During rainy season, the fall is more voluminous, but can become yellow and dirty-looking; in August, when I saw it, it was simply stunning, rivaling Iguaçu Falls, perhaps not in volume, but at least in grace. Sturdy trekkers will love the half-hour climb down to the foot of the waterfall (one hour back), but be forewarned: the inclines are abrupt. (Also, the route back may be deceiving because it doesn't look the same going—just stick to the wall on the right.) The fall is actually a big lake, which you can only see from the base, and the water and surrounding air are always cold, no matter the season. The canyon itself is a natural wonder, embraced by a forest and accentuated by vertical backdrops of red rocks. A snack bar serves beer, snacks, and *galinha com arroz* (chicken with rice) for $2.

Cachoerinha (Little Waterfall)

Eight kilometers before you reach the city of Chapada (and an easy one-hour trek from Véu de Noiva) is this smaller waterfall. The *mata* here is being reforested by locals, since destruction of this environment could endanger the entire microsystem of the Pantanal. Walking down an idyllic woody path, you'll come upon a small waterfall jutting out of a rocky embankment; facing it is a most idyllic beachlet. A thatched-roof restaurant surrounded by a mixture of rain forest and cerrado is a perfect place to let the sound of crashing rivulets wash over you. It's also a great place to sun, but weekends are packed. The path to the left above the waterfall goes to Véu de Noiva.

Insider Tip

Buses that run between Cuiabá and Chapada dos Guimarães do not stop at the above sites; in fact, you'll see little of the marvelous countryside from a bus. The Expeditours travel agency in Cuiabá offers tours of the area, or you can take the bus to Chapada and sign up for treks at Eco Turismo, off the main square. Anyone who plans to travel the swampy Pantanal by boat, truck, or foot should absolutely make time to enjoy these contrasting environs between Cuiabá and Chapada. (For more options see under Chapada dos Guimarães.)

Mirante

Considered the "picturesque" geodesic center of South America, this magnificent rocky cliff and mountain range is felt by many to be a point of high magnetic energy and one of the best places to sight **UFOs**, particularly at night. At the very least, on a clear day you can see Cuiabá—50 kilometers to the southwest. Do take the exhilarating walk down the rocky path to the right, until you reach the 700-meter drop-off plateau; the trip back up is tiring but worth it. Hopefully, the litter marring the landscape has been picked up; be careful with cigarettes since fires start fast. Near the rock formations there is a large amount of burned land that can't be attributed to any reason other than human carelessness.

Parque Nacional

Founded about three years ago, the park covers about 33,000 hectares but is a national park in name only (the government does little to nothing to maintain it). Eco Turismo is the only agency that conducts tours to the park's wonderful **Cidades das Pedras**, seven "cities" of rock formations situated among the gnarled trees of the *cerrado*. During the rainy season, this route, which must be navigated by truck or four-wheel drive, is considerably less dusty than in dry season, and more animals, such as pigs, foxes, jaguars, tapirs, wolves and coatis can be seen scurrying over the landscape. But even dry season is exciting. In August, the stunted cerrado lends an other-worldly air to the forbidding rock formations, which can look variously like sacrificial altars, alligators, or Indian faces. Animals do approach at times; we clocked an *emu* (ostrich) running chase in front of our truck at 80 kilometers an hour. Many of the rocks are over 3 million years old; on their side you can often see stratification lines where the ocean left its indelible marks. It's even possible to find chips of hematite and crystals embedded in the ground, as well as fossils engraved with fish shapes.

At the **Nascente do Rio Claro**, you can walk to the edge of a 350-meter cliff and witness an awesome vista of rivers and plateaus that could keep you mesmerized for days. The most unforgettable site I saw here is the **Casa de Pedra**, a natural house of stone situated over a running stream that was surely the home of native peoples thousands of years ago. I dream of making an overnight camp-out here; the nearby waterfalls boast such clean water you could probably safely drink it. Our final trek in Chapada took us down a slightly torturous descent to what must be the most perfect cove in

Brazil—a gorgeous waterfall embraced by a thumb-sized strand of beach, behind which is a craggy outcropping of rock.

Insider Tip

If you have rugged desires, do arrange a two- to three-day trekking expedition through this region, which could include camping out at one of the above sights. Backpacks are required, but all other equipment, tents, and food are supplied. Wear good hiking boots, take your swimsuit, and dress in layers (nights get nippy).

THE CAVES

Eco Turismo's trek to the Caverns is not to be missed. In late August we start out by jeep over a rollicking dusty road hugged on one side by flat dry plains and on the other by tall willowy soyfields. Just at the moment I think we're in Oklahoma, we begin to pass miles of burnt land and scorched trees, and as the road turns into white sand, it winds around countryside that looks like the aftermath of World War III. As Jorge parks his truck, seemingly in the middle of nowhere, we hop out, following his energetic lead for 20 minutes up a torturous hill. At the first cavern, armed with flashlights, we wade through a dark gallery, feeling our toes squish into ankle-high mud. Apparently, native peoples lived here thousands of years ago, their spirits nearly still palpable. The hot afternoon sun calls us out and we start trekking again, this time through a sudden crop of rain forest obscuring the second cave. Another dry forest leads us into a humid one in a matter of a few feet, our arrival greeted by a raucous outburst of birds. The climax of the hike is Blue Lake (not exactly the luminescent color of its name), provocatively set inside an outcropping of rock connected to a swimmable tunnel. After taking a dip, we beat a fast path back to the car since the terrain is too rough to negotiate after dark. As the moon rises, the ride back to Chapada on the dark highway turns even eerier, evoking the kind of atmosphere where any moment you expect to see strange colored lights pulsing in front of you. What we actually do witness is the spontaneous combustions of fires exploding all along the highway, making us even more aware of the fragility of the landscape.

WHERE TO STAY

Chapada is a rustic town; so are the hotels. Fortunately, with such cool temperatures, air conditioning is not necessary. No pousada or hotel in Chapada has telephones inside the room.

Expensive-- **$27–$32**

Moderate -- **$10–$20**

Inexpensive --- **Under $10**

Pousada da Chapada

Rodovia MT-251, kilometer 63, Estrada Chapada dos Guimarães/ Cuiabá, 2 kilometer, ☎ *791-1171. Reservations: SP* ☎ *(11) 231-4511; FAX 791-1299.* The nicest hotel in Chapada is unfortunately 800 meters from the city (not walking distance), but the hotel provides free transportation. The red-tile, white stucco complex of four buildings retains a frontier colonial charm. Apartments, with raw wood furniture, are spacious, and tiled floors cut down on dirt. The deluxe suite, which sleeps four, is unusually elegant. On premises is a playground and outdoor pool, and a restaurant that serves all three meals. The owner also runs the Fazenda Porto Joffre in the Pantanal, as well as the Selva Turismo travel agency. Singles with fan run $27, doubles $32, double the price for air conditioning. Fielding's readers receive a 10 percent discount. (38 apartments.)

Moderate. No Cards.

Rios Hotel

Rua Tiradentes, 333; ☎ *791-1126.* Among the lesser-priced hotels, Rios rates as the best. A block from the bus station and near the telephone company, it looks like a private residence. Families stay here, as do the kind of hippie clientele that sport feather earrings. Bathrooms are reasonably clean. Prices are rated according to the presence of air conditioning and TV. Singles with air conditioning run $17, doubles $22. (18 apartments.)

Inexpensive. Cards: V.

Hotel Turismo

Rua Fernando Corrêa, 1065; ☎ *791-1176.* From the street, this small hotel looks like a residential house, complete with crowing roosters; the rooms are simple and clean, if overpriced. The dining room serves lunch and dinner (a small breakfast of fruit, bread, and coffee). Sunday features all-you-can-eat *comida caseira* (home-cooked). Air-conditioned rooms with minibar and TV run about $25, with fans $20. (14 apartments.)

Moderate. No cards.

Pensão do Povo

Rua Fernando Corrêa, 825. Located behind the church, Chapada's cheapest rooms are for those who don't care what bites them after they drop dead asleep. One communal bathroom for most rooms; two apartments have private bath. Some rooms have four beds, but no phones. About $3 a night.

Cheap. No cards.

WHERE TO EAT

Taberna Suiça

Rua Fernando Corrêa. Friday, Saturday, and Sunday. Open only on the weekends, but insiders consider this to be the best restaurant in town for international cuisine. Friday serves only dinner.   *Inexpensive. No cards.*

Nivio's Tour Restaurante

Praça Bispo Dom Wunibaldo, 631; ☎ *791-1206.* Don't let the word "tour" discourage you. This Portuguese-styled house with blue-tiled walls and white stucco arches offers a veritable feast. No one ever knows what will be served, but it's invariably a full table with two main courses and several side dishes of vegetables and rice. Saturday features *feijoada*. There's also a short list of French and German wines. Rates per person run $4–$5.

Inexpensive. No Cards.

Véu de Noiva Restaurante

Rua Penna Gomes, 535. Daily 11:00 a.m.–10:00 p.m. Grungy walls and a cracked stone floor, but the ambiance is very *caseira* in this one-room house. If temperatures rise too high inside, you can sit outside on the veranda on a residential side street overlooking the public swimming pool. (The natural water is piped in from the Prainha River 200 meters away.) Chicken and rice dishes are excellent, as is the *prato feito* (meal of the day) for about $2.50 per person. *No cards.*

Costelão

Road to Cuiabá, 2 kilometer (Aldeia Velha); ☎ *791-1102. Daily 11:00 a.m.–3:00 p.m., 7:00 p.m.–9:00 p.m.* Good barbecue styled in a typical *gaúcho* house. *No cards.*

Amarelinho

Rua Dom Wunibaldo. Daily lunch and dinner. Regional food.

Gaia Bar

Off the main plaza. This green-and-orange house is the denizen for the local "Green People," who are still reading Herman Hesse. Outsiders are sometimes scowled at, but yell out "Preserva natureza!" and you'll be fine.

Borboleta Casa de Chá

Rua Fernando Corrêa, 446-B; ☎ *321-5307.* A civilized tea house in this dirty-boots wilderness is definitely refreshing. Indulge in *bolos* (cakes), *docinhos* (sweets), and *salgadinhos* (salty pastries), washed down with tea or cold beer.

SHOPPING

Achei Novidades

Praça D. Wunibaldo. Daily 8:00 a.m.–8:00 p.m. Next to the Gaia bar off the main *praça*, this is the city's premier crafts store featuring jewelry made by the Xavantes Indians (situated about 1250 kilometers from Chapada) and pottery from the Carajas tribe in the state of Pará. Other great buys are homemade liqueurs with *pequi cristalizado* (a tree typical of the *cerrado*). You can also buy modern art from regional artists. *No Cards.*

HEALERS

Chapada, like Cuiabá, has a strong Green movement, as well as a New Age/alternative health community. If you ask around, you can easily meet students of various gurus (like Rajneesh, called Osho here), Zen meditators, yoga enthusiasts, massage therapists, acupuncturists, and even psychic healers. There may also be a few lingering souls who speak Esperanto. The small brochure-like magazine *Tempo de Crescer!* lists various professional holistic practitioners and organizations in the Cuiabá-Chapada region.

HANDS-ON CHAPADA DOS GUIMARÃES

ARRIVAL

The **Rodoviária** (bus station) is located at *Rua Cipriano Curvo;* ☎ *791-1280.* Buses run regularly between Cuiabá and Chapada dos Guimaráes, starting at 7:30 a.m., 8:00 a.m., 10:00 a.m., noon, 2:00 p.m., 3:00 p.m., 4:00 p.m., and 7:00 p.m., and returning at 6:00 a.m., 9:00 a.m., noon, 1:00 p.m., 1:30 p.m., 2:00 p.m., 4:00 p.m., and 6:00 p.m. Buses also run to Brasilândia, Paranatinga, and others.

CLIMATE

Between April–October, which is the dry season, temperatures average between 68 and 75 degrees fahrenheit, but temperatures can rise over 50 degrees in just a matter of hours. The hottest months in the Pantanal are December–February, when temperatures average between 110°F–112°F. During dry season, it's important to drink lots of liquids to avoid dehydration. Starting in November, weather alternates between torrential rains and scalding sun. The most animals can be seen in December and January.

CREDIT CARDS

Chapada seems to have trouble processing **American Express** cards. A few businesses take **VISA**. (See *Money Exchange* below.)

MONEY EXCHANGE

Do come with a full stash of cruzeiros. You'll be hard put to find anyone who will accept dollars or credit cards. Even the Banco Brasil will not exchange dollars, though it is rumored the **Hotel Turismo,** located on *Rua Fernando C. da Costa, 1065,* ☎ *791-1176,* will .

TAXIS

There's only one taxi in Chapada.

Eco Turismo
> ☎ *791-1393* to find out who owns it that week.

TELEPHONE

Posto Telefônico
> *Rua Tiradentes, 390.*

TRAVEL AGENCY

Eco Turismo Cultural
> *Praça Dom Wunibaldo, 464;* ☎ *(85) 791-1393, 791-1305.* One of Chapada's premier trek agencies is owned by Jorge Belfort Mattos Jr., a university professor who, despite his Santa Claus girth, scampers up and down steep hills like a master. All his trips last between four and six hours, including transportation, light lunch, and water. Three main tours include the Parque Nacional (with the Véu de Noiva), the Caverna Aroe Jari with the Lagoa Azul, and the Cidades das Pedras (City of Rocks). Exciting two- to five-day packages, from $100–$282, including breakfast and one meal a

day, can also be arranged (accommodations at Hotel Pousada or Turismo).
Five-day tours include city tour and geodesic site, caverns, National Park,
Cidades das Pedras, and horseback riding. *Cards: V only.*

WHEN TO GO

July

Winter Festival mid-month.

SURVIVING BRAZIL

Gold mining on an Amazon tributary

BEFORE YOU GO

ACCOMMODATIONS

Where you stay in the Amazon will depend on your budget, your port, and your individual lifestyle—be it rough to luxurious. Accommodations can run from the fantasy resort hotel to first-class jungle lodges with air conditioning to primitive bungalows teetering on stilts in the middle of a lake. Lodging in urban areas vary according to the size and class of the city. In the city of Manaus proper, you can find not only a palatial resort (Hotel Tropical) complete with its own zoo and excellent high-class restaurants, but also numerous middle-ranged hotels with adequate cleanliness and service. The city of Belém also has numerous hotels of middle-of-the-road quality, the flagship property being the Belém Hilton. In Santarém, however, hotels are on the cutting edge of "iffy," with the exception of the Tropical (owned by Varig Airlines), although it is not comparable in any fashion to that of the Tropical in Manaus. Particularly in the Amazon, any lodging less than three stars (according to the Brazilian rating system established by EMBRATUR, the official tourist board) should be approached with caution; you might find greasy walls, grimy bathrooms, and suspicious-looking creatures roaming the floors. In essence, a 3-star hotel in the Amazon is not equivalent to a 3-star hotel in more fashionable cities like Rio de Janeiro and São Paulo.

During Carnaval and other regional folklore festivals (such as Belém's Círio festival in October), reservations for rooms should be made several months in advance.

Also note that prices may fluctuate during high and low season, but do not hesitate to ask for discounts. Anything can be bargained in Brazil if it is done tastefully.

Excellent package deals for accommodations can be made through various private tour companies that you will find listed under "Package Deals" below and under *Specialty Tours* in the back of the book. If you fly on Varig Airlines, you can receive a ten percent discount on Varig hotels, and often a transfer to the airport. (Varig hotels can be found in Manaus, Santarém and Iguaçu Falls).

For more information about accommodations in Brazil in general, do see my other book *Fielding's Brazil.*

AIR TRAVEL TO BRAZIL

International flights from the United States to Brazil run between five and 12 hours, depending on where you leave from and where you arrive.

Flying **Varig Airlines** (☎ *800-468-2744*), Brazil's national carrier, is one of the best ways to start off your Brazilian vacation. While other airlines may be cheaper, Varig is known throughout the travel industry as one of the best carriers in the world—consistently providing punctual arrivals, excellent food, and cheerful, efficient service. Executive class seats are considerably more comfortable than tourist class, and their meals (along with those of first class) include extensive hors d'oeuvres and desserts; one might even complain that there is too much food! Films (generally two) shown throughout the long flights are usually the latest releases. Best of all, the Brazilian flight attendants give you the opportunity to try out your Portuguese and will answer any questions you may have about traveling.

From North America, Varig offers wide-body services to Brazil through 5 gateways: New York, Atlanta, Miami, Los Angeles, and Toronto. From Miami, there are 17 weekly flights, including daily nonstops to both Rio and São Paulo, plus one flight each to Manaus, Belém (continuing on to Fortaleza), and one to Recife and Salvador. From New York, there are eight weekly nonstop flights to Rio and/ or São Paulo. Los Angeles operates six weekly flights to Rio and São Paulo, three via Lima, one via Manaus. In addition, Varig flies three times weekly from Los Angeles to Tokyo. For Canadian travelers, there are six weekly flights from Toronto.

The cheapest fare Varig offers is an excursion package, with a minimum stay of 7days (maximum 21 days), with the ticket purchased 14 days in advance (LA–Rio: $849; Atlanta–Rio: $739; NY–Rio: $1215). Another excursion package (minimum seven days, maximum 21 days, 14day advance purchase), must be combined with a land tour, hotel, or package booked through Varig. About $100 can be saved during low season, which runs August 8–December 9, and January 11–June 20. First-class tickets in any season run about $4960; executive class about $3230 (leaving from NY).

Varig passengers traveling to Rio de Janeiro, Brasília, Porto Alegre and Curitiba may now reserve a cellular phone to use during their stay, with more cities being added. Daily rental fees, minimum usage fees, and security fees are all waived; renters receive a 10 percent discount on all calls. Reservations for the service must be made 72 hours in advance through a travel agent or Varig.

United Airlines (☎ *800-241-6522)* offers nonstop flights from New York and Miami to Rio. Although rates fluctuate depending on season, the lowest ones are awarded for 14-day advance purchase and a minimum stay of 21 days (maximum 90 days). Highest rates are generally between December and January. A New York-Rio roundtrip runs about $1210 in low season (with advance purchase).

American Airlines (☎ *800-433-7300)* flies Miami-Rio nonstop (for about $1148 coach low season) and New York-São Paulo nonstop ($1300). This requires a three-week minimum stay (90-day maximum), 14-day advance purchase. Low season runs August 8–December 9.
For information about packaged vacations and discount flights, see "Package Deals" below.

Aerolinas Argentinas (☎ *800-333-0276)* flies Miami-Rio nonstop for $1180 coach low season) and New York-São Paolo (through Buenos Aires). This

requires a 14-day advance purchase, 7–21 day stay.
For information regarding cruises to Brazil, see *Specialty Tours*.

VASP (☎ *800-732-8277*), *(212) 753-3600; 800-732-8277*. In 1994, this Brazilian-owned carrier opened up intercontinental flights between the U.S. and Brazil. There are no direct flights to the Amazon, but on Sundays you can fly from Miami to Recife (in the Northeast of Brazil, a fine tourist stop), and catch a connecting flight to Manaus. (For more information about Recife, see my other book *Fielding's Brazil*. For more information about connecting flights and invaluable "air passes," see below under "Air Travel Within Brazil.") VASP also offers direct flights from New York to São Paulo (a big haul from Manaus) twice a week, and a connecting flight through Miami on Saturday.

AIR TRAVEL WITHIN BRAZIL

Brazil is a *big* country (as the musician Caetano Veloso once said, "kinda *too* big"), and the distances between major cities are enormous. If you are planning to visit more than one city in Brazil, do seriously consider buying **Varig's Brazil Airpass**. For a basic cost of $440, you receive one to five flight coupons (six if Santarém is included), which allows you to make that many flights within a 21-day period. (You are also allowed to make two connections via any of the following cities: Brasília, Fortaleza, Manaus, Recife, Rio, Salvador and São Paulo.) Additional coupons can be purchased for $100 each. Do note that you must plan your itinerary carefully, as some cities, especially in the Northeast, will require several connections. Also, the Airpass must be purchased outside Brazil (though you need not be flying internationally on Varig), and it may be used only on domestic Varig flights. It is not valid on the Rio/São Paulo shuttle between Congonhas and Santos Dumont airports. Nevertheless, this Airpass, depending on your itinerary, can save you hundreds of dollars, since domestic travel within Brazil is extremely expensive.

VASP also just instituted its own Brazil Air Pass (also for $440), which allows you to fly to five different Brazilian cities. It must be bought outside of Brazil.

Other airlines within Brazil are **Transbrasil**, **TAP** and **Taba**, but airfare bought within Brazil can run into hundreds of dollars. Transbrasil flights are usually at night and connections aren't always convenient.

For travel by bus, car and train within Brazil, see "Travel Within Brazil" below.

BEST TIME TO VISIT

Anyone interested in Brazil must experience Carnaval *ao vivo* at least once in his life—whether it's in Rio, Salvador, Recife, or a folkloric city like São Luis (for dates, see *Carnaval*). Do avoid July, a school vacation month, when hotels are packed and rates excessive. Regional folkloric festivals are great fun, such as the beer-swilling Oktoberfest in Blumenau (October), Círio de Nazaré in Belém (second Sunday of October), and Bumba-meu-boi in São Luis (June). New Year's Eve in Rio and Salvador offers huge processions of white-clad celebrants who perform ceremonies on the beach. Wine-tasting in the state of Rio Grande do Sul is best done January–March while the grapes are still on the vine. The best time to visit the Amazon and Pantanal is in August. (For more information on climatic conditions and when to visit, see the "Hands-On" section of each city.)

Before you visit the Amazon, you must decide if you are a wet person or a dry person. I've never been to the Amazon during the wet season (October-April); just the thought of all that soppy, squishy mud and rain-rain-rain sends me back to my hammock. June-August was a fine time for me personally, the *terra firme* is firm, the mud is mud, not soup, and the heat is bearable. But don't let me influence you. Some people love to experience the raininess of the forest, but do go prepared with ponchos and rain boots, etc.

CHOLERA

Cholera was declared epidemic in Brazil in 1992, but it need not scare away informed tourists. Long called the poor people's disease, it largely attacks populations with untreated sewage and no access to clean drinking water. Unless you are traveling in rural areas and/or drinking tap or river water, you stand almost no risk of getting sick. The U.S. Centers for Disease Control also recommend that all visitors to Latin America avoid consuming ice, salads, tap water, foods sold by street vendors, raw fish, and cooked food served cold. For more information, see the chapter *Health Kit for the Tropics.*

CONSULATES

The **Brazilian Consulate General** in the U.S. is located at *630 Fifth Avenue, New York, NY 10020;* (☎ *212-757-3080).* Brazilian consulates are also located in Chicago, Houston, Los Angeles, Miami, San Francisco, Washington D.C., and Puerto Rico. Visas may be obtained from these offices, as well as general information.

In England, the embassy is located at: **Embassy of Brazil** *(32 Green St., London WTY 4AT England)*.

For American consulates in Brazil, see "Hands-On" in each city.

CUSTOMS

Upon arrival from international flights, all foreign visitors pass through customs—usually a quick and painless process. It is a good idea not to look like a raving maniac or a "hippie"-type person who might be carrying drugs. Follow the crowd to the inspection site and have your passport, visa and card of embarkation ready for viewing by the passport inspector. (On the flight over, the flight attendant will have handed you this card—a declaration card—to fill out. Guard it with your life and do not lose it under any circumstances (documents seem to mysteriously disappear on jungle expeditions or fall into grungy rivers). You must show it to the airline check-in attendant upon departure. Best bet is to attach it securely to your passport and tuck your passport into a safe, waterproof pouch.

Besides clothing and personal belongings, travelers to Brazil may carry a radio, a tapedeck, a computer, a typewriter and cameras for their personal use only. Though luggage is usually not inspected, it will be difficult, for example, to explain why you personally need ten radios, if discovered. Also permitted is $500 in gifts (an additional $1000 in taxable gifts), and $300 of duty-free goods (liquor, cigarettes, etc.) bought at the airport.

DOCUMENTS

A valid passport is required for entering into Brazil, and you must also obtain a visa prior to arrival. Visas may be obtained in person at the Brazilian Consulate (for addresses in the U.S., see below under "Consulates," or you may write the head consulate in New York). You'll need one 2" x 2" photo (black-and-white or color), your passport, and your airline ticket (or itinerary confirmed by your travel agent), as well as a completed and signed application. Tourist visas obtained in person are free; those transacted by a messenger cost $10; you may also use local visa service agencies.

Tourist visas last 90 days, renewable for a second 90 days. If you plan to stay longer, do not, under any circumstances, forget to renew your visa at the nearest Federal Police office or immigration office in Brazil. If you are late, you will be fined and given 8 days to leave the country, unless you are a fast talker with a keen sense of theatrics. It's rumored that offenders are placed on a computerized list that makes returning to the country difficult.

Business visas may be obtained by showing a passport (valid for at least six months), photo, completed application, and a letter from your company detailing the purpose of your trip. Business visas are processed in 24 hours and cost $30 ($40 by messenger).

If you need to stay longer than six months (three-month visas are only renewed once, for a six-month limit), you must prove you are financially able to remain in the country without working. Check with the Federal Police or immigration office to determine your applicability.

You should also carry with your passport the official record of your vaccinations, particularly if you are planning to go into the jungle. If you become sick or if an epidemic breaks out, a physician can determine your susceptibility. If you pass into bordering countries, you may be required to show it.

Brazilians love letters of introduction, so if you are doing special research, collect as many signed references as you can. Business cards are also impressive and prove you are a serious professional.

JET LAG

International flights from New York and Miami usually leave at night and arrive in Rio between 7:00 a.m. and 9:00 a.m. Although there are no remarkable differences in time zones from most U.S. destinations (see "Time Zone"), you may be exhausted from fidgeting in your seat all night long. For tips to combat travel stress, see *Health Kit for the Tropics.*

LANGUAGE

Brazilians are not at all like the French when it comes to foreigners speaking their native tongue. In fact, Brazilians will deeply appreciate the slightest effort you make to speak in Portuguese, even if it's a garbled mess. In general, Spanish is a help, but it will only get you so far. Brazilians have the uncanny ability to *understand* Spanish, although if you speak only Spanish, you will be floored when you first *hear* Portuguese—the rhythm, accent and sensibility are totally different, although more than a few words may be similar. (Written Portuguese, on the other hand, is much easier for Spanish-speaking travelers to decipher.)

Even if you speak Portuguese, you will find that regional accents vary profoundly. Southerners actually speak with a kind of cowboy twang, and Northeasterners speak extremely fast and clipped. Sometimes even Brazilians don't understand each other, and actors from the interior have been known to undergo diction classes before they're allowed on stage or screen.

Still, it's very possible to travel throughout Brazil without any facility in Portuguese or Spanish. Just make sure all your travel arrangements are made in advance, and join group tours rather than wander around alone in the backcountry. In fact, Brazil without Portuguese (or even "*Portu-Spanglish*"), can be a great international adventure. In southern cities like Blumenau, Nova Petrópolis, and Gramado/Canela, German is spoken as a second language, and throughout the southern wine country in Rio Grande do Sul, many of the Italian-born families are well versed in their mother tongue. There is also a large Japanese-speaking community in São Paulo.

As for finding English-speakers in Brazil, if you stay at five-star and four-star hotels, you are sure to discover receptionists who do, as well as at some travel agencies in Rio, Salvador, São Paulo, and Manaus. Usually, at least one person at a city or state tourist information center speaks English. *Fluent* English, however, is another matter. Although many can understand English because of the huge influx of foreign music and film, Brazilians have little opportunity to practice speaking and, hence, are extremely shy. If you are speaking English to anybody in Brazil (no matter how fluent they may *seem*), speak slowly (but do not shout!), use simple words and grammar, and be on the lookout for misunderstandings. Brazilians tend to mix up *he* and *she*, and often confuse negative constructions. They also speak more through body language than through words.

MONEY

Traveling to Brazil with a large amount of cash is risky (because once it's stolen, it's gone). As of summer 1994, the value of the currency—now the *real*—was not as wildly fluctuating as in the past, but do check its current status before you go. However, it's still your best bet to exchange only small amounts at a time, and carry as well a variety of credit cards and traveler's checks. Credit cards (the most widely accepted are MasterCard and Diner's Club, followed by American Express) can be used at most five- and four-star hotels, but not all restaurants accept cards (particularly American Express) because the delay in payment causes them to lose money. Clothing stores and boutiques often give discounts if you pay in Brazilian currency or dollars, and/or charge 20 percent extra if you pay by card.

If you are traveling into the interior (in the Amazon, that's any city but Manaus), make sure you have exchanged enough money to pay for everything in Brazilian currency because you will be hard pressed to find anyone who will accept traveler's checks or dollars.

Unless you are staying at a top-notch hotel in Manaus with a safe in the room or a reliable one at the reception, don't leave valuables and/or money there while you go on a jungle adventure. If you have to trek through the jungle with your stash, you must carefully water-proof all money and documents and either carry them in a securely belted waistpouch (inside your clothes) or find some way to indelibly glue the kit-and-kaboodle to your body. (Don't feel insulted, but I feel obligated to remind you that you don't want to lose your passport in the middle of the jungle.) Just stay aware: given the nature of jungle expeditions, you may be forced to leave gear behind on a barge, canoe, etc. when you venture into the forest, and sad to say, not all guides, just-met traveling companions, and locals can always be trusted. Judge the situation accurately and take precautions.

If you run out of money while traveling, the easiest way to receive extra funds is through cash advances on your credit card, but note that you can only receive the money in Brazilian currency. Remember to bring personal checks with you to facilitate this negotiation. American Express will cash up to US $1000 on green cards and $5000 on gold once a week, exchanged at the official tourist rate (offices can be found in Rio, São Paulo, Manaus, and Salvador). Banco do Brasil also handles money forwarded on Visa. In New York the **Brazilian American Cultural Center** (☎ *212-730-1010*) does make transfers in dollars to Brazil.

It's best to have already exchanged some Brazilian currency (small bills) before you arrive to pay for airport tips and taxis. There is usually an exchange house or bank in the airports of major cities.

PACKAGE DEALS

The cheapest way to get to Brazil is to buy your transcontinental ticket through a wholesaler. These independent operators and travel agents buy tickets in bulk and sell them at discounted rates and/or arrange package tours that include ground transportation, hotels, transfers from airports, and stops in several cities. Many agencies work on an FIT system, which allows them to contour a package vacation according to your specific needs. Carnaval packages often include tickets to the Sambódromo parade. Do note that prices from year to year can change drastically, depending on inflation in Brazil (and in the U.S.!), as well as the agency's ability to obtain discounts. Your best bet is to call around to many operators and find the lowest price for your particular itinerary. Three reliable wholesalers are:

The Brazilian American Cultural Center *20 West 46th Street, New York, NY 10036; (☎ 212-730-1010) or toll free 800-222-2746* is not only a wholesaler but a membership club that requires a $20 fee. The BACC membership allows you to take advantage of round-trip fares that are sometimes $400 below fares listed by the airlines. Included in the membership fee is also a subscription to *The Brasilians*, the organization's newspaper, which gives up-to-date news from Brazil. For a $15 fee, BACC will also secure a visa for you. You must first request an application, then mail them the completed form with one 2" x 2" photo and a check or money order payable to BACC. The company will then process your papers through the Brazilian Consulate. This service is especially good for travelers who don't live near a consulate.

Ladatco *2220 Coral Way, Miami, FL 33145; (☎ 800-327-6162)* A specialist in Latin American travel, Ladatco has been in business for 26 years. President Michelle Shelburne offers numerous packages (one 14-day itinerary includes Salvador, Rio, Brasília, Manaus, and a stay in the jungle). She can also arrange discounts on air travel and tailor-make any agenda.

Ipanema Tours *8844 West Olympic Blvd., Suite C, Beverly Hills, CA 90211 (☎ 800-421-4200)* offers a five percent discount to clients, 10 percent to travel agents on all international flights. The agency handles all of South America and can custom-tailor itineraries. Carnaval packages are also available.

For more package tours, charters, and cruises, see *Specialty Tours* in the back of the book.

PHOTOGRAPHY

Film and developing often costs twice as much in Brazil as it does in the States, so stock up before you go. Carry all film in a protective lead-lined bag to protect it from damaging x-rays at airport security stations and take it out of your hand luggage before you pass through any metal detectors in airports. Do not pack expensive equipment in checked baggage; it could get damaged or stolen. In the rain forest, keep film well protected from moisture and humidity.

SAFETY

Brazil has received an undeserved reputation for being dangerous. True, in the big cities such as Rio, São Paulo, Salvador and Recife, you must exercise extreme caution and not walk around like a neon sign for robbers. In general, this means carrying as little money on your person as possible, not wearing jewelry (leave gold watches at home), and not brandishing expensive-looking cameras. Don't leave valuables strewn about your hotel room; do use the safe inside your apartment or at the receptionist's desk. Take taxis, especially at night, and don't exchange money with people you meet on the street. Use your common sense.

As you move into the interior, away from the big cities, you'll happily discover laid-back, crime-free areas. In some cities, like Nova Petrópolis in Rio Grande do Sul, the residents don't even bother to lock their car doors. The trick is to look like you have nothing to steal.

You can do a lot for your own safety by becoming an expert traveler. This means double-checking your airline schedules, keeping a consistent check on your passport and travel documents, and carrying your cash, credit cards, traveler's checks and ID in separate places. Never carry your wallet in a back pocket. Carry backpacks in front of you. Invest in a money bag that straps inside your clothes around your stomach, chest, or ankle.

And don't think crime only happens in Brazil. There's been a rash of airport thefts reported in the U.S.; the most targeted ones are Kennedy, LaGuardia, Newark, Boston, Miami and Los Angeles. Entire bags have been stolen, or relieved of packed cameras, laptops, credit cards, portable phones, jewelry, scuba equipment and even golf clubs. For protection, don't carry expensive-looking luggage or attach American Express platinum card tags. Buy adequate locks and use them. Pack only clothes and carry anything that is valuable with you on board. The motto is: If you don't want to lose it, don't check it.

VACCINATIONS

Yellow fever vaccination is highly recommended if you are visiting rural areas or the Amazon jungle. Immunizations for hepatitis and typhoid are suggested for rural and jungle travel. It's always a good idea to update tetanus vaccinations. For in-depth information, see *Health Kit for the Tropics* in the back of the book.

WHAT TO PACK

Before going to Brazil, it's important to check the climate of the areas you will visit (see each region) and also consider whether you will be spending most of your time in metropolises, small back-road towns, or the jungle. In very hot weather, tropical clothing (light cottons or silks) are *de rigueur*. Businesspersons in Brasília and São Paulo wear suits and dresses, but in general, jeans and T-shirts are the fashion, all worn with a sexy, stylish flair. In fact, most Brazilian fashion feeds on extreme seduction—skirts are very short, pants are tight (or very baggy), and tops for women are skimpy. Think anti-dowdy. Although you may not want to do as Brazilians do, it is a good idea for safety's sake not to look like a tourist. This means don't even think about wearing a loud, garish tropical shirt, any T-shirt with BRAZIL or I LOVE RIO blazoned across it, or any large handbag that looks like you're carrying a microwave oven. Instead, invest in a waist-pouch to carry your small necessities (cheap ones can be bought from street vendors in Ipanema and Copacabana in Rio) and/or consider carrying your money in a body pouch underneath your clothing.

For most Americans, what to wear on a Brazilian beach is a dilemma. If you want to look like a Brazilian, probably no bathing suit you can buy in the States will be small enough. Simply, most Americans on the beach look like they are either dressed for winter or wearing a diaper. On the other hand, if you are anything but petite, most Brazilian bathing suits will not fit you, or at least certainly not cover what you are used to covering. One option for women is to buy a large scarf and tie it native-style around your waist; you can also buy adjustable bathing suit tops that can regulate the amount of flesh you expose. Fair-skinned travelers, however, should give real consideration to coverups for skin protection; the tropical sun is much more intense than it seems.

What you wear on your feet is a prime factor in determining your trip's pleasure quotient. Many of Rio's streets are cobblestone or uneven pavement, and you won't be happy in anything that has a high heel. Flat, lightweight tennies or well-grounded walking shoes are best, though Brazilian women do wear high heels at night (okay if you take cabs). A pair of sturdy sandals is also important, as well as a cheap pair of beach sling-ons. Cowboy boots tend to be too hot (not to mention bulky to pack), but fashionable Brazilians have taken to the miniboot, the kind that just grazes the top of your jeans. If you run, you'll want to throw in your jogging shoes to join the throngs that turn out dusk and dawn in nearly every seaside city.

Brazilians live to dress up at night. They take hours after work getting ready to go out for dinner, even though they may end up looking nonchalantly casual in an open shirt and nice slacks, or a short sexy dress. Only in the very elite restaurants are men required to wear ties; a jacket is sufficient in most cases. If you are going out with Brazilian friends, they will, upon meeting you, check out just how fashionable and coordinated you look, even in the smallest city. If you're going high society, matching shoes and bag is expected, and fashionable (if fake) jewelry is a must. No matter what one's social class, in Brazil taking care of one's physical appearance is a sign of self-respect.

I discuss jungle attire at more length in the "Amazon Survival Kit" in the Amazônia section, but do note that at some point you will have to come out of the jungle, and Brazilians don't take kindly to muddy, smelly, wild-looking barbarians, no matter how great their jungle stories are. Make sure you bring an extra pair of pants or a skirt, a clean pair of shoes, and a nice shirt, if you want to partake of anything in the city that's civilized.

WHILE YOU'RE THERE

AIRPORT TAX

You will be charged US $18 for international flights (if you stay in Brazil over 24 hours) and US $1–$3 on local flights, payable when you check in. To facilitate matters within Brazil, have small change in Brazilian currency ready.

AIRPORT TRANSFER

Taxis are always available at airports. Buses into the city are much cheaper, but are awkward if you're juggling lots of luggage, and they may not drop you at your hotel's front door. Special taxis can often be obtained at a central post near the exit of the airport, where you pay in advance, then give your receipt to the driver. These special taxis generally cost about 10 percent more than the regular fare but are considered safer and are guaranteed to get you to your destination. Have the name and address of your hotel readily available. Some hotels, especially those booked through package deals, will provide transfers to and from the airport, so check in advance.

BRINGING HOME BRAZIL

Varig Airlines is entirely accommodating when it comes to traveling home with a *berimbau*—a large, one-stringed instrument attached to a round gourd. Wrap the bow separately in heavy packing paper and send it through with your luggage. Carry the gourd with you as hand luggage.

U.S. Customs allows returning residents of the United States to bring home duty-free articles totaling up to $400. This includes up to 100 cigars, 200 cigarettes (from one carton), and one liter (33.8 fluid ounces) of alcoholic beverages. When shipped, gifts up to $50 in fair retail value may be received by friends and relations in the U.S. free of duty and tax.

Among prohibited articles considered injurious to the public welfare are: absinthe, liquor-filled candies (where prohibited by law), narcotics, obscene articles and publications, and switchblades (unless you are a one-armed person who uses a switchblade knife for personal use). Most fruits and vegetables are either prohibited from entering the country or require an import permit. Meat, livestock, poultry, and their byproducts (sausage, paté) are either prohibited or restricted from entry, depending on the animal disease condition in Brazil.

If you are traveling with medicines containing habit-forming drugs or narcotics (i.e., cough medicine, diuretics, heart drugs, tranquilizers, sleeping pills, depressants, stimulants, etc.), you must properly identify all drugs, carry only the quantity you will normally need, and have ready a prescription or written statement from your personal physician confirming you are under a doctor's care and in need of these drugs for your personal health while traveling.

Plants, cuttings, seeds and certain endangered species either require an import permit or are prohibited from entering the U.S. Wildlife and fish are subject to certain import and export restrictions, prohibitions, and quarantine requirements. All ivory and ivory products—except antiques—made from elephant ivory are prohibited. If you are contemplating purchasing articles made from wildlife, such as tortoise shell jewelry, leather goods, or other articles from whalebone, ivory, skins, or fur, contact—before you go—the U.S. Fish and Wildlife Service, Department of the Interior, Washington, DC 20240.

BUSINESS HOURS AND HOLIDAYS

Most businesses and stores open at 9:00 a.m., break for lunch between noon and 2:00 p.m., and reopen from 2:00 p.m. to 5:00 p.m. Monday–Friday. Shops in Ipanema and Copacabana in Rio tend to open 9:00 a.m.–1:00 p.m. on Saturday. Banks are open 10:00 a.m.–4:30 p.m. Monday–Friday. Many businesses close up shop for the five days of Carnaval leading up to Ash Wednesday. Museums throughout the country are generally closed on Monday.

Businesses, but not restaurants, shut down completely for the following Brazilian holidays. (As in the States, some offices may shut down not on the official date, but on the Monday closest to it, for a long weekend.)

January 1 --------------	**New Year's**
Carnaval ----------------	**5 days leading to Ash Wednesday**
March/April ------------	**Good Friday and Easter Sunday**
April 21 -----------------	**Tiradentes' Day**
May 1 --------------------	**Dia do Trabalho**

June 10 ----------------- Corpus Christi

September 7 ---------- Independence Day

October 12 ------------ Nossa Senhora da Aparecida (Our Lady of the Apparition)

November 2 ----------- Dia dos Finados (All Soul's Days)

November 15 ---------- Proclamation of the Republic

December 25 ---------- Christmas (most restaurants closed)

CLIMATE

Brazil's climate varies according to latitude and elevation. Seasons are opposite to the Northern hemisphere; winter runs June–September and summer, November-March. Average temperatures during the summer ranges from 25–40 degrees C (75–100 degrees F). Warm tropical weather extends north from Rio de Janeiro throughout most of the year. South of Rio–in the states of São Paulo, Santa Catarina, Paraná and Rio Grande do Sul–the climate is temperate with warm summers and cold winters, with occasional snowfall in the far south.

COMPUTERS

Laptop computers should be carried on board airplanes with you in your hand luggage, but *don't ever* send them through a Brazilian x-ray machine. Otherwise, you may find your entire program and files wiped out, as I did. Travelers headed for the rain forest should protect the computer and diskettes from humidity and moisture by wrapping the case in an extra plastic bag.

CONSULATES

In the case of *any* emergency (health, safety), immediately contact your own consulate in the nearest city.

CURRENCY EXCHANGE

One of Brazil's ways to handle inflation is to knock off zeroes from its present currency and change its name. At press time, the currency is the *cruzeiro real*, though it may have changed by the time you read this. Contrary to popular belief, there is really no longer a black market for exchanging currency in Brazil. There are, however, three levels of exchange: the *oficial*, or official rate, which Brazilians pay to buy air tickets and foreign currency; the slightly higher tourist rate called *dólar turismo*, generally offered to tourists at official exchange offices called *câmbios*, and the even higher parallel rate, called *dólar paralelo*, which is so rarely made available to tourists that it's not worth thinking about. Rates vary daily, and you should check the newspaper before exchanging money.

The safest places to exchange money are at banks or at officially recognized *câmbios*, where you may be taken to a back room to make the transaction in private. Exchanging money on the street with people you don't know is asking for trouble; you might as well just give your wallet away. Hotel employees, especially in five-star properties, are generally honest, but check the newspaper first for the official tourist rate. Hotel exchange houses usually give the lowest rate around, so try to avoid them, though they are often more convenient. Do note that traveler's checks often receive a slightly lower rate than the tourist dollar because of the paperwork involved.

One word of advice

Travelers have been known to ruin their trips obsessing over the exchange rate and how to get the best deal. Frankly, it's not worth it, but there are some guidelines to keep you sane: exchange only small amounts at a time (for two or three days' expenses); exchange in reputable places and keep the receipts; use a pocket calculator and be clear how many dollars you are spending on a purchase; exchange money in big cities, where you will get better rates. At some point you will have to give up and realize it's a gambler's game, and often the amount you would be saving adds up only to a few dollars. At last call, remember you are in Brazil for a good time.

CUTTING COSTS

Traveling at off season is the best way to save money since most hotels offer discounts if you ask. Other tips include: join a pre-packaged tour; take full advantage of your hotel's large "American" breakfast and skip lunch; forego a hotel with a pool in a seaside city; rent a room without a view; buy an air-pass for travel within Brazil; and carry a map so you won't get cheated by taxi drivers. Soda, bottled water, and candy bars in your minibar can run up to $2 each; make a stop at a neighborhood store or bar and stock up. If you need to travel with your own bottle of scotch or whiskey, buy some at the duty-free shop before you leave the States. Don't use credit cards, to avoid the surcharge. Make overseas telephone calls direct or at the public phone company. Lunching at a *rodízio* (an all-you-can-eat steak house) could last you all day. Regularly verify all meal checks and hotel bills for accuracy; "mistakes" are often made. Become well acquainted with the currency before using it so you won't confuse the bills.

DISEASES

Brazil now has the third largest number of recorded HIV infections in the world (about 1 million people infected, twenty percent of them women). Among the factors contributing to its proliferation are a large amount of bisexual activity, heterosexual anal sex, an active gay population, a lack of efficient blood testing practices, and the sharing of needles, particularly in the upper class, where drugs were deemed fashionable in the late 1970s and 1980s. Young prostitutes who come down from the *favelas* often believe in magical potions made by the Indians or think using a bidet is sufficient for cleansing germs. Despite a television blitz campaign warning about the danger of unsafe sex, and the omnipresence of Benetton billboards featuring enormous multicolored condoms, few couples take preventive measures. Brazilian men often refuse to use condoms out of ignorance or inconvenience, and women are loath to press the issue. Furthermore, the quality of Brazilian condoms is vastly inferior to the ones you may be familiar with, and prone to breakage.

A foreign traveler's best bet is to pack a sufficient supply of American condoms, use them unstintingly, and give the leftovers to Brazilian friends, who will be delighted to receive them. If you must buy condoms in Brazil, they can be found in most pharmacies, under the name *camisinha* or *camiseta de Vênus* (note the word *camiseta* alone means T-shirt).

For information regarding jungle diseases, see the *Health Kit* in the back of the book.

DOCTORS AND PHARMACIES

If you have a medical emergency, ask your concierge to recommend a doctor (some five-star hotels have doctors and nurses on call). If the problem is extremely serious, contact your consulate and ask for help in returning home as quickly as possible. Simply, Brazilian hospitals tend to be overcrowded and not up to American standards.

The good news: if you find a competent doctor (usually referred by a friend or your concierge, and they do exist!), he/she will probably give you more time than their American counterparts, exhibit more gracious behavior, and even call you at home to follow up on your condition. Frankly, all private health care I received in Brazil, from traditional western medicine to more oriental practices, turned out to be excellent.

If you travel with prescription drugs, carry a copy of the prescription with you (for customs and emergency refills), but be sure to pack more than enough of your own supplies. Do note, however, that many drugs that are available only through prescription in the States are available over the counter in Brazil, though their quality can't be vouched for. Other products, such as homeopathic remedies (Bach Flower Remedies, in particular) require a prescription from a certified practitioner.

Receiving prescription drugs (or even vitamins) from home while in Brazil is often tricky. All overseas packages are opened, and you will be required to pick up the box at a government agency, as well as show three copies of the prescription and a letter from the doctor stating why these products cannot be bought in Brazil. (To the country's credit, a care-package of vitamins I never picked up in Rio was actually returned to my mother, the sender—totally intact!—a mere 12 months later.)

Shiatzu and acupressure practitioners are well trained in Brazil and provide excellent service. Make sure, however, that any needles have been disinfected before they are used on your body, or carry your own.

DRIVING

No room for contest—Brazilian drivers are maniacs. (Is there a better reason why the Formula One races are held in Rio?) They ride on each other's bumpers, turn left from right-hand lanes, run stop signs and red lights, and most of all, love to swoop down and park on the sidewalk next to your foot. Unless you have the mind of a madman, I wouldn't suggest driving a great deal in Brazil unless you are settling down there and have no choice. Outside the large cities, which usually have paved and/or cobblestone streets, roads run from passable in the South to awesomely hazardous in the Pantanal, where four-wheel drive is an absolute necessity.

If you insist on renting a car, you will find car-rental agencies in most airports and in all major cities. Officially, you are required to have an international driver's license, but a few extra bucks might curtail that requirement. Gas in Brazil is more than twice the cost in the U.S., while the state-subsidized alcohol is slightly less.

Pedestrians should note that the police in Rio advise drivers not to stop at red lights at night to avoid being held up. So whenever you're crossing the street, look both ways several times and keep an eye out for speeding cars. Pedestrians in Brazil do not have the right of way.

ELECTRICITY

Electric voltage is not standardized in Brazil. What we consider "house current" in the States can generally be found only in Manaus and some five-star hotels. The general current is 127 volts, while the city of Brasília uses 220 volts. Plugs have two round holes, so if you want to use hairdryers, shavers, or other appliances from home, you will need a converter kit that has an adapter. Check your appliances before you leave: some have a switch that can be turned to 110- or 220-volt current (110-volt appliances work normally on 127-volt current.) Computers should always be used with a surge protector because they draw more power.

Most five- and four-star hotels supply hairdryers in the bathroom, or you can ask for one. Just check the voltage before plugging anything in. One warning: even with a converter, my electric steamer pooped out after only a few weeks.

FLIGHTS

You must confirm all flights at least 24 hours in advance, and international flights, 48 hours; otherwise you will risk losing your reservation. And keep a check on the weather at your destination. Some of the planes flying between Northeastern destinations and in the Pantanal are small.

HAIR SALONS

Excellent hair salons and barbershops can be found in most five-star hotels in big cities, though not in the Amazon. I would suggest not getting your hair colored or permed anywhere in Brazil. Products tend to be harsher than their American counterparts, and my own hair actually started to fall out from a combination of bad products and overbleaching from the tropical sun. Manicures are cheap (about $2–$5), but bring your own utensils; I never saw any disinfecting equipment that satisfied me. And don't be startled—Brazilian manicurists have a way of globbing polish all over your fingers, then cleaning up the residue later, but the final result is usually excellent.

LUGGAGE DAMAGE

Luggage has been known to get damaged on the finest airline carriers. Reports may be made to an airline official at the airport, but unless the bag is totally dysfunctional, you are better off biting the bullet, especially if you are not staying long in that city. In general, suitcases are taken to be repaired, not exchanged, a delay that could cause you even greater grief.

Do make sure that all luggage (hand and checked) is well identified with your name and home address.

MAIL

On a good day, it takes about five days to a week for a letter from Rio to reach New York. On a bad day, it might take a few years. Anyone sending packages to Brazil should note that all packages are opened by post office officials and that strict restrictions apply.

The easiest way to mail an envelope is to hand it to your concierge, who will mail it for you or sell you stamps at a small markup. There are usually post offices in major airports. Postcards from Brazil to the States cost about $1 to mail, as do letters up to 20 grams. Express post, registered mail, and parcel service operate both domestically and internationally.

NEWSPAPERS

Most major cities have at least one newspaper, if not two, which will offer listings of local events in music, theater, film, and dance. *O Jornal do Brasil* is Rio's version of the *New York Times*, as is *A Folha de São Paulo* in São Paulo. In Rio, São Paulo, and Brasília, it is relatively easy to locate the *International Herald Tribune*, the *Miami Herald*, and the *Wall Street Journal*, as well as international versions of *Newsweek* and *Time* magazines. A daily English-language newspaper, the *Latin America Daily Post*, circulates in Rio and São Paulo. I've even glimpsed copies of *Musician* and *Downbeat* magazines in Rio—for more than twice the price. At larger newsstands and airport bookshops you can find other foreign newspapers and magazines, and possibly some paperback novels in English.

POLICE

Contrary to popular belief, the police in Brazil can often be helpful, especially in Rio, where special forces maintain watch over the beaches. If you are in trouble, don't hesitate to approach one even if he doesn't speak English; he will find someone who does. (I was saved during Carnaval by one charming officer who made sure I got to my proper samba school.) If you are the victim of petty theft (camera, wallet, etc.), the best thing to do is notify the concierge and manager of your hotel. Filing a complaint with the Federal Police may be a waste of time unless you want to file an insurance claim.

Don't get nervous if you see armed policemen stopping cars on the street or highways near *favelas* (slums). They are most probably making routine searches for drugs.

RESTROOMS

Memorize this phrase: *"Onde fica o toalete?"* ("On-gee fee-cah oh twah-letch-ee?") That will get you a finger pointed to the nearest restroom. Women's restrooms (also called *banheiros*) are usually marked *M* for *mulher*, and, for men, *S* for *senhor*. Adequate facilities can be found at most restaurants, and if you are not trailing sand, the more casual ones will probably let you use them without dining. Toilet paper is not uniformly present in public restrooms, so I'd suggest carrying your own supplies (like Handiwipes) or snitching a few sheets of tissue from your hotel room. Bus stations usually have clean facilities, with an elderly woman handing out a stiff, torturous paper for a few cents. Most hotel rooms come with regular toilets, as well as European-style bidets. If you're camping out, you'd better go prepared with something other than leaves.

SHOPPING

Fine clothes, though stylish, have become extremely expensive in Brazil, often costing more than comparable items in the States. Centers of fashion are Rio and São Paulo, which boast extremely modern shopping malls, as well as chic neighborhood boutiques. Best buys are leather shoes and bags, particularly if you take advantage of end-of-season sales (look for the words *promoção* or *liquidação*).

Most native crafts can be bought in Rio, but they will usually cost twice as much as they do in their states of origin. Unabashed bargaining is expected at open-air markets and bazaars, but use discretion in finer stores and boutiques, although you might be able to wrangle discounts on large purchases, such as jewelry, if you speak to the owner or manager.

TAXIS

Taxi drivers have long been notorious, but are slowly being educated that their honest service deeply affects tourism, and thus the country's economy. Here are some tips for avoiding being carried miles out of your way and stiffed for an outrageous fee.

- Know where you're going and have your destination written in Portuguese on a piece of paper, as well as the best route there, recommended by your concierge.

- Because of inflation, rates are constantly changing, but up-to-date prices must be displayed on a chart pasted on the back window. See that the taxi meter, located in the front seat next to the wheel, starts when you do, and check the chart yourself at the end of the ride. A surcharge is collected on Sunday and after 10:00 p.m., so check the second table of prices.

- If you are returning to your hotel, call out to the porter to verify the charge, or hail a policeman if you see one.

- Special air-conditioned taxis, which are safer, are usually found lined up in front of fine hotels, but they invariably run almost twice as much as the normal fee. Rates are determined in advance, so ask.

- Hire a car and guide for the day or by the hour.

- Attend nighttime shows with tour groups, which provide transfers by private coach.

- If you're hailing your own cab, stand on the curb and point your index finger down to the ground, not up!

- Always carry the name, address, and telephone number of your hotel tucked inside your shoe in case your wallet or purse gets stolen.

TELEPHONES

The phone line in Brazil has a mind of its own. Many numbers seem perpetually busy, and you can be suddenly disconnected for no apparent reason. Be patient. Local calls can be made from your hotel usually free of charge (though do check ahead of time), but you can also make them from city streets at phone booths that require tokens. You can obtain these tokens, called *fichas*, quite cheaply at any newsstand; buy at least two packs of five at one time, since each *ficha* lasts only for about three minutes. When you first pick up to dial, put two or three in at once, since disconnections come fast and without warning.

☎ Calling Brazil/Calling Home

It's cheaper to call Rio from the States than vice versa. Since AT&T offers no weekend rates, the best time to make a call to Brazil from the States is between midnight and 8:00 a.m.: a 10-minute call from New York to Rio costs about $7.59; between 6:00 a.m. and midnight about $9; and between 8:00 a.m.–6:00 p.m., about $11.86. In Brazil, the same Rio-New York call runs about $26 during the week (all hours), with a 20 percent discount on Sunday. Some five-star and four-star hotels offer direct dialing; when the hotel operator becomes involved, calls can often take up to a half hour or more to place. Hotels often charge up to 25 percent service fee or more for international calls; to save money, patronize the city phone company called EMBRATEL, where you will be directed to a private booth and given a key that opens the phone. You pay the receptionist after you make the call. Phone companies operate at most airports as well.

☎ To Brazil

From the States, dial 011-55, followed by the area code and number.

☎ Within Brazil

For direct-dial: 0 plus the area code plus the number. For collect calls (not in a hotel): dial 107.

☎ From Brazil

For direct international calls to: **U.S.** 00-1-area code-number; **Great Britain** 00-44-area code-number; **Ireland** 00-353-area code-number; **Australia** 00-61-area code-number. For collect calls: dial the International Operator, 000111.

Direct calls from Brazil to the U.S. and Canada run about $4 per minute before 8:00 p.m., about $3 after 8:00 p.m., and Sunday until 8:00 p.m.

TIME ZONE

Brazil has three time zones, though most of the country is located three hours behind Greenwich Mean Time. This region occupies eastern Brazil and parts of central (including Rio de Janeiro, Salvador, São Paulo, Brasília, Recife, and Belém.) That means when it's noon in New York, it's 2:00 p.m. in Rio de Janeiro. The second zone, which is 4 hours behind GMT, encompasses the states of Mato Grosso and Mato Grosso do Sul and most of Brazil's north (such as Manaus, Corumbá, Rio Branco, Porto Velho, Cuiabá, and Campo Grande). Far-western Brazil (Acre and the western edge of Amazonas) are five hours behind GMT. For Daylight Savings Time, clocks go forward an hour on the second Sunday in November and are set back on the second Sunday in March. The city of Belém is not in the habit of following this schedule, so double check your flight schedules.

TIPPING

There are no service taxes charged in Brazil, but most hotels and restaurants add a 10 percent service charge unless otherwise specified (look for the sign *não taxa de serviço* or *serviço não incluso*). If none is added, or if you want to leave more, feel free—remember, you're in a third-world country where maids, waiters, manicurists, porters, and other service people barely subsist on minimum wages.

In Rio and Salvador (and most anywhere, actually), especially if you are sitting at a sidewalk café, street children or beggars may ask you for money or food. Follow your conscience, but be aware that the request is sometimes a ploy to divert your attention while a third party lifts your belongings.

On a good tour, tip a guide between $1 and $5 (half-day tours). They usually make very low wages, despite being multilingual and well educated. Do note that they probably receive commissions from any stores they steer you to.

TRAVEL WITHIN BRAZIL

Bus

Bus travel through the country can be an invigorating way to see the countryside, if a little demanding. Most buses are not air-conditioned, but the breeze is refreshing, and the tickets are cheap. Sharing the bus with you may be chickens and other small animals that are riding with their owners (I have yet to see a pig). In most cases, seats are reserved by numbers, which are taken seriously. Ask for a seat next to the window *(janela)*, which is generally cooler. Buses stop frequently, about every three or four hours, and bus terminals, with snack bars, casual restaurants, newsstands and bathrooms, can provide colorful glimpses of native life. A viable trip by bus is down the southern coast from Rio to the seaside cities of Ubatuba and Guarujá. Another well trod bus trip is the Rio-São Paulo route, which is about 6 hours, for $25. Reservations for buses should be made as far as possible in advance, especially on weekends and during high season.

Custom-designed, air-conditioned buses called *leitos* are more expensive but luxurious, sporting reclining chairs for overnighters and sandwiches and cookies in cardboard boxes. The Salvador-Ilhéus route in the state of Bahia is an excellent overnight trip.

In seaside cities, such as Salvador, Maceió, Natal and Recife in the Northeast, **special tourist buses** take bathers down the main beach drag to the various beaches.

City buses are boarded from the back and payment in exact change is given to the cashier, who sits in the rear. You exit from the front. City buses, however, are usually not the best form of transportation for a first-time tourist. They are almost always packed, and crime is prevalent.

Train

There are few trains in Brazil, and you are generally better off taking the bus. A few daily trains run between Rio and São Paulo, and two trains weekly between Rio and Belo Horizonte.

TRAVELING WITH KIDS

Brazil is an extremely family-oriented country. High chairs are available in numerous restaurants, and many hotels do not charge for children under five. Baby-sitters are often available at resort-style hotels, whose private grounds and excellent security make them ideal for families. Best examples of this kind of resort-hotel are the Rio Sheraton in Rio de Janeiro, Nas Rocas Resort in Búzios (near Rio), the Transamérica Hotel and Praia do Forte in Bahia, and the Pratagy Eco-Hotel in Maceió. Kids love the jungle lodges in the Amazon and would do well taking a lazy boat trek through the Pantanal. However, a child who goes on an adventure tour must be accompanied by an adult, and should be old enough to take directions without misinterpreting or balking.

Throughout the book, suggested activities geared especially for children are highlighted.

WATER

For health reasons, you must drink *only* bottled water wherever you go in Brazil. Even in small towns, you will be able to order it at bars or in restaurants; even Amazon jungle lodges serve bottled water. If you are camping, you must carry your own; you're asking for cholera and any other number of diseases if you drink river water, or in some cases tap water, purified or not. Most hotel rooms are supplied with bottled water in the minibar. Avoid brushing your teeth with tap water. For more tips, see *Health Kit* in the back of the book.

WOMEN ONLY

I have yet to accurately nail the quality of machismo in Brazil. It is more charming, more subtle, yet at times more brutal than in other Latin American countries. More and more women are working outside the home, but a woman's first responsibility is still to her family, and she is rarely allowed the freedom to come and go as freely as a man. Consequently, a foreign woman traveling alone in Brazil is still a point of enormous intrigue. Blondes, in particular, seem to evoke the same kind of fantasies that darker-hued women inspire in Northerners, but pinching is rare (more common are intense stares and lighthearted flirtation). How you dress and carry yourself will determine how you are received. If you don't want undue attention, you might consider wearing a fake wedding ring, although this will only slow down action, not stop it. In no circumstances, should you go off into dark places with a man you do not know, or traipse off alone into the jungle with only a male guide. On the plus side, women traveling alone are often treated with great deference; old ladies will be glad to watch your luggage at bus stations while you use the bathroom. Just use your head about whom to trust. If you are traveling to São Paulo or Rio, the Caesar Park Hotel is especially attentive to single women, as is the Tropical hotel in Mauasu, as well as the southern states of Brazil are particularly hospitable, in the European fashion.

YOUTH HOSTELS

For a list of youth hostels and addresses throughout Brazil, write: **Youth Hostels Contej** *(Estácio de Sá/ Rua Vinícius de Moraes 120/ Rio de Janeiro, Brasil).*

SPECIALTY TOURS

Chapada dos Guimaraes, Mato Grosso

Specialty tours, especially through the Amazon, are often the easiest and safest way to travel. The following agencies, most of them based in the U.S., are all reputable, but do take precautions. Cancellations and price changes are a way of life in Brazil; you might even consider taking out insurance *against* cancellation. And do read the fine print of any contract; usually you are required to take responsibility for your own health and property.

Brazil Nuts
79 Stanford St., Fairfield, CT 06430; ☎ *(203) 259-7900, or toll free (800) 553-9959.* Owner Adam Carter is a passionate Brazilophile who offers

packaged tours of Rio, the Pantanal, the Amazon, Carnaval in Salvador, and others. Independent travelers can also take advantage of the "Rio Like a Native" program on a day-by-day basis, that includes various excursions to tourist sights and evening performances. To contact the office in Rio upon arrival, call ☎ *255-6692.*

International Expeditions

One Environs Park, Helena, Alabama 35080; ☎ *(205) 428-1700.* This company usually offers trekking journeys through the Amazon basin in Peru, but may have now extended trips into Brazil.

ICS Scuba and Travel

5254 Merrick Road, Suite 5, Massapequa, NY 11758; ☎ *(516) 797-2133, (800) 722-0205.* This company specializes in scuba expeditions throughout the world, including an extensive program in Fernando de Noronha. (For more information, see the section on Fernando de Noronha.)

Special Expeditions

720 Fifth Avenue, New York, NY 10019; ☎ *(212) 765-7740; (800) 762-0003.* This company, aimed at the more adventurous tourist, offers remarkable 16-day voyages aboard the 80-passenger M.S. *Polaris* from Manaus to Ciudad, Venezuela, traversing a thousand miles on the Amazon. Cost begins at $5030 per person, double occupancy, including everything but airfare.

Ecotour Expeditions

P.O. Box 1066, Cambridge MA 02238; ☎ *(617) 876-5817.* A three-year-old company, Ecotour offers a nine-day Amazon journey with three meals a day, including a tour of Manaus. The cost is about $1895 (plus airfare to Brazil).

Rainforest Alliance

270 Lafayette Street, Suite 512, New York, NY 10012; ☎ *(212) 941-1900.* One of the leading organizations dedicated to the preservation of the rain forest lead small trips on the Amazon. An 80-passenger ship cruises up the Amazon to Iquitos, Peru, departing from Manaus. All trips are conducted by Alliance staff members and local naturalists. For more information contact Paul Ewing.

International Study Tours

225 W. 34th Street, Suite 913, New York, NY 10122; ☎ *(212) 563-1327; (800) 833-2111.* IST offers educational and cultural tours of Brazil to tourists of all ages. Trips include a rain forest expedition out of Manaus (or a combination package including Manaus, the Pantanal, Iguaçu Falls and Rio) "Carnaval of Cultures" 12-day tour of Rio, Salvador, and Recife to explore samba and Afro-Brazilian lore; and an "Art in Brazil" tour, including stops in Rio, Brasília and Ouro Preto. Trips run from 7–13 nights. Lecturers are professors from universities in Brazil.

The American Museum of Natural History Discovery Tours and Cruises

Central Park West at 79th Street, New York, NY 10024; ☎ *(212)*

769-5700. The museum offers a cruise down the Amazon on the M.S. Polaris. Lectures are given by a team from the museum. The prices range from $5700–$9600 (air included).

New York Botanical Garden
Travel program/New York Botanical Garden, Bronx, NY 10458-5126; ☎ (212) 220-8700, FAX (212) 220-6504. Special Amazonian tours for groups of 8–20 are planned for the early dry season of each year. Cruises are taken on a small river boat built especially for the program, accompanied by guides who lecture on the botanical aspects of jungle life. Fee, including roundtrip airfare from Miami to Manaus, all meals, transfers, expeditions and reading material, is $2495.

Brazilian Views, Inc.
201 East 66th Street, Suite 21G, New York, New York 10021; ☎ (212) 472-9539. This New York-based specialty consulting firm has previously offered serveral types of expeditions including a 10-day birdwatching tour in the Pantanal, a (four-day minimum) fishing expedition to the Pantanal, a garden tour of Brazil and Argentina, sponsored by four South American garden clubs and a decorative fiber arts and folk crafts tour of the cities of Belém, Recife, Salvador, Belo Horizonte, Rio de Janeiro and São Paulo. Write for more current information.

F & H Consulting
2441 Janin Way, Solvang, CA 93463; ☎ (800) 544-5503, FAX (805) 688-1021. This extremely reputable firm, co-owned by Claudio Heckmann, a native-born Brazilian, works exclusively with five-star hotels in Brazil and Brazilian-owned properties. He also acts as the coordinator for the Brazilian Tourism Information Center in the U.S. Contact F & H for the most up-to-date information on resort facilities, spas and private islands and the Ariau Jungle Tower outside Manaus.

Brazilian Roots
Rua do Riachuelo, 44, 4th floors (downtown). Rio de Janeiro, RJ Brasil 20.230-014; ☎ (21)252-2759, FAX 232-9643. Owned and run by two black Brazilians prominent in video, radio and politics, this is a service promotion company specializing in international trade and tourism. The agency designs, plans and executes international events and also offers special "Ethnic Cultural Tours" featuring the Afro-Brazilian culture of Brazil. They are skilled in bringing large groups of Afro-American tourists to Brazil.

Expeditours
Rua Visconde de Pirajá, 414, loja 1120 (11th floor); ☎ (21)287-9697, FAX 521-4388. The leading eco-tour agency in Brazil offers expeditions for all levels of expertise, with dozens of options for hiking, trekking, boating scuba, and sailing throughout Brazil. Owner André von Thuranyi can custom design sojourns into the Amazon forest, float you through the Pantanal, or introduce you to some of the most secluded islands in the country. The company also has made a systematic study of all the major ecosystems

in Brazil and can provide experts in many fields, such as botany, bird-watching and herbism to accompany individuals or groups. Expeditour guides are hearty fellows who will take risks if you push them. The agency also offers tours to remote places like Gabriel da Cachoeira in the Amazon. Write for their extensive brochure.

TRAVEL AGENCIES/TOUR OPERATORS

Abreu Tours

317 E.34th Street, New York, NY10016; ☎ *(212)532-6550, FAX (212) 532-7153.* Handles groups of 15 or more on a custom basis. Also specializes in Portugal.

Go To Rio Tours

551 Fifth Ave., New York, NY 10176; ☎ *(212) 682-5310, FAX (212) 963-2398.* Arranges FITs and groups throughout Brazil, with 24-hour guides and special requests. Also Amazon packages. Carnaval packages, minimum five night, average is nine nights.

Equitable Travel

654 Madison Ave., New York, NY 10176; ☎ *(212) 682-5310, FAX (212) 486-0783.* Arranges trips for individuals, particularly businessmen.

Panavian Travel

25 W. 45th Street, New York, NY 10036; ☎ *(212)719-2270, FAX (212) 719-2273.* Discount airfares using Tower Airlines (747) and Vasp (767).

Tourlite

551 Fifth Ave., New York, NY 10176; ☎ *(212) 599-3355, FAX (212) 370-0913.* Handles package tours and airfare. The "Carioca" package (Rio only) runs 6–14 nights, with airfare and three-star accommodation, for about $899 (five-star available). The "Ecological" packages include three days in Manaus, two days in a river lodge, and two days in Belém, including hotel, airfare, transfer and half-day city tours.

Transbrasil

500 Fifth Ave;, New York, NY 10110; ☎ *(212) 944-7374, FAX (212) 944-7458.*

OCEAN LINE CRUISES

The following companies offer cruises that make port in various Brazilian cities, including Rio de Janeiro, Manaus, Recife, Salvador and Santarém.

Holland America Line

300 Elliott Avenue West, Seattle, WA 98119; ☎ *(206) 681-3535.*

Odessa America Cruise Company

250 Old Country Road, Mineola, NY 11501; ☎ *(516) 747-8880.*

Ocean Cruise Lines

1510 S.E. 17th Street, Fort Lauderdale, FL 33316; ☎ *(305) 764-3500 or (800) 556-8850.*

Regency Cruises
260 Madison Avenue New York, NY 10016; ☎ (212) 972-4499.

Royal Viking Line
95 Merrick Way, Coral Gables, FL 33134; ☎ (305) 447-9660; for reservations ☎ (800) 422-8000; for brochures ☎ (800) 448-4785.

Sun Line Cruises
1 Rockefeller Plaza, Suite 315, New York, NY 10020; ☎ (212) 397-6400 or (800) 872-6400, outside New York City.

Also see "Travel Agencies" under "Rio Hands-On" and in the various "Hands-On" sections of each city in Amazônia and the Pantanal.

LANGUAGE

It's often been said that Portuguese is one of the sexiest languages in the world. If you are planning to spend any time in Brazil, it's well worth studying it seriously, even for a few months. Those who do are usually deeply moved by the sensuosity of the cadences and the vibrant vowel sounds—surely the secret behind the beauty of Brazilian music. Accents notwithstanding, continental Portuguese (that which is spoken in Portugal), varies only slightly in word usage, although natives from Portugal are constantly lamenting the damage Brazilians have wrought on the mother tongue over their 500-year history. (Brazilians, for their part, consider their contributions enlivening.) Among other things, Brazilians have usurped a lot of Tupi, Arabian, and French words, not to mention English phrases, particularly in the field of advertising. Don't be surprised if, in the middle of a whirl of Portuguese, you suddenly hear more familiar words like "know-how," "marketing," "design," "outdoor," and "brainstorm" —all somewhat mangled by the Portuguese accent. (For more information, see under "Language" in the Directory.)

The easiest way to reap a smile from a Brazilian is to learn one choice phrase of slang and use it at just the right time.

Slang	
Cool, neat (literally, legal)	Legal! (leh-gow)
How great!	Que legal!
Really, really great!	Tri-legal!

Slang

How neat!	Bacana!
What a joy! Neat! Cool! Fantastic!	Jóia!
Wow! No kidding.	Puxa! (or Puxa vida!)
Oh, my gosh (literally, Our Lady)	Nossa Senhora (or Nossa)
Keep cool.	Fica frio.
Keep it going. Chill out.	Fica numa nice.
expert (adjective)	craque
You said it!	Falô!

Super (and even hiper, which is bigger and better) can be added to any word in Portuguese, i.e., supermercado (supermarket), hipermercado (even bigger supermarket), super legal (better than great), and super bonita (really beautiful).

Proverbs

These three proverbs should cover almost any situation you will encounter in Brazil.

Don't create a tempest in a teacup.	Não fazer tempestade em copo d'água.
One who doesn't have a dog hunts with a cat (in other words, make do with what you have).	Quem não tem cão caça com gato!
A man is a devil that no woman can deny, but every woman wishes for a devil to take her away.	O homem é um diabo não há mulher que o negue, mas toda mulher deseja que um diabo a carregue.

Airplane/Customs

Have you anything to declare?	Tem alguma coisa a declarar?
One suitcase of mine is missing.	Faltame uma mala.
Smoking is not allowed.	É proibido fumar.
I feel air-sick.	Sinto-me enjoado(a).

Common Questions and Phrases

Where is the bathroom?	Onde fica o toilete (banheiro)?
Flirting Hello	Alô
Hi, hey	Oi
Oops	Opa
Bye	'Tchau (as in ciao)
Good-bye	Até logo
Good morning	Bom dia

Common Questions and Phrases

Good afternoon	Boa tarde
Good night (good evening)	Boa noite
What's your name?	Qual é seu nome?
My name is . . .	Meu nome é . . .
How are you?	Como vai?
I'm fine, thank you.	Bem, obrigado(a).
Thank you (very much).	Obrigado (muito).
You're welcome.	De nada.
Excuse me (apology).	Desculpe.
Excuse me (to pass by someone in your way).	Com licença.
Where are you from?	De onde você é?
I'm from . . .	Sou de . . .
Do you speak Portuguese/English/Spanish?	Você fala português/inglês/espanhol?
I don't speak Portuguese.	Não falo português.
Do you understand?	Você entende?
I don't understand.	Não entendo.
Please speak more slowly.	Por favor, fale mais devagar.
How do you say . . . ?	Como se diz . . . ?
What do you call this in Portuguese?	Como se chama isto em português?
What does "—" mean in Portuguese?	Que quer dizer "—"?
Want to go out with me?	Quer sair comigo?
Want to have a drink?	Quer tomar alguma coisa?
You're very beautiful.	Você é muito bonito (a).

Insider Tip

Gosto de você *is perhaps the most misunderstood phrase in Brazilian Portuguese. Depending on the tone, the body gesture, and the look in the eye, it can variously mean* I like you *(you're a nice person),* I like you a lot *(I hope we see other again),* I really like you a lot *(let's be friends for life), or* I really, really like you a lot *(do you want to go to bed with me?).*

Direction

left	esquerda
right	direita
here	aquí
there (where you are)	aí

Direction

over there or yonder	lá
pull	puxe
push	empurre

Brush-offs for Street Punks

Leave me alone.	Deixe-me em paz.
Go away.	Vá embora.
Don't touch me.	Não me toque.
Don't bother me.	Não me chateie.
Don't bother me (stronger).	Não enche.
Help!	Socorro!

Date

Monday	segunda-feira (written as 2a)
Tuesday	terça-feira (3a)
Wednesday	quarta-feira (4a)
Thursday	quinta-feira (5a)
Friday	sexta-feira (6a)
Saturday	sabado
Sunday	domingo
weekend	fim de semana
yesterday	ontem
today	hoje
tomorrow	amanhã
the day	o dia
the month	o mês
the year	o ano

Numbers*

1	um/uma	17	dezessete
2	dois/duas	18	dezoito
3	três	19	dezenove
4	quatro	20	vinte
5	cinco	21	vinte e um
6	seis	30	trinta

Numbers*

7	sete	40	quarenta
8	oito	50	cinquenta
9	nove	60	sessenta
10	dez	70	setenta
11	onze	80	oitenta
12	doze	90	noventa
13	treze	100	cem
14	quatorze	101	cento e um
15	quinze	500	quinhentos
16	dezesseis	1000	mil

*Numbers in Portuguese use periods instead of commas, and commas instead of periods. For example, cr $3.500,75.

Time

What time is it?	Que horas são?
At what time?	A que horas?
How long does it take?	Leva quanto tempo?
When?	Quando?
Which day?	Que dia?

Official time in Brazil (buses, airplanes, etc.) is reported on a 24-hour system. Midnight is meia noite; one, two, three o'clock in the morning is uma hora, duas horas, três horas, etc., until noon, which is meio dia. One o'clock in the afternoon is reported as treze horas, two o'clock as quatorze horas, etc. In general conversation, use the 12-hour system (i.e., you'll meet for dinner at oito horas (eight o'clock).

at 1:00 AM	a uma hora
at 3 PM (official)	às quinze horas (15:00 hours)
an hour from now	daqui a uma hora
yesterday	ontem
today	hoje
tomorrow	amanhã
this week	esta semana
last week	semana passada

Dining

Waiter	Garçon
Maitre d'	Maitre
The menu, please.	O cardápio, por favor.
What's the specialty?	Qual é a especialidade da casa?

Dining

I don't eat meat/fish.	Não como carne/peixe.
A little more.	Um pouco mais.
The bill, please.	A conta, por favor.
Is service included?	O serviço está incluido?
I want a receipt.	Quero recibo, por favor.
I want my change.	Quero meu troco, por favor.
The meal was superb.	A refeição estava ótima!
I'm full.	Estou satisfeito (a).
breakfast	café da manhã
lunch	almoço
dinner	jantar
a napkin	um guardanápio
a plate	um prato
a glass	um copo
a cup	uma xícara

Beverages

mineral water	água mineral
carbonated	com gás
noncarbonated	sem gás
coffee	café
tea	chá
milk	leite
black coffee in demitasse	cafezinho
soda pop	refrigerante
beer	cerveja
draft beer	chopp
wine	vinho
red wine	vinho tinto
white wine	vinho branco
with ice	com gelo
without ice	sem gelo

Cover/Condiments/Hors d'Ouevres

cover	couvert
bread	pão
butter	manteiga

Cover/Condiments/Hors d'Ouevres

salt	sal
pepper	pimenta
sugar	açúcar
oil	azeite
vinegar	vinagre
sauce	molho
without sugar	sem açúcar

Fruits

fruits	frutas
apple	maçã
banana	banana
grapes	uvas
lemon	limão
melon	melão
orange	laranja
pear	pêra
strawberries	morangos
juice	suco
orange juice	suco de laranja
smoothie with fruit, juice, often milk and sugar	vitaminas

Seafood

seafood	frutos do mar
codfish	bacalhau
crab	siri
marsh crab	caranguejo
lobster	lagosta
octopus	polvo
oysters	ostras
shrimp	camarão
sole	linguado
squid	lula

Beef

beef	bife
chicken	frango/galinha
chops	costeletas
goat	bode
ham	presunto
lamb	carneiro
pork	porco
rabbit	coelho
sausage	linguiça
turkey	peru
veal	vitela
barbecue	churrasco
all-you-can-eat	rodízio

Vegetables

salad	salada
carrot	cenoura
cucumber	pepino
green beans	vagens
lettuce	alfaçe
tomato	tomate
cooked vegetables	legumes cozidos

Beans and Pasta

bean	feijão
pasta	massa

Money

cash	dinheiro
credit card	cartão de crédito
traveler's cheque	traveler's check (cheque de viagem)
exchange house	câmbio
I want to exchange money.	Quero trocar dinheiro.
Do you exchange money?	Você troca dinheiro? (dólares)

Money

What is the exchange rate?	Qual é o câmbio?
Can you cash a traveler's cheque?	Pode trocar um traveler's check (cheque de viagem)?

Getting Around/Directions

Where is the . . . ?	Onde é o (a) . . . ?
I want to go to . . .	Quero ir para . . .
How can I get to . . . ?	Como posso ir para . . . ?
Does this bus go to . . . ?	Este ônibus vai para . . . ?
Please, take me to . . .	Por favor leve-me para . . . ?
airport	aeroporto
bathroom	toilete
beach	praia
bus station	rodoviária
bus stop	ponto de ônibus
embassy/consulate	embaixada/consulado
gas station	posto de gasolina
supermarket	supermercado
market/ street market	mercado/ feira
street arts fair	feira hippie
movies	cinema
police station	delegacia de polícia
post office	correio
subway station	estação de metrô
theatre	teatro
train station	estação de trem
Please stop here.	Por favor pare aqui.
Please wait.	Por favor espere.
I want to rent a car.	Quero alugar um carro.

Driving

Danger	Perigo
Dangerous bend	Curva perigosa
Service station	Posto

At the Doctor's Office

Call for the doctor.	Chame o médico.
I have a . . .	Estou com dor . . .
headache	de cabeça
sore throat	de garganta
stomach ache	de estômago
toothache	de dente
backache	nas costas
I have a bad sunburn.	Estou queimado(a) do sol.
sunstroke	insolação
food poisoning	intoxicação alimentar
I have a fever.	Estou com febre.
I sprained my arm/ankle.	Torci o braço/o tornozelo.
injections	injeções
cough medicine	xarope
aspirin	aspirina
tablets	comprimidos
ointment	pomada
tonic	tônico
vitamins	vitaminas
I need to go to the hospital.	Preciso ir ao hospital.

At the Hotel

I have a reservation.	Tenho uma reserva.
I want to make a reservation.	Quero fazer uma reserva.
I want to see the room.	Quero ver o quarto.
I want to talk to the manager.	Quero falar com o gerente.
a single room	um quarto de solteiro
a double	um quarto de casal
double room with bath	quarto de casal com banheiro
triple	triplo
with air conditioning	com ar condicionado
minibar	frigobar
safe	cofre
key	chave
What time is breakfast served?	A que horas é o café da manhã?
Can you wake me up at seven?	Pode me acordar às sete horas?
I need another pillow/blanket.	Preciso de outro travesseiro/cobertor.

At the Hotel

Where can one hire a car?	Onde se pode alugar um automóvel?
The air conditioning/ central heating is not working.	O ar condicionado/ aquecimento central não está funcionando.
Does that include all service and taxes?	Estão incluídos o serviço e o imposto?
Where is the manager?	Onde está o gerente?
I enjoyed my stay.	Gostei da estadia.
Thank you for your help.	Obrigado/a pela sua ajuda.

Shopping

Brazilian salespeople, especially those barely out of their teens, are sometimes overly eager to help. To have some breathing space, it's absolutely necessary to learn the password "Só olhando," or "just looking." Other helpful phrases are:

How much?	Quanto?
How much does it cost?	Quanto custa?
That's too expensive.	É muito caro.
I want something cheaper.	Quero alguma coisa mais barata.
Can I try this on?	Posso provar?
I want to buy (this).	Quero comprar (isto).
Do you sell film?	Vende filme?
batteries	pilhas
cassette	fita cassete (k-7)
Where can I buy . . . ?	Onde posso comprar . . . ?
postcards	cartões postais
soap/shampoo	sabonete/xampu or champoo
toothpaste/sunscreen	pasta de dente/filtro solar
stamps	selos
condom	camisinha
newspaper	jornal
shoe store	sapataria
These shoes do not fit me.	Estes sapatos não me servem.
What size do you take in shoes/clothes?	Qual é o tamanho/número que calça/que veste?
This color does not suit me.	Esta cor não me fica bem.
This coat is tight on me.	Este paletó está apertado.
silk	seda
cotton	algodão

Clothes		
suit	terno	
skirt	saia	
jacket	casaco	
dress	vestido	
trousers	calça	
swimsuit/bikini	maiô/ fio dental/tanga	
blouse	blusa	
raincoat/umbrella	capa de chuva/guarda-chuva	
girdle/stockings/panties/bras	cinta/meias/calcinha/soutien	
socks/nightgown	meias/camisola	
tie/shirt	gravata/camisa	

HEALTH KIT
FOR THE TROPICS

JET LAG

Overnight overseas flights to Brazil (nine hours from New York to Rio) can easily cramp your style by the time you arrive. The time change from the East Coast is minimal (two hours); it's the long hours spent cramped in a seat, the night of lost sleep, and the rich food and drinks that may get you down. Here are some tips to minimize discomfort:

- Minimize alcohol before and during flights.
- Avoid large meals for several hours after landing to shrink your stomach to its normal size.
- Chew gum slowly only to relieve ear discomfort.
- Avoid gas-producing and greasy foods.
- Eat small portions starting two hours before takeoff. Eat high-fiber foods to avoid constipation.
- Drink one pint of liquid for every three flying hours to counteract the dryness of the cabin. Best are water and fruit juices.
- Use eyedrops for dry eyes and take off your contact lenses.
- Eat simply and sparingly the first few days in Brazil.

TRAVELER'S DIARRHEA

Traveler's diarrhea is not preordained, though few escape it. It's usually caused by ingesting contaminated food and water or by placing your contaminated fingers in your mouth. The rule for all travelers: Boil it, cook it, peel it, or forget it. Also:

- Avoid street foods, shellfish, and any uncooked or undercooked foods. Be careful which restaurants you choose. Deluxe international hotels are usually your best bet, since most use modern refrigeration, purify local water, protect foods from insects, wash vegetables in chemical solutions and cook food properly.

- Eat only fruit with thick skins that you peel yourself. Don't drink milk in Brazil after noon (since it is rarely refrigerated and is delivered only in the morning).

- Avoid salads and uncooked vegetables. Do not eat raw fish or meat and avoid shellfish.

- Wash your hands always before eating. Germs are picked up through handling money, souvenir shopping, door knobs, sand and ocean, etc. In remote areas, carry your own soap, toilet tissue and handiwipes.

- Drink only bottled water. The carbonation in water (*água com gas*) acidifies it and kills microorganisms that may have gotten into the water prior to boiling. Be suspect of juices or fruit drinks not prepared in your presence.

- Minimize the water you swallow when swimming.

- Use bottled water when you brush your teeth (found in the minibar).

If you do get Montezuma's Revenge, minimize food intake for several meals and drinks lots of liquids. Medications that you should pack are Pepto Bismol (over the counter), Imodium (over the counter), Bactrim (prescription), and Lomotil (prescription). If you have bloody stools or fever, feel unusually weak, or if your symptoms continue for three days, see a doctor immediately. Dehydration is a severe risk. Drink fruit juices, carbonated soft drinks, or mix eight ounces of carbonated or boiled water with a quarter-tablespoon of baking soda alternated with a mixture of orange juice, a half-teaspoon of honey or corn syrup and a pinch of salt. Drink alternately from each glass until thirst is quenched and supplement with carbonated beverages, water or boiled tea. (Information courtesy of the Centers for Disease Control, Atlanta, GA.)

TIPS FOR DRINKING WATER

- Always order mineral water (*sem gás*, without gas, or *com gás*, with gas). Insist it be opened in front of you.

- Avoid ice cubes in any drink; they are usually made from tap water. If you must have ice, put them in a small, clean, leak-proof bag inside your glass.

- Tie a colored ribbon around the bathroom faucet to remind yourself not to drink tap water.

- Carry an electric immersion coil for boiling water—to brush teeth or make tea or coffee. You will most likely need a current converter and a plug adapter available in department stores and travel boutiques.

- Carry a small (unbreakable) bottle of chlorine bleach or tincture of iodine to disinfect water when boiling is not feasible. Add two drops of five percent chlorine bleach or five drops of two percent tincture of iodine to a quart of clear water. Let stand for 30 minutes. Commercial tablets available in the U.S. to disinfect water are Halazone, Globaline and Potable-Agua.

- Travelers using filters to purify river water may find them hopelessly clogged with sediment and thus be forced to drink river water straight—a perfect way to contract amebiasis. Best to take a safe water supply with you.

IMMUNIZATIONS

Yellow fever is endemic in the northern half of Brazil, Vaccines are recommended for those going to jungle or rural areas. Suggested, but not required are hepatitis and typhoid immunizations when traveling to areas of sub-standard sanitation outside the usual tourist routes. Persons working extensively in the countryside and on working assignments in remote areas should be vaccinated. Tetanus shots should always be updated.

MALARIA

Malaria is transmitted by the bite of the female Anopheles mosquito, which feeds from dawn to dusk. You can also get malaria from blood transfusions, or from using contaminated needles and syringes. Not every mosquito carries malaria, but one bite can give you the disease. The Centers for Disease Control in 1995 believes that all travelers to the Amazon Basin will be exposed to what is called chloroquine-resistant malaria. The recommended prophylactic is mefloquine, taken weekly and continued for four weeks after leaving the malarious area. You can also carry a treatment of Fansidar or doxycycline alone, taken daily. If you are pregnant or are planning to fly a plane or undertake any task requiring fine coordination, you should not take mefloquine since small doses have been known to cause dizziness and/or gastrointestinal upset.

OTHER BUG-TRANSMITTED DISEASES

Other mosquito-transmitted diseases found in jungle areas are: **dengue fever** (flulike symptoms, with rash, over in about a week; antibiotics do not help and no vaccine available; beware of hemorrhaging); **leishmaniasis** (avoid sandfly bites which attack most frequently at dusk and dawn); **filariasis** (caused by larvae of worms injected into the body through the bite of a mosquito; usually only heavier exposure causes symptoms; treat with Hetrazan); **onchocerclasis** (a form of filariasis, or river blindness, borne by flies that breed in rivers; if parasites invade the eyes, total blindness can occur; treat with Ivermextin early); and **Chagas' disease** (spread by the reduid bug usually found on roofs and walls of native huts). For more information, see the *International Travel Health Guide* by Stuart R. Rose, M.D.

PREVENTION

Cut down on your chances of catching mosquito-transmitted diseases by protecting yourself. Search your sleeping quarters and bed for hidden insects. Use insecticides, preferably pyrethrum-based, in your living and sleeping quarters (RAID Formula II Crack and Crevice Spray is good). And protect your bed (if outdoors) with mosquito netting (spray the inside of the netting with RAID Flying Insect Spray).

Mosquito and tick bites can be reduced greatly by using the appropriate repellants. Insect repellants with a DEET percentage between 35 and 50 is recommended. Clothing may be sprayed with DEET-containing repellants and the insecticide permethrin, available in many states as Permanone, or PermaKill 4 Week Tick Killer. If you are using a mosquito net, spray it with the same product. A good, lightweight, compact mosquito net well suited for the vagabond traveler is "The Spider." Contact **Thai Occidental**, *5334 Yonge Street, Suite 907, Toronto M2N 6M2, Ontario, Canada;* ☎ *(416) 498-4277, price $69.95.*

CHOLERA

Cholera is an acute diarrheal disease caused by bacteria found in water contaminated by sewage. Although there have been serious outbreaks of cholera during the last few years in many Latin American countries, including Brazil, few Western travelers ever get seriously ill. Most illness occurs in native people who are undernourished and who regularly ingest large amounts of contaminated water. The main symptom is explosive, though painless diarrhea, which if left untreated, may lead to fatal dehydration. Treating loss of fluids immediately is primary to recovery. A good idea is to carry Oral Rehydration Salts mixture distributed by the World Health Organization, which you should mix with safe drinking water and consume after every loose stool. If you can't drink enough to replace lost fluid because of vomiting or weakness, get to a hospital immediately. The best prevention is to pay attention to what you eat and drink.

OTHER DISEASES

Schistosomiasis

Wading or swimming in fresh water can put you at risk for this disease, caused by parasitic blood flukes called schistosomes. The tiny larvae of these creatures bore into the skin and mature within the body. Some people disregard the initial symptom—a rash at the site of penetration—but 4–12 weeks later, fever, malaise and coughing, along with diarrhea, usually sets in abruptly. It's often curable, but if left untreated can progress to more severe stages.

Hepatitis A

This disease can be transmitted by person-to-person contact or by contaminated food, water, or ice. The flulike symptoms don't appear typically for 2–6 weeks and are soon followed by jaundice. The CDC recommends a gamma globulin vaccination for each three-month period. There's no specific treatment and normally healthy people recover on their own, but do see a doctor.

Hepatitis B

Travelers to the Amazon basin are at high risk for hepatitis B. Vaccinations are not required, but the CDC recommends one for health-care workers, long-term travelers, or anyone expecting to have intimate relations with locals in rural areas. The virus is transmitted through the exchange of blood products, daily physical contact, and sexual intercourse. The vaccine involves a series of three intramuscular doses, which should be begun 6 months before travel; the series should be begun even if it cannot be completed before travel begins.

Typhoid Fever

Travelers in Brazil are at risk for typhoid fever when in small cities, villages, and rural areas. Although not required, the CDC recommends a vaccination for those straying from the regular tourist itinerary or staying more than six weeks. The disease is transmitted through contaminated food and water. Currently, the vaccine only protects 70–90 percent of cases, so continue to drink only boiled or bottled water and eat well-cooked food, even if you've taken the vaccination.

AIDS

As of press time, Brazil does not require foreign travelers to take AIDS tests. For a free four-page leaflet on how to travel abroad and not bring home acquired immuno-deficiency syndrome, write **Global Programs on AIDS, World Health Organization**, *Avenue Appia, 1121; Geneva 27, Switzerland.* (Also see "Diseases" under Directory)

OTHER INFORMATION

For the most current information on traveling to tropical countries, contact the **Centers for Disease Control**, ☎ *(404) 332-4559*, using a touch-tone phone 24 hours a day. A recorded voice will direct you through a menu of information.

For an excellent bimonthly newsletter on travel precautions, write **Traveling Healthy**, *108-48 70th Road; Forest Hills, NY 11375.*

An excellent 51-page booklet published by the **American Society of Tropical Medicine and Hygiene** discusses such topics as pre-trip preparations, immunizations, malaria prevention, traveler's diarrhea, etc. Write: Karl A. Western, MD c/o **ASTMH**, *6436-31st Street, N.W., Washington, D.C. 20015-2342. Price $4.00.* Everything you need to know about the latest travel-health requirements worldwide (updated annually) can be found in *International Travel Health Guide,* by Stuart R. Rose, M.D. Published by **Travel Medicine, Inc.**, *351 Pleasant Street, Suite 312, Northhampton, MA 01060.*

POST-TRIP CHECKUPS

Many specialists feel there is no reason to have a post-tropics checkup if you are feeling well. In some cases, however, symptoms don't appear for weeks, months, or a year after the trip; you may even suffer intermittent attacks followed by periods of subsidence. The incubation period for malaria varies from five days to a month, and longer in some cases. In its initial stages, it causes flulike symptoms, and if treatment is delayed, it can become potentially fatal. If you have any of the following symptoms, don't delay seeking immediate medical attention:

- gastrointestinal distress (if diarrhea, loose stools, abdominal pain, or excessive flatulence continues for a week or more, you could be harboring parasites);

- fever (never ignore fever coming out of the tropics—it could be malaria, schistosomiasis, roundworms, hepatitis A, or a sign of tuberculosis);

- rashes, change in skin pigmentation, or swelling;
- persistent coughs, possibly due to parasitic worms in the lungs or tuberculosis;
- unexplained weight loss. In all cases, it is best to go to a tropical disease specialist straightaway.

To find a specialist in your area call the local health department or the tropical disease unit of a nearby hospital. The new **International Society of Travel Medicine**, *Box 150060, Atlanta, GA 30333;* ☎ *(404) 486-4046,* should have a list of specialists. (To request a nationwide directory of tropical disease specialists, send a stamped, self-addressed business-size envelope to **Dr. Leonard C. Marcus**, *148 Highland Avenue, Newton, MA 02165.*

BOOKS AND FILMS

BOOKS

Luso-Brazilian Books

Box 170286, Brooklyn, NY 11217; ☎ (718) 624-4000, toll free ☎ (800) 727-LUSO, FAX (718) 858-0690. This is one of the leading distributors of Brazilian and Portuguese-oriented material. Write for a free catalogue.

Photography

Manor, Graciela, text, and Mann, Hans, photos. *The Twelve Prophets of Aleijadinho*. Austin & London: University of Texas Press, 1976. Black and white photos, a short text and a poetic essay by Carlos Drummond de Andrade on the character of Minas Gerais as seen through the eyes of the Baroque sculptor Aleijadinho.

Verger, Pierre. *Historical Center of Salvador (Centro Histórico de Salvador 1945–1950)*. Rio de Janeiro: Câmara Brasileiro do Livro, 1989. Black and white photos by a French documentary photographer in the 1940s whose reminiscences are still fresh.

Bruce Weber. *O Rio de Janeiro*. New York: Knopf, 1986. A sensual photographic journal by one of the world's leading photographers.

History

Alden, Dauril., ed. *Colonial Roots of Modern Brazil*. Berkeley: University of California Press, 1973.

Burns, E. Bradford. *A History of Brazil*. New York: Columbia University Press, 1980. Perhaps the most readable history of Brazil readily available in bookstores.

Conrad, Robert Edgar. *World of Sorrow: The African Slave Trade in Brazil*. Baton Rouge & London: Louisiana State University Press, 1986. A rich resource of details and culture, particularly helpful for anyone writing an historical novel.

Diffie, Bailey W. A *History of Colonial Brazil 1500–1792.* Malabar, Florida: Robert E. Krieger Publishing Co., 1987.

Freyre, Gilberto. *Order and Progress: Brazil from Monarch to Republic.* Berkeley and Los Angeles: University of California Press, 1986. A three-volume masterpiece by the premier Brazilian sociologist.

Freyre, Gilberto. *The Mansions and the Shanty: The Making of Modern Brazil.* Berkeley and Los Angeles: University of California Press, 1986.

Freyre, Gilberto. *The Masters and the Slaves: A Study in the Development of Brazilian Civilization.* Berkeley and Los Angeles: University of California Press, 1986.

Maxwell, Kenneth. *Conflicts and Conspiracies: Brazil and Portugal 1750–1808.* Boston: Cambridge University Press, 1973. Interesting analysis explaining why Brazil adopted a monarchical system of government instead of fragmenting into numerous separate states like other areas in Latin America.

Street Life

De Jesus, Maria. *Child of the Dark: The Diary of Carolina Maria de Jesus.* New York: Penguin, 1963. An extraordinary diary of a poor woman living in a São Paulo ghetto, written originally on scraps of paper. After her writings were discovered by a journalist, they were first serialized in the newspaper, then made into an instant bestseller. Nothing more honest and direct exists to describe the day-to-day struggle of living in a *favela.*

Dimenstein, Gilberto, introduction by Rocha, Jan. *Brazil: War on Children.* London: Latin America Bureau, 1991. One of Brazil's most outstanding journalists investigates the tragic world of underaged pimps, muggers, prostitutes and petty criminals—all homeless children who live in fear of sudden death at the hands of vigilantes.

Trevisan, João, translated by Martin Forman. *Perverts in Paradise.* London: GMP Publishers, 1986. Written by one of the founders of the Brazilian gay movement, this is a fascinating, if severely biased, history of the development of homosexuality in Brazil, from the Papal Inquisition to today's pop music idols. A provocative analysis of how homosexuality dovetails with the Brazilian traits of extravagance and social repression is followed by a startling interview with a gay *candomblé* priest. Write: GMP Publishers, LTD., P.O. Box. 247, London N15 6 RW, England.

Native Peoples

Davis, Shelton H. *Victims of the Miracle: Development and the Indians of Brazil.* Boston: Cambridge University Press, 1977, reprinted in 1988. An anthropologist examines contemporary Indian policy in Brazil and discusses the devastation wrought on tribal life by highway construction and mining.

Hemming, John. *Amazon Frontier: The Defeat of the Brazilian Indians.* London: Macmillan London Ltd., 1987. Covering the period from the mid-18th century to the early 20th century, this compelling analysis explains how and why native cultures fell into demise. The author is Director and Secretary of the Royal Geographic Society.

The Amazon

Head, Suzanne and Heinzman, Robert, editors. *Lessons of the Rainforest.* San Francisco: Sierra Club Books, 1990. Essays from 24 leading authorities (biologists, ecologists, economists, and political activists), all committed to finding alternatives to rain forest decimation.

Hecht, Susanna and Cockburn, Alexander. *The Fate of the Forest: Developers, Destroyers and Defenders of the Amazon.* New York: Harper Perennials, 1990. A deeply informed and searing work exploring the history of the rain forest from the conquistadors to the goldminers to the military dictatorship. It also sheds new light on the role of Chico Mendes and other activists.

Miller, Cristina G. and Berry, Louise A. *Jungle Rescue: Saving the New World Tropical Rain Forests.* New York: Atheneum, 1991. A thought-provoking and entertaining book for children, explaining the complexities of the rain forest and its relationship to the Western Hemisphere.

Lamb, F. Bruce. *Wizard of the Upper Amazon, The Story of Manuel Córdova-Rio.* Boston: Houghton-Mifflin, 1975. Written by a Peruvian healer held captive by Amazonian Indians, this is a mesmerizing document of life in a South American tribe, including descriptions of *ayahuasca* rituals—a hallucinogenic tonic made from two Amazonian plants.

Lewis, Scott, preface by Robert Redford. *The Rainforest Book: How You Can Save the World's Rainforests.* Los Angeles: Living Planet Press, 1990. An extremely easy-to-read book that explains how rain forests are being destroyed, why we should preserve them, and what we can do.

Kane, Joe. *Running the Amazon.* New York: Knopf, 1989. A must-read for anyone looking for arm-chair adventure, this eyewitness account of traversing the Amazon River was written by a formerly office-bound journalist whose pretrip naiveté was matched only by his unexpected fearlessness.

Matthiessen, Peter. *The Cloud Forest.* New York: Penguin, 1961, 1989. Zen master Matthiessen crisscrossed 20,000 miles of South American wilderness, from the Amazonian rain forests to Machu Picchu and Mato Grosso. Stylish, ironic, and insightful.

Popescu, Petru. *Amazon Beaming.* New York: Viking, 1991. When world-class photographer Loren McIntyre was kidnapped by an Amazonian tribe, he found himself descending, unwillingly, into another level of perceptual reality that ultimately changed his life. This amazing "Twilight Zone" story is told with style by Romanian filmmaker Petru Popescu.

Shoumatoff, Alex. *The Rivers Amazon.* San Francisco: Sierra Club Books, 1978 and 1986. A staff writer for the New Yorker and a premier commentator on Brazilian affairs resolved to spend his thirtieth birthday in the Amazon. His reminiscences of negotiating headwaters, mosquitoes, exotic vegetation and wildlife, as well as all manners of *bureaucratic* red tape lie somewhere between poetry and science.

Pantanal

Banks, Vic. *The Pantanal: Brazil's Forgotten Wilderness.* San Francisco: Sierra Club Books, 1991. Photojournalist and cinematographer Vic Banks chronicles his lively adventures in the Pantanal, accompanied by photos of the region. Also included is a good overview of the political dilemmas of the region.

Art and Architecture

Epstein, David. *Brasília: Plan and Reality. A Study of Planned and Spontaneous Urban Development.* Berkeley: University of Press, 1973.

Holston, James. *Brasília: The Modernist City. An Anthropological Critique.* Chicago & London: University of Chicago Press, 1989.

Music

McGowan, Chris and Ricardo Pessanha. *The Brazilian Sound.* New York: Billboard Books, 1991.

Perrone, Charles. *Masters of Contemporary Brazilian Song: MPB 1965–1985.* Austin: University of Texas Press, 1989.

Roots and Culture

Amado, Jorge. *Bahia de Todos Os Santos (Guia de ruas e mistérios).* A mystical guide to Salvador's streets and icons by Brazil's foremost novelist. (Portuguese)

Religion

Brumana, Fernando Giobellina and Elda Gonzales Martinez. *Spirits from the Margin: Umbanda in São Paulo.* Stockholm: Wicksell International, 1989.

Bastide, Roger, translated by Helen Sebba. *The African Religions of Brazil: Toward a Sociology of the Interpretation of Civilizations.* Baltimore and London: Johns Hopkins University, 1960. The leading analysis of Brazilian religious cults by a noted French social scientist.

Galembo, Phyllis. *Divine Inspiration: Benin to Bahia.* New Mexico: University of Albuquerque Press, 1993. An exquisite photo album with a foreward by David Byrne and various essays celebrating the ritualistic "theater" of African and Afro-Brazilian trance cult religions. The folklore-rich photos help explain how African traditions, as living elements transmitted orally, were adapted in Brazil without losing their sacred fire.

McGregor, Pedro. *Jesus of the Spirits.* New York: Stein & Day, 1966. An interesting analysis of African myths and ritual and their influence on the religious beliefs of Brazilians.

O'Gorman, Frances. *Aluanda: A Look at Afro-Brazilian Cults.* Rio de Janeiro: Livraria Francisco Alves Editora S.A., 1979.

St. Clair, David. *Drum & Candle.* New York: Doubleday, 1971. An American journalist made a personal investigation into the psychic/spiritual side of Brazil and came out a believer.

Wofer, Jim. *The Taste of Blood: Spirit Possession in Brazilian Candomblé.* Philadelphia: University of Pennsylvania Press, 1991.

Samba/Carnaval

Guillermoprieto, Alma. *Samba.* New York: Random House, 1990. A marvelous account of one year in the life of Rio's Mangueira samba school, written by a former journalist with the soul of a poet.

Gardel, Luis. *Escolas de Samba.* Rio de Janeiro: 1967. Subtitled "A Descriptive Account of the Carnival Guilds of Rio," this book is a bit out of date, but the historical details of Carnaval are interesting. (The English edition is available in Rio's best book stores; try the one next door to the Copacabana Palace Hotel).

Dance

Bira, Almeida. *Capoeira: A Brazilian Art Form: History, Philosophy, and Practice.* Berkeley: North Atlantic Books, 1986. The student of one of the great capoeira masters of the 20th century and now a master teacher himself in California, the Brazilian-born author writes poignantly about the history, philosophy, and form of the country's premier martial art. The book is filled with legends, songs and tricks of the trade—valuable for anyone interested in ethnocultural studies.

Cuisine

Rojas-Lombardi, Felipe. *The Art of South American Cooking.* Harper Collins, 1991. Innovative Latin cooking by the late Peruvian owner of The Ballroom restaurant in New York City. Recipes for Brazilian delicacies are superb.

Health

Rose, Stuart R., MD. *International Travel Health Guide.* Northampton: Travel Medicine, Inc., 1991. Written by a physician who is a member of the AMA and the American Society of Tropical Medicine and Hygiene, this book gives excellent advice about traveling in third-world countries and tropical jungles. Specific guidelines for individual countries, including Brazil, are denoted in detail.

Guides

The Best of São Paulo. Hard-cover pocket-size guide written by a native Paulistano. Price, including shipping and handling, is $10. Write to: Editora Marca D'Agua, *Avenida Cidade Jardim 427 #124, São Paulo, Brazil 01453;* ☎ *(11) 881-0753, FAX (11) 883-5965.*

Humor

O'Rourke, P. J. *Holidays in Hell.* New York: Vintage, 1989. An irreverent and world-weary foreign correspondent for *Rolling Stone* reports from hellholes and other fun spots around the world. His chapter about driving on third-world roads is required reading for anyone heading for the Amazon or Pantanal.

FILMS

Black Orpheus

Directed by Marcel Camus, with music by Antônio Carlos Jobim and Luis Bonfá, this stunning movie retells the Orpheus tale through the eyes of a carioca streetcar conductor who figuratively descends into hell to save the woman he loves. A lush, if fantastical, view of Carnaval during the 1960s. Portuguese with English subtitles. (Available from Luso-Brazilian Books, see address above.)

At Play in the Fields of the Lord

Directed by Hector Babenco, this 1991 film preserves the moral intelligence of Peter Mathiessen's 1965 novel but loses some of the adventure. Aidan Quinn plays a nerdy evangelist sent to convert an Amazonian tribe, which is also being invaded by a half-Cheyenne mercenary with his own savior complex. The footage of the jungle near Belém is colossal.

Medicine Man

New York magazine called this film "the most enjoyable bad movie in some time"—a big, messy emotional drama starring Sean Connery as a research scientist obsessed with finding a cure for cancer in the Amazon jungle. The shots of Connery and his sidekick, Lorraine Bracco, swinging over the forest on cables are exciting, but her jungle attire is all wrong.

Blame It on Rio

Michael Caine plays a businessman in São Paulo seduced by the nubile virgin daughter of his best friend. The film gives a beautiful view of Grumari Beach, but the token toplessness is not authentic to the region. Anyone going to Rio for the first time might tolerate the horrible script for the cultural glimpses of *candomblé, capoeira,* and samba.

Flying Down to Rio

This 1933 music and dance extravaganza featuring Fred Astaire and Ginger Rogers is unabashedly fun, especially the chorus line dancing samba on the wings of the airplane. Unfortunately, the music is more mariachi than Brazilian.

The Emerald Forest

A marvelous, near-mythical tale of an Amazonian Indian who tries—literally—to scale civilization. The score alone is superb, and the clash between the white and native cultures is thought-provoking.

RAIN FOREST INFORMATION

Organizations involved in saving tropical rain forests include:

Arctic to Amazonia
P.O Box 73, Stafford, VT 05072. An educational organization devoted to constructive, nonviolent change in the world by facilitating dialogue between indigenous and nonindigenous peoples, particularly regarding social justice and the environment. Publishes *Arctic to Amazonia Report*, available with a $25 annual membership.

Conservation International
1015 18th Street NW, Suite 1002, Washington, D.C. 20036.

Friends of the Earth/U.S.
218 DD, SE Washington, DC. 20003.

Greenpeace
1436 U Street NW, Washington, DC 20009.

National Resources Defense Council
40 W. 20th Street, New York, NY 10011.

Rainforest Action Network (RAN)
450 Sansome, Suite 700, San Francisco, CA 9411. A grass-roots activist environmental organization working with indigenous land-based peoples in struggles to protect their rain forest homelands and cultures from rampant rain forest destruction. Available with a $25 annual membership is *World Rain Forest Report* quarterly, with monthly action alerts.

Rainforest Alliance
270 Lafayette St, Suite 512, New York, NY 10012.

Sierra Club
730 Polk Street, San Francisco, CA 94109.

World Wildlife Fund/U.S
Panda House, Godalming, Surrey GGU 7 1 XRR United Kingdom.

COICA
(Coordinating Body for the Indigenous Peoples' Organizations of the Amazon Basin) Jiron Almagro 614, Lima 11, Peru.

Amanaka's Amazon Network
339 Lafayette Street, #8, New York, NY 10012; ☎ (212) 674-4646, FAX 274-1773. A nonprofit organization that sponsors an annual Amazon Week to promote public dialogues between Amazon leaders and their U.S. supporters. Amanaka also publishes a quarterly newsletter on Amazon-related issues. Volunteer programs are available for those who want to commit themselves to political and social activism. Letter writing campaigns and civil protests initiated by Amanaka have already had far-reaching consequences in the region.

SELECTED DISCOGRAPHY

The following records were selected with regard to quality and availability. Recent releases have been emphasized. Stars represent Fielding's choice.

Singer/Songwriters

★ Ben, Jorge. *Benjor.* Tropical Storm/WEA, 1989.

Ben Jorge and Gilberto Gil. *Gil Jorge.* Polygram/Verve, 1975.

Ben, Jorge. *Live in Rio.* Warner Bros., 1992.

★ Bethânia, Maria. *Álibi.* BR/Philips, 1988 (rpt.)

Bethânia, Maria. *Memória da Pele.* BR/Philips, 1989.

Bethânia, Maria. *Personalidade.* Polygram/Brazilian Wave.

Biglione, Victor. *Baleia Azul.* Tropical Storm/WEA, 1989.

★ Bonfá, Luiz. *Non Stop to Brazil.* Chesky Records, 1989.

★ Bosco, João. *Odilê Odila.* Polygram/Verve, 1991.

Buarque, Chico. *Construção.* BR Philips, 1980.

Buarque, Chico. *Malandro.* Barclay, 1985.

Buarque, Chico. *Personalidade.* Polygram/Brazilian Wave, 1987.

Buarque, Chico. *Vida.* BR/Philips, 1980.

Carlos, Roberto. *Roberto Carlos.* BR/CBS, 1986.

Djavan. *Lilás.* CBS, 1984.

★ Djavan. *Luz.* BR/CBS, 1982.

Djavan. *Não é Azul, Mas é Mar.* CBS, 1987

Djavan. *Seduzir.* World Pacific, 1990 (rpt).

★ Gil, Gilberto. *Dia Dorim Noite Neon.* Tropical Storm/WEA, 1985

Gil, Gilberto. *Parabolic.* Tropical Storm, 1992.

Gil, Gilberto. *Raça Humana.* Tropical Storm/WEA, 1984.

★ Gil, Gilberto. *Realce.* Tropical Storm, 1979.

Gil, Gilberto. *Um Banda Um.* Tropical Storm, 1982.

Gilberto, João. *Chega de Saudade.* BR/EMI, 1959.
Gilberto, João. *Interpreta Tom Jobim.* BR/EMI, 1985.
★ Gilberto, João. *The Legendary João Gilberto.* World Pacific, 1990.
Gilberto, João. *Live in Montreaux.* Elektra/Asylum, 1987.
★ Gonzaga, Luiz. *O Melhor de Luiz Gonzaga.* BR/RCA, 1989.
Gonzaguinha, É. World Pacific, 1990 (rpt.)
★ Horta, Toninho. *Diamond Land.* Polygram/Verve, 1988.
Horta, Toninho. *Moonstone.* Polygram/Verve, 1989.
Joyce. *Language and Love.* Verve, 1991.
Joyce. *Music Inside.* Verve, 1991.
Lins, Ivan. *Awa Yió.* Reprise, 1991.
Lins, Ivan. *Harlequin.* GRP, 1986.
Lins, Ivan. *Love Dance.* Reprise, 1989.
★ Lins, Ivan. *O Talento de Ivan Lins.* EMI. Maria, Tânia. Bela Vista. Capitol, 1990.
Maria, *Tânia.* Love Explosion. Concord, 1984.
★ Moraes, Vinícius de & Toquinho. *Vinícius e Toquinho.* BR/Philips, 1985.
★ Nascimento, Milton. *Anima,* 1982.
★ Nascimento, Milton. *Ao Vivo.* Polygram, 1983.
★ Nascimento, Milton. *Clube da Esquina 2.* BR/EMI, 1978.
★ Nascimento, Milton. *Geraes.* BR/EMI, 1976.
★ Nascimento, Milton. *Milagre dos Peixes.* Intuition Records, 1992 (reissued).
Nascimento, Milton. *Missa dos Quilombos.* Polygram/Verve, 1982.
Nascimento, Milton. *Txai.* CBS, 1992.
Nascimento, Milton. *Yuareté.* CBS Discos, 1987.
Toquinho. *Canta Brasil.* CGD, 1989.
Toquinho. *Made in Coração.* Elektra, 1990.
Toquinho e Vinícius. *Personalidade.* Polygram/Brazilian Wave.
Valença, Alceu. *7 Desejos.* EMI, 1992.
★ Veloso, Caetano. *Cinema Transcendental.* BR/Philips, 1979.
★ Veloso, Caetano. *Circuladô.* Elektra, 1992.
Veloso, Caetano. *Estrangeiro.* Elektra/Musician, 1989.
★ Veloso, Caetano. *Personalidade.* Polygram.
★ Veloso, Caetano. *Totalmente Demais.* Verve, 1987.
Vila, Martinho da. *Martinha da Vida.* CBS, 1990.
Viola, Paulinho da. *O Talento de Paulinho da Viola.* EMI Odeon.

Singers

Alcione. *Emoções Reais.* RCA, 1990.
Alcione. *Fogo da Vida.* RCA, 1985.
Andrade, Leny. *Embraceable You.* Timeless Records, 1991.
Barbosa, Beto. *Beto Barbosa.* BR/Continental, 1988.
Belém, Fafá de. *Atrevida.* BR/Som Livre, 1986.
★ Calcanhoto, Adriana. CBS Discos, 1992.
Caram, Ana. Rio After Dark. Chesky Records.
Carvalho, Beth. "Das Bênçãos que virão com os novos amanhã." RCA, 1985
Carvalho, Beth. *O Carnaval de Beth Carvalho and Martinho da Vila.* BMG, 1990.
Caymmi, Nana. *Atrás da Porta.* BR/CID, 1977.
★ Costa, Gal. *Bem Bom.* RCA, 1985.

★ Costa, Gal. *Gal Canta Caymmi.* Verve, 1976.

Costa, Gal. *Personalidade.* Polygram/Brazilian Wave.

Gilberto, Astrud. *Astrud Gilberto Plus the James Last Orchestra.* Polydor, 1987.

Kenia. *Initial Thrill.* MCA, 1987.

Leão, Nara. *Personalidade.* Polygram/The Best of Brazil.

Lee, Rita. *Rita Lee.* BR/Som Livre, 1986 (rpt.).

Matogrosso, Ney. *Matogrosso & Mathias, vol. 14.* Chantecler.

Menezes, Margareth. *Kindala.* Mango, 1991.

Menezes, Margareth. *Elegibo.* Mango, 1989.

Miranda, Carmen. *Carmen Miranda.* BR/RCA, 1989.

★ Monte, Marisa. *Marisa Monte.* BR/EMI, 1988.

Purim, Flora. *Midnight Sun.* Virgin Records, 1988.

Purim, Flora. *Queen of the Night.* Sound Wave Records, 1992.

Ramalho, Elba. *Personalidade.* Polygram/The Best of Brazil series.

Regina, Elis. *Elis.* BR/Philips, 1988 (rpt.).

★ Regina, Elis. *Elis & Tom.* Verve, 1974.

★ Regina, Elis. *Essa Mulher.* WEA Latina, 1988

★ Regina, Elis. *Fascinação.* BR Philips, 1988.

Regina, Elis. *Falso Brillhante.* BR/Philips, 1988 (rpt.).

Regina, Elis. *Nada Será Como Antes.* Fontana, 1984.

Regina, Elis. *Personalidade.* Polygram/Brazilian Wave, 1987.

★ Regina, Elis. *Samba Eu Canto Assim.* 1983.

★ Sá, Sandra. *Sandra!* BMG Ariola Discos, 1990.

Simone. *The Best of Simone.* Capitol Records, 1991.

Rock

Baby Consuelo. *Sem Pecado E Sem Juízo.* BR/CBS, 1985.

★ Cazuza. *Burguesia.* BR/Philips, 1989.

Kledir. *Kledir Ao Vivo.* Som Livre, 1991.

Lobão. *Sob O Sol de Parador.* BMG/RCA, 1989.

Paralamas do Successo. *Bora Bora.* Capitol/Intuition, 1989.

Paralamos do Successo. *Selvagem?* EMI, 1989.

RPM. *Rádio Pirata Ao Vivo.* BR/CBS, 1986.

Gaúcho

Borghetti, Renato. *Renato Borghetti.* BR/RCA, 1987.

Gaucho da Fronteira. *Gaitero, China e Cordena.* Chantecler.

Gildo de Freitas. *Successos Imortais de Gildo Freitas.*

Minas School

Azul, Paulinho Pedra. *Sonho de Menino,* 1988.

Azul, Paulinho Pedra. *Uma Janela Dentro dos Meus Olhos,* 1984.

Franco, Tadeu. *Captivante.* Barclay, 1983.

★ Franco, Tadeu. *Animal.* Barclay, 1989.

Guedes, Beto. *Viagem das Mãos.* EMI, 1987.

Guedes, Beto. *Alma de Borracha.* EMI, 1986.

Instrumentalists

Airto, Moreira. *Samba de Flora*. Montuno Records, 1988.

★ Moreira, Airto. *Identity*. Arista, 1975.

★ Moreira, Airto and Flora Purim. *The Colours of Life*. W. Germany/In + Out, 1988.

★ Assad, Sérgio and Odair. *Alma Brasileira*. Elektra/Nonesuch, 1988.

Alameida, Laurindo & Carlos Barbosa-Lima, Charlie Byrd. *Music of the Brazilian Masters*. Concord Picante, 1989.

Alemão (Olmir Stocker). *Longe dos Olhos, Perto do Coração*. Happy Hours Music.

Banda Savana. *Brazilian Movements*. Libra Music (Denmark)

Barbosa-Lima, Carlos & Sharon Isbin. *Brazil, with Love*. Concord, 1987.

Biglione, Victor. *Victor Biglione*. Tropical Storm, 1987.

★ Castro-Neves, Oscar. *Maracujá*. JVC, 1989.

★ Castro-Neves, Oscar. *Oscar!* Living Music. 1987.

Cayymi, Dori. *Brasilian Serenata*. Qwest/Warner, 1991.

★ Elias, Eliane. *Eliane Plays Jobim*. Blue Note, 1990.

Elias, Eliane. *So Far So Close*. Blue Note, 1989.

★ Favero, Alberto. *Classical Tropico*. Tropical Storm/WEA Latina, 1989.

★ Gandelman, Leo. *Leo Gandelman*. Secret Records, 1989.

★ Geraissati, André. *Dadgad*. Tropical Storm/WEA, 1989.

Gismonti, Egberto. *Amazónia*. EMI, 1991.

★ Gismonti, Egberto. *Dança das Cabeças*. ECM, 1977.

Gismonti, Egberto. *Dança das Escravos*. ECM, 1989.

★ Gismonti, Egberto. *Sol do Meio Dia*. ECM, 1978.

Gismonti, Egberto and Nana Vasconcelos. *Duo Gismonti-Vasconcelos*. Jazz Bühne Berlin/Repertoire Records, 1990.

★ Jobim, Antônio Carlos. *Passarim*. Polygram/Verve, 1987.

Jobim, Antônio Carlos. *Personalidade*. Polygram/Brazilian Wave.

Jobim, Antônio Carlos. *Urubu*. BR/WEA, 1985 (rpt.).

★ Jobim, Antônio Carlos & Gal Costa. *Rio Revisited*. Verve, 1989.

Lyra, Carlos. *Carlos Lyra: 25 Anos de Bossa Nova*. 3M, 1987.

Tiso, Wagner. *Baobab*. Antilles/Island, 1990.

Silveira, Ricardo. *Sky Light*. Polygram/Verve, 1989.

Vasconcelos, Naná & the Bushdancers. *Rain Dance*. Antilles/Island, 1988.

Compilations

Alô Brasil. Tropical Storm/WEA Latina, 1989.

Afro Brasil. Verve, 1990.

Bahia Black Ritual Beating System. Island Records, 1992.

Black Orpheus (soundtrack). Verve, 1990 (rpt.).

Brazil Classics 1: Beleza Tropical, compiled by David Byrne. Luaka Bop/Sire, 1989.

Brazil Classics 2: O Samba, compiled by David Byrne. Luaka Bop/Warner, 1989.

Brazil Classics 3: Forró, etc., compiled by David Byrne. Luaka Bop/Warner, 1989.

Brazil Classics 4: The Best of Tom Zé, compiled by David Byrne. Luaka Bop/Sire, 1990.

Brazil is Back. Braziloid Records, 1987.
Brazilian Groove: Melting Pot. Lux Music Corp., 1994.
Djavan, João Gilberto, Toninho Horta. Capitol Records, 1990.
Lambada Brazil, featuring Caetano Veloso and Margareth Menezes. Polygram, 1990.
Nordeste Brazil. Verve, 1991.
Samba Brazil, Verve, 1991.
Sampler '89. Tropical Storm/WEA, 1989.
Sounds of Bahia Volume 2. Sound Wave records, 1991.
★ *Violões.* Banera. (São Paulo), 1991.
For Brazilian-influenced recordings by non-Brazilians, check out the releases of Stan Getz, Pat Metheny, Basia, Chick Corea, Ella Fitzgerald, Manhattan Transfer, Dave Grusin, Lee Ritenour, Sara Vaughan, Weather Report, and Paul Winter, among others.
Best cities to buy and hear music in Brazil are Rio and São Paulo (all genres), Belo Horizonte (especially the Mineiro School), Fortaleza (*forró and lambada*), Salvador (*afoxé*), Recife/Olinda (*forró*).

Best Samba Recordings

Escolas de Samba Enredo. Sony Music. Collection with 10 CDs, each dedicated to one of the great samba schools in Rio—from Portela to Beijo Flor, with famous interpreters like Beth Carvalho, João Bosco, and others.
Olodum, O Movimento. Continental/Warner. The famous percussion band from Bahia, which made international headlines with Paul Simon.
A História da Musica de Carnaval. Collector's. Eight cassettes with rare recordings of sambas and marches extracted from 78s, compiled by the famous musicologist José Maria Manzo. For more information, call in Rio ☎ *(21) 239-6367.*

INDEX

Get the latest travel & entertainment information faxed instantly to you for just $4.95*

The new Fielding's fax-on-demand service.

Now get up-to-the-minute reviews of the best dining, lodging, local attractions, or entertainment just before your next trip. Choose from 31 U.S. and international destinations and each has five different category guides.

Take the guesswork out of last-minute travel planning with reliable city guides sent to any fax machine or address you choose. Select just the information you want to be sent to your hotel, your home, your office or even your next destination.

All category guides include money-saving "best buy" recommendations, consensus star-ratings that save time, and cost comparisons for value shopping.

Fielding's Cityfax™ now combines the immediacy of daily newspaper listings and reviews with the wit and perspective of a Fielding Travel Guide in an easy-to-use, constantly updated format.

Order a minimum of two or all five category guides of the destination of your choice, 24 hours a day, seven days a week. All you need is a phone, a fax machine, and a credit card.

5 different category guides for each destination

❶ Restaurants

❷ Hotels & Resorts

❸ Local Attractions

❹ Events & Diversions

❺ Music, Dance & Theater

Choose from 31 destinations

1 Atlanta	18 New York City
2 Baltimore	19 Orlando
3 Boston	20 Philadelphia
4 Chicago	21 Phoenix
5 Dallas	22 San Diego
6 Denver	23 San Francisco
7 Detroit	24 San Jose/Oakland
8 Hawaii	25 Santa Fe
9 Houston	26 Seattle
10 Kansas City	27 St. Louis
11 Las Vegas	28 Tampa/St.Pete
12 L.A.: Downtown	29 Washington DC
13 L.A.: Orange County	
14 L.A.: The Valleys	**INTERNATIONAL**
15 L.A.: Westside	30 London
16 Miami	31 Paris
17 New Orleans	

* Order each category guide faxed to you for $4.95, or order all five guides delivered by U.S. Priority Mail for just $12.95 (plus $3.50 shipping and handling), a savings of $8.30!

Fielding's Cityfax™

CALL: 800-635-9777 FROM ANYWHERE IN THE U.S.
OUTSIDE THE U.S. CALL: 852-172-75-552
HONG KONG CALLERS DIAL: 173-675-552

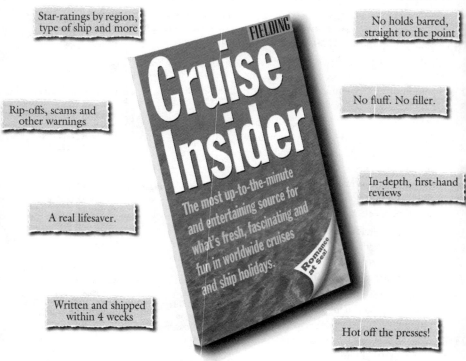

Order Your Fielding Travel Guides Today

BOOKS	$ EA.
Amazon	$16.95
Australia	$12.95
Bahamas	$12.95
Belgium	$16.95
Bermuda	$12.95
Borneo	$16.95
Brazil	$16.95
Britain	$16.95
Budget Europe	$16.95
Caribbean	$18.95
Europe	$16.95
Far East	$19.95
France	$16.95
Hawaii	$15.95
Holland	$15.95
Italy	$16.95
Kenya's Best Hotels, Lodges & Homestays	$16.95
London Agenda	$12.95
Los Angeles Agenda	$12.95
Malaysia and Singapore	$16.95
Mexico	$16.95
New York Agenda	$12.95
New Zealand	$12.95
Paris Agenda	$12.95
Portugal	$16.95
Scandinavia	$16.95
Seychelles	$12.95
Southeast Asia	$16.95
Spain	$16.95
The World's Great Voyages	$16.95
The World's Most Dangerous Places	$19.95
The World's Most Romantic Places	$16.95
Vacation Places Rated	$19.95
Vietnam	$16.95
Worldwide Cruises	$17.95

To order by phone call toll-free 1-800-FW-2-GUIDE
(VISA, MasterCard and American Express accepted.)

To order by mail send your check or money order,
including $2.00 per book for shipping and handling (sorry, no COD's) to:
Fielding Worldwide, Inc. 308 S. Catalina Avenue, Redondo Beach, CA 90277 U.S.A.

**Get 10% off your order by saying "Fielding Discount"
or send in this page with your order**

Favorite People, Places & Experiences

ADDRESS:	NOTES:

Name

Address

Telephone

Name

Address

Telephone

Name

Address

Telephone

Name

Address

Telephone

Name

Address

Telephone

Name

Address

Telephone

Name

Address

Telephone

Favorite People, Places & Experiences

ADDRESS:	NOTES:

Name

Address

Telephone

Name

Address

Telephone

Name

Address

Telephone

Name

Address

Telephone

Name

Address

Telephone

Name

Address

Telephone

Name

Address

Telephone

Favorite People, Places & Experiences

ADDRESS:	NOTES:

Name

Address

Telephone

Name

Address

Telephone

Name

Address

Telephone

Name

Address

Telephone

Name

Address

Telephone

Name

Address

Telephone

Name

Address

Telephone

Favorite People, Places & Experiences

Name

Address

Telephone

Name

Address

Telephone

Name

Address

Telephone

Name

Address

Telephone

Name

Address

Telephone

Name

Address

Telephone

Name

Address

Telephone

Favorite People, Places & Experiences

ADDRESS:	NOTES:

Name

Address

Telephone

Name

Address

Telephone

Name

Address

Telephone

Name

Address

Telephone

Name

Address

Telephone

Name

Address

Telephone

Name

Address

Telephone

Favorite People, Places & Experiences

ADDRESS:	NOTES:

Name

Address

Telephone

Name

Address

Telephone

Name

Address

Telephone

Name

Address

Telephone

Name

Address

Telephone

Name

Address

Telephone

Name

Address

Telephone

Favorite People, Places & Experiences

ADDRESS:	NOTES:

Name

Address

Telephone

Name

Address

Telephone

Name

Address

Telephone

Name

Address

Telephone

Name

Address

Telephone

Name

Address

Telephone

Name

Address

Telephone

Favorite People, Places & Experiences

ADDRESS:	NOTES:
Name	
Address	
Telephone	
Name	
Address	
Telephone	
Name	
Address	
Telephone	
Name	
Address	
Telephone	
Name	
Address	
Telephone	
Name	
Address	
Telephone	
Name	
Address	
Telephone	

Favorite People, Places & Experiences

ADDRESS:	NOTES:

Name

Address

Telephone

Name

Address

Telephone

Name

Address

Telephone

Name

Address

Telephone

Name

Address

Telephone

Name

Address

Telephone

Name

Address

Telephone

Favorite People, Places & Experiences

	ADDRESS:	NOTES:

Name

Address

Telephone

Name

Address

Telephone

Name

Address

Telephone

Name

Address

Telephone

Name

Address

Telephone

Name

Address

Telephone

Name

Address

Telephone

Favorite People, Places & Experiences

ADDRESS:	NOTES:

Name

Address

Telephone

Name

Address

Telephone

Name

Address

Telephone

Name

Address

Telephone

Name

Address

Telephone

Name

Address

Telephone

Name

Address

Telephone